Praise for *Gr*

"*Gritos* is an intimate look at Gilb's growth as a writer grappling with a desire to stay true to his working-class roots, and at the same time expose the powerful talent he has for penetrating, honest and emotional writing about cultural misconceptions, family relationships, manual labor and American literature."
—Paul S. Flores, *San Francisco Chronicle*

"A challenging, thought-provoking series of pieces rooted in an outsider's perspective."
—Sharyn Wizda Vane, *Austin American-Statesman*

"A splendid and touching and intelligent work that demonstrates the difficulties of becoming an artist when coming from modest means . . . *Gritos* is a book serious readers need to read. Gilb's voice is one too seldom heard."
—Eric Miles Williamson, *Houston Chronicle*

"Gilb's first book of essays reads like told stories, as choppy, authentic, and captivating as his much-loved fiction and National Public Radio commentaries. . . . His essays tackle the fantastic, the ridiculous, and the racially charged with a conversational style that, smiling, holds all accountable for these absurdities and wrongs."
—Mary Wiltenburg, *The Christian Science Monitor*

"[Gilb] has an uncanny, near magical ability to paint almost three-dimensional word pictures. . . . He is adept at stripping away facades to reveal the essence of the human condition."
—Geoff Campbell, *Fort Worth Star-Telegram*

"A rough-hewn gem of brutal honesty . . . The honesty and often-spectacular prose of these essays make them essential to anyone who wishes to challenge the too-often exclusive and esoteric status of American literature. These essays are truly gritos into the hot sun: primal, heart-wrenching as well ecstatic and often explosive." —Sergio Troncoso, *El Paso Times*

"Gilb captures the dusty southwestern landscapes of the working-class Latino. The author's rise from—and ties to—that uncompromising world gives these essays added depth."
—Steve Kurutz, *Details*

"Full of sentiments that are not only not heard enough, but often aren't heard at all. Subjects as novel as cockfighting, Cormac McCarthy, and lawn-care blues are tackled."
—Chad Hammett, *Southwestern American Literature*

"They're in your face, these essays. . . . They've got so much attitude and arrogance, so much candor, bias and raw emotion, and so much authentic material that you're snagged. . . . They're bold and convincing, full of life, and they revel in the wonder of writing." —Christine Wald-Hopkins, *Tucson Weekly*

"Even those not inclined toward essays will find Dagoberto Gilb's *Gritos* irresistible. . . . Gilb writes as though he were pouring out his heart at the kitchen table over a cup of coffee and a smoke. The prose . . . is tenaciously honest, and the pugnacious intelligence behind the swagger makes this collection resonate."
—Mike Shea, *Texas Monthly*

GRITOS

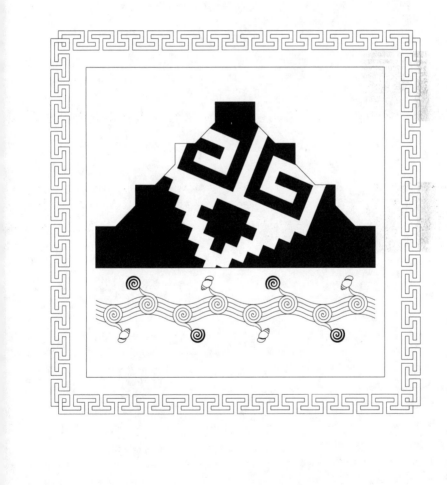

GRITOS

Essays by
Dagoberto Gilb

Illustrated by
César A. Martínez

Grove Press / New York

Published simultaneously in Canada
Printed in the United States of America

These pieces have previously appeared, sometimes in slightly different form, in the following periodicals, to which grateful acknowledgment is made:
Harper's Magazine: "Blue Eyes, Brown Eyes" (published as "Blue Eyes, Brown Eyes: A Pocho's Tour of Mexico")
The New Yorker and *Las Mamis* (Knopf, 2000): "Mi Mommy" (published as "I Knew She Was Beautiful"), "Spanish Guy"
The New York Times: "Steinbeck" (published as "Sentimental for Steinbeck")
San Francisco Chronicle: "Un Grito de Tejas"
The Los Angeles Times: "Documenting the Undocumented" (published as "Ebb and Flow Colors Our World")
San Antonio Express-News: "The Donkey Show" (published as "Found Art: *Boystown*")
Latino USA: "Eulogy for Don Ricardo Sánchez"
The Threepenny Review: "Northeast Direct" "Me Macho, You Jane" (published as "Machismo")
The Washington Post Magazine: "Victoria" (published as "Nice Like a Kiss")
The Washington Post Book World: "This Writer's Life" (published as "The Writing Life")
The Nation: "*The Border Trilogy* by Cormac McCarthy"
ANQ: "Note on Lit from the Americas"
Balcones: "Los Gallos"
Texas Monthly: "Vaya con Dios, Rosendo Juarez" (published as "Juarez and Peace")
The Carpenter (magazine of the United Brotherhood of Carpenters): "Work Union"
The Texas Observer: "Pride," "010100," "Get Over It, Good Brown Man," "L.A. Navidad," "I Want to See a Fortune-teller," "What I Would Have Said about the State of Texas Literature," "M'ijo Goes to College," "Rite of Passage," "Bullfights, Vegetables, Death," "Eulogy for Don Ricardo Sánchez," "Living al Chuco," "If You Were a Carpenter," "Books Suck," "Poverty is Always Starting Over," "My Landlady's Yard," "El Paso"
These pieces were also first read by the author for National Public Radio's *Fresh Air:* "I Want To See a Fortune-teller," "M'ijo Goes to College," "Rite of Passage," "Wyoming Eats Coyote," "Poverty is Always Starting Over," "Books Suck," "Bullfights, Vegetables, Death"
"Pride" was first published in "It Ain't Braggin' if It's True," catalog for the Texas State History Museum

FIRST GROVE PRESS PAPERBACK EDITION

Library of Congress Cataloging-in-Publication Data

Gilb, Dagoberto.
    Gritos : essays / Dagoberto Gilb
      p. cm.
    ISBN 0-8021-4127-7 (pbk.)
      1. Gilb, Dagoberto, 2. Authors, American—20th century—Biography.
    3. Mexican American authors—Biography. 4. Mexican Americans—Civilization.
    5. Mexican Americans in literature. I. Title.
    PS3557.I296G75 2003
    813'.54—dc21   2002044688

Grove Press
841 Broadway
New York, NY 10003

04   05   06   07   08   10   9   8   7   6   5   4   3   2   1

Contents

III. THE WRITING LIFE

IV. WORKING LIFE AND LA FAMILY

Introduction

Several months ago I had taken notes, which apparently I've lost, for this introduction. I'd written them on a page of one of those yellow pads. It's that I had stacked these essays and reread most of them and had ideas bubbling up through an excited friction of thinking about so many years of my own words in front of me—and of, Do I have a book here? I still remember the way I scribbled the words over the paper. As always, I started out neat, but I don't tend to follow the blue lines when I use the pen. I write in different handwriting sizes, depending on when I do it (at night, if I wake up with the need, I like to turn on a Magnum flashlight, and my lettering is really small) and how much room I have left. If I don't like a line, I don't cross it out, I just take it from the point where I want to start over and go again. I write above words, below them. I write from the bottom toward the top, I write along the right side, sideways on the left, any way up and down the page, the paper itself turned to suit, letting the rollerball ink seek the open range of blank space. I draw lines to separate the "threads." That yellow page, as I would now describe it, looked a little like several crumpled wrappers and bags on a table. As though I'd stayed up doing this, not eating dinner, so I'd gone over to Taco Cabana all solito and hungry around two in the

morning and bought a couple of bean and cheese burritos and
filled a couple little copitas de chile (a few—I like too much in
mine) and a side (large) of guacamole. Those salsitas leaked on
the drive back, so the bag was a little wet and torn at the bottom, but there were napkins to wipe that up after I'd set it down.
I'd put the bag on the table, and I'd turned on the tube—I get
free HBO!—and I got out a can of sparkling water from the
refrigator and cut wedges of limon and tomato I had in the refrigerator, too. Because I love to eat tomatoes. So I had a paper
plate to cut it on, a sharp knife. A jalapeño. Some pepper. Salt
which I know I know is bad for me. I like this easy meal very
much, I admit it. You know the scene—a mess when it's going,
one swoop or two to the trash, and a sponge wipe when it's over.

I don't believe I threw that page of notes away. It's got to
be around, but I have no idea where right now, and at this point,
I have to get on with the introduction without those first in-
sights. My life on the whole feels a lot like the mess on that lost
page and on the table, the mess of me losing it and me hurrying
to write this still, both the "I Love Life" good and the "I Keep
Screwing Up" bad of it. I don't know why. I'm always trailing
behind what I want to do and into what I have to do right now,
going too fast, too much going by—or is it too slow, am I dwell-
ing too long on the going by?—but no matter, this happens, that
happens, I have to respond to this, and now that is getting out of
my reach as I am moving, certainly moving, another rent and
year and job, but then I *am* moving, and look at all the surprising places I get to go and see, the people I never imagined knowing I get to know. And then, you see, I did get a couple of pieces
done, and look, here is this book. Though for the most part, I
feel pushed by forces I react to: with few exceptions, for instance,
I wrote the essays in *Gritos* because I was asked to, because there
was, to be straight up, a money offer involved—I do recognize
the craze in me that even if I would say this is not what I chose,

it's true that I am doing it and I've closed my eyes and I am smiling in its pleasure, those winds blowing into me—I don't resist the ride as I give in to it. And this often leads me, and my "writing career," too far away. Leads me to places where I forget where I was before. Forget where I put things before I went off. Which also causes me not to have a usual or continuous place where this belongs, where that is stored. I don't possess much, and yet I still can misplace the few things I have. I can't find the page of notes.

When I turned this collection in, I had the essays arranged chronologically, from the most recent to the oldest, which makes up almost a twenty-year span. Being real creative, I thought this sequence was the most direct way to read about me as a young, innocent carpintero, raising a family, so happy with that, a man who wrote and dreamed of being a writer but told no one about it when he was or wasn't on a high-rise; to me as a man who is now considered a writer but has to tell people he was once a carpenter those other years, as though *that* was a dream, as though it was the same as a summer job so many academically programmed writers think of as their "work" past. From a union carpenter, simpleminded in his want, digging for the mysteries of writing success, pounding out stories to stand up a career, to a complicated writer stunned by the blow of publication, the simplicity once it happened, what it is and is not, what it does and does not change. . . . Well, that sequencing wouldn't have worked. The arrangement you see here, suggested by a young Grove editor, Morgan Entrekin's assistant, Daniel Maurer, is now more reader-friendly. It shows concerns in a layout more logical—more intelligent—than mine was or I could have been aware of.

Some of the pieces aren't as good as others. Some probably aren't any good at all. I'm sure I don't have to say that. A couple are odd. It was my decision to keep what's here. I wanted the collage of what crossed typewriter, which became computer keyboard, the different ways that my obsessions carried me into different formats and frames. Broken, chipped, ugly. Wide, tall, short. A couple I wanted to include because, unmelodic as the writing itself might be, I felt banged loud what doesn't get heard enough. I wanted to say, There, I have it right there, see?

The larger story herein is about a fight for recognition, which seems personal but I say is not only. I know that what I write is almost always personal. Even when I try to write outside my head, there I am again. But it's not my intention to inflate my own self. One easy explanation is that I don't feel the authority to be objective, to use a commanding third-person address, even with essays. I call this technique of mine first-person stupid: it's not my fault I don't know everything (maybe it really is, but whatever) (see how I do it?), or very much, I can account to you only what I know, I'm trying only to be as honest (and easy) as I can, and what can I tell you that you would listen to oh-so-smart me? With the exclusion of the one piece that comes from my journals (though even it, I would argue as such an unbiased reader, I don't think is about me alone), the one that begins a journey out of a construction-site hole to a literary award, my want is show an experience that, yes, is passing through me, but no, is not only "mine." And much of what is not mine, what I have found, still find, that I battled, has changed very little: even after all these years, people like me are unseen, patronized, so out of the portrait of American literature. It seems impossible that so many of the writers I have known—and yes, me, too—with a decent record of publications by usual standards, still fight a battle for acceptance, that we are a product of an ongoing American story that is not foreign, not only about a dark exotic people, not only fascinating as so much is "south of the border," not just about the poor and dangerous other side of the tracks. When you look around at the lands of the West, the names of the mountain ranges and the rivers, the names of states and cities, you can realize without even a history lesson that a Spanish-speaking culture has long been here.

Years ago, when my home was El Paso, I visited with a magazine editor in Austin, and he wanted to take me to lunch at a Tex-Mex restaurant, his favorite. Austin has lots of them, but oddly enough, because the food is so popular, many do not employ Mexican people as waiters or waitresses, not to mention Mexican or Mexican-American clientele. I needed some water, and when I caught the attention of a busboy cleaning a table near us, I asked him if he wouldn't mind getting me a glass. I like talking to people, so when he got back, I also asked him where he was from, how long he'd been here, what he thought of the town, the usual, and we even laughed a little. Austin, for me, was a new, if odd place, because I still thought of Texas as a mix of Mexican and American cultures and people. But then, to my surprise, I caught something nonverbal from that editor, a genuinely nice guy, as his eyes were taking in light. He was seeing things anew, seeing yet another Mexican busboy and watching the Mexican cooks, too—we were close enough that we could hear them talking. It was, I realized, the first time he'd gotten this perspective, the first time he'd ever noticed these people in his favorite restaurant. We were so deep in the country which was once Mexico, now so colonized, that the people themselves were no longer visible. I simply could not have imagined how distant, how faraway, El Paso culture was in Austin.

It's wild and free, the wide open, when Jack Kerouac romanticizes his love affair with a Mexican girl. Katherine Anne Porter can love Mexico and be considered sophisticated and haunting. But people of Mexican descent themselves, when they write, that's another genre, something tangential to the American story. My own experience with the magazine of the Texas State, *Texas Monthly,* makes it clear that, according to it, Mexican-Americans still aren't yet ready to be part of highbrow Texas culture. Look over its archives and you'll find a winky apartheid vision of the people—firey food, spicy music, and maybe a hot Chicano boxer or sexy Tejana singer who works not from the brain but out of native juices, instincts, roots.

Not surprisingly, this perception isn't limited to the region. Being from the West is always a handicap: literature is published in the East, and literary figures come from there, and it's literary characters, wild as stallions and flooding rivers, who are western. Some years ago, Jonathan Franzen, in a well-known article published in *Harper's,* couldn't find a single writer of importance who was not from the historically dominant culture. For people like me, essays such as his are as distant as ones on British literature—which actually has seen non-Anglo Salman Rushdie catapulted into prominence.

Too little has changed since I went to college. A couple of new voices, a couple of new faces. No children from those working in restaurants and hospitals, paving the streets, building houses, cooking food, wearing hard hats, driving delivery trucks and wearing tool bags, washing windows, sewing, bagging trash and bagging groceries, typing and filing, answering office phones, picking fruit, picking vegetables, picking nuts, fitting parts, bolting, welding, sweeping, waxing. Where I am from, the West, the Southwest, Texas, it's as though Mexican and Chicano culture were there like oranges and lemons and pecans, like agave or ocotillo or yucca—go ahead and love the tacos and enchiladas and tequila, love the colors, love the music, love the furniture, love the architecture, love the landscaping, but . . .

That story glues these essays together—and it isn't mine at all. It is a story about being here, in this country, in America, from a territory that was America before it was in the United States—an American culture, a Chicano culture, the one that is right here, where it was long before it was cartoonized into images from Frito Bandido and Taco Bell.

I, too, am guilty. For years, I had fallen in line with the Franzens and *Texas Monthly*s who would dismiss and demand better quality. I would say that we do have to work harder, make it better than what we have. I'd put aside so much of my own consistent experience of rejection and kept producing, and I'd go, Sure, I'm mediocre, they're right. It's the basis of all respectable, self-loathing writers that what we do is worthless and lousy. Gradually, however, I began to watch and read what got published, and then I'd be like, I'm supposed to accept that I'm *more* mediocre than *that*? No, I am not. It's a lot like the first time you got into a luxury car and you thought it was about the people who owned it. What they've done, the accomplishment. No, it's that they have money, they can afford it without working any harder, often even less hard. It's like this: they say, He went to Harvard, that's why. You go, Yeah, wow, that is impressive, I can't imagine going to Harvard. What's not said is that he went to Harvard because he went to a prep school in Massachusetts or Rhode Island, where recruiters sought him out, and where this prep school spent time teaching SAT tests. His parents were rich enough to afford that, and they went to Harvard, too, and Harvard gives incentives to the children of alumni. His parents inherited . . . and so on. It never ends, and how can we ever catch up? This attitude of mine is, of course, nasty and arrogant, yet another reason to have a head shake at me—no, not at me, away from me, when I'm not looking.

I am guilty, too, because I don't think I'm smart enough. Flawed in a couple of personal areas, I wish I could claim to be better here, I wish instead of wanting to collapse and watch HBO (even, I admit, those cheap judge shows), I could read another book. I know those kinds of writers. My God, they are so brilliant and articulate. I even know a couple who are genuises. But what I hope might be seen is what gets undervalued: not only has writing saved my life, projected it into New York and Wash-

ington, D.C., and European fantasylands I'd never know otherwise, it has offered me joy and fun. There are limits to how much
that might be seen in these essays. I assure you, every one of them
has given me such pleasure and satisfaction, the same kind I had
when I used to cut wood with my skilsaw and drive nails and
build, watch a building rise huge, a fun of the kind that trowels
the back of a tile with adhesive and sets it in, a pattern mount-
ing. Each word is a rock I've placed personally into a wall—five
go in and I pick through a pile and find another, shift them all
around until it's right. I've chipped and nicked at most so they
look to me like good sentences, good paragraphs. If I don't think
of myself as the smartest, I do feel a strength in my working of
the craft, so that every time I finish something, I'm maybe too
proud of myself, can hardly believe I did it, that I could. The
words are beyond my own physical self or nature, because I was
not born to be a writer, I've just done it anyway. Often this work
is outright fun, almost as fun as a good construction job where
we were all muscles sweating and laughing and building shit and
getting paid at the same time—living and working—except writing work is alone, only an imaginary crew. Sometimes you see
that laughter in these essays, but even when it's not haha, when
it's like the drudgery of any job, it's still so good when it's finally
gone through, completed—that pleasure, that joy.

    Gritos. When I turned in this collection, my publisher wasn't
sure about that title. That's because it was thought the title translated as "shouts." A part of me liked that it would be what people
who don't know the Mexican tradition of a grito would think
when they looked it up in a Spanish-English dictionary. If you
don't know, yeah, right, it's a shout, a yell. But it's not. The most
famous grito is the one from Father Hidalgo, *el grito de Dolores,*
declaring Mexico's independence from Spain—defiance and freedom. A grito is what a coyote does—an animal wail of need, sin-

gular and for the group. A grito is the "¡Viva!" at a wedding or a political rally—joy and support. A grito is most known when mariachis sing, that loud, extemporaneous howl of triumph, or the sad—and loud, it has to be loud—lament of love lost, the orgasmic agony of love found. I wanted this collection to be all of those.

I

CULTURE
CROSSING

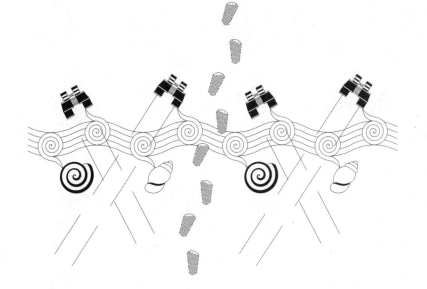

My Landlady's Yard

It's been a very dry season here. Not enough rain. And the sun's beginning to feel closer. Which, of course, explains why this is called the desert. Why the kinds of plants that do well enough in the region—creosote, mesquite, ocotillo, yucca—aren't what you'd consider lush, tropical blooms. All that's obvious, right? To you, I'm sure, it's obvious, and to me it is, too, but not to my landlady. My landlady doesn't think of this rock house I rent in central El Paso as being in the desert. To her, it's the big city. She's from the country, from a ranch probably just like the one she now calls home, a few miles up the paved highway in Chaparral, New Mexico, where the roads are graded dirt. She must still see the house as she did when she lived here as a young wife and mother, as part of the city's peaceful suburbs, which it certainly was thirty years ago. She probably planted the shrubs and evergreens that snuggle the walls of the house now, probably seeded the back- and front-yard grass herself. And she wants those Yankee plants and that imported grass to continue to thrive as they would in all other American, nondesert neighborhoods, even if these West Texas suburbs moved on to the east and west many years ago, even if the population has quadrupled and water is more scarce, and expensive, than back then.

So I go ahead and drag around a green hose despite my perception that *gold,* colorless and liquid, is pouring out onto this desert, an offering as unquenchable and ruthless as to any Aztec deity (don't water a couple of days and watch how fast it dries away). Superstitions, if you don't mind my calling them that, die hard, and property values are dependent on shared impressions. I'm not ready to rent and load another U-Haul truck.

With my thumb over the brass fitting and squeezed against the water, I use the digits on my other hand to pluck up loose garbage. You've heard, maybe, of West Texas wind. That explains why so much of it lands here on my front yard, but also a high school is my backyard: the school's rear exit is only a dirt alley and fence away from my garage, and teenagers pass by in the morning, during lunch, and when school lets out. I find the latest Salsa Rio brand of Doritos, Big Gulp Grande cups, paper (or plastic or both) bowls with the slimy remains of what goes for cheese on nachos from the smiley-faced Good Time Store two blocks away, used napkins, orange burger pouches, the new glossy-clean plastic soda containers, waxy candy wrappers from Mounds and Mars and Milky Way. Also beer cans and bottles, grocery-store bags both plastic and paper, and fragments from everything else (believe me) possible.

I'm betting you think I'm not too happy about accumulating such evidence. You're right. But I'm not mentioning it to complain. I want the image of all the trash, as well as the one of me spraying precious water onto this dusty alkaline soil, to get your attention. Because both stand for the odd way we live and think out here, a few hundred miles (at least) from everyplace else in the United States.

My green grass in the desert, for instance. My landlady wants thick, luxuriant grass because that's the way of this side of the border, and this side is undeniably better, whatever misconception of place and history and natural resources the desire for that image depends on. It's not just her, and it's not just lawns. Take another example: a year ago about this time, police cars squealed onto the asphalt handball and basketball courts on the other side of the school fence to regain control of a hundred or so students lumped around a fight, most of them watching, some swinging baseball bats. What happened? According to the local newspaper, the fight broke out between a group of black students, all of them dependents of Fort Bliss military personnel (as their jargon has it), and a group of Hispanic students. "Hispanic" is the current media term for those of descent from South of the Border. Even around here. Which is the point: that even in this town—the other side of the concrete river considered the official land of Spanish-language history and culture—the latest minority-language terminology is used to describe its historic, multigenerational majority population. With the exception of one high school on the more affluent west side of town, Anglos are the overwhelming minority; at the high school behind my backyard the ratio must be ten to one. Though Mexico has been the mother of this region, and remains so, it's the language and understanding of The North that labels the account of the school incident: "Hispanic" students, black dependents of GIs.

If green grass is the aspiration, the realization of an American fantasy, then the trash is from the past, the husks of a frontier mentality that it took to be here, and stay, in the first place. Trash blowing by, snared by limbs and curbs and fences, is a display of what was the attitude of the West. The endlessness of its range. The ultimate principle of every man, woman, animal, and thing for itself. The meanness required to survive. The wild joy that could abandon rules. The immediacy of life. Or the stupidity of the non-Indian hunter eating one meal, then leaving behind the carcass. Except that vultures and coyotes and finally ants used to clean that mess up. The remains of the modernized hunt don't balance well in nature or its hybrid shrubs, do not biodegrade. And there are a lot more hunters than before.

Trash contradicts the well-tended lawn. And in my neighborhood, not all is Saint Augustine or Bermuda. Hardy weeds sprout and grow tall everywhere, gray-green century plants shoot stalks beside many homes. El Paso is still crossing cultures and times, the wind blows often, particularly this time of year, the sun will be getting bigger, but the pretty nights cool things off here on the desert. Let me admit this: I'd like it if grass grew well in my backyard. What I've got is patchy at best, and neglected, the brown dirt is a stronger color than the green. So the other day, I soaked that hard soil, dug it up, threw seed grown and packaged in Missouri, covered it with peat humus from Menard, Texas, and I'm waiting.

Documenting
the Undocumented

Those of us who have grown up and lived on the southern-desert border of the United States have heard many brutal stories—betrayal, theft, rape, and death—of men and women who journeyed far and were stopped so very close to its line of crossing. These are the meanest, most horrific asides to a larger story of what some want to describe as an invasion of people from the outer side, from Mexico, whose name tag changes depending on the times and the speakers—wets, illegals, aliens, undocumented, immigrants. Sometimes just saying "Mexicans" can be heard, and meant, like a dirty word.

All countries have borders, and everyone knows them well. Mexico itself has a southern border it worries about. Protecting its citizens' work is one of the intrinsic functions of a nation. France, such a cliché of liberality in matters sensual and intellectual, is one of the most restrictive about letting nonnatives find employment. But not every border is natural. Most are marked by historical contrivances. In El Paso, Texas, what is now called the Chamizal National Memorial is really an area of land that the Rio Grande swung north and south of on its course to the Gulf of Mexico. The monument and park symbolize the cooperation—both flags whipping in an unencumbered wind on either side of a cemented river—between the countries sharing the international boundary.

I am just back from Andalucía—that word derived from the Arabic *Al Andalus.* So much of what is considered architecturally spectacular about this region of southern Spain is what remains of the culture that came up from south of it. The fountains and their courtyards, the love for and worship of water, the lines of orange trees crisscrossing patios and plazas, the idea of a central patio itself, all Moorish. The palace arches and grounds of the Alhambra in Granada, the startling interior columns in the Mezquita of Córdoba, the Alcázar's fortress walls and towers in Sevilla and the bone-carving complexity of the Giralda of the cathedral there, a minaret before it was a Christian bell tower. The radiant *azulejos,* what decorates all the envied rooms of these masterpiece buildings and most of southern Spain, the glazed ceramic tile that we now consider a Spanish style when we remodel our bathrooms and kitchens: it, too, Arabic in origin.

The Moors arrived in 711 and by 929 had established Córdoba as the capital of Andalucía, having taken the region from the Visigoths who themselves had conquered it from the Romans, there since the 200s. It wasn't until 1492, when the Catholic monarchs Isabel and Ferdinand defeated Granada, the last Moor stronghold, that Arabic political power was finally expunged. They had been there eight centuries.

It has been a little over 150 years since the Treaty of Guadalupe Hidalgo was signed, shifting the governmental power and property that once was Mexico's to the United States. That land includes what we call the Southwest—Arizona and New Mexico—as well as California, Nevada, Colorado, and Texas. For two centuries previous, before the Pilgrims, before a tea party or Paul Revere, Spanish was the primary language of these lands. Spanish words have named the mountains, the rivers, and the cities. Spanish architecture still dominates and identifies the cultural landscape. What is most loved about the West—from its art and the rainbow of colors used in it, to the food, those spices, chiles, and tortillas, from horseback riding to barbecuing—is Mexican.

Those people who cross that political border are not crossing a cultural one. The language spoken in the communities that harbor these "immigrants" is nothing like, say, one of a Turk's commuting to Germany. *Mejicanos* go to the first historical communities in a city, often within walking distance of the oldest churches, where several generations lived before the English-speaking world sprawled.

Those people who risk everything to cross the border do so to work, to earn money for poor families. They take the hardest jobs and the lowest wages and, once employed, offer in return an almost overly romanticized pride and patriotism.

Over twenty years ago, I worked as a carpenter on a HUD housing project in what was still only a desert El Paso. Even for El Paso, the pay wasn't so good—at least the contracter didn't let it be. The guy I partnered with was there with two brothers who worked together. They were from a small town between Juárez and Chihuahua, and it was their first time on this side of the border. One of the things we talked about as we worked was the possibility of the INS raiding this job site. I liked him, so I told him to say, if he was asked, that he was from El Paso, not from the United States. You know, to be local, you have to sound local. The INS knows it makes people nervous (though not the employers), and it counts on mistakes. I taught my partner phrases that would make him sound like a bilingual Chicano. And when the migra did come one day in their green van, as many of the workers scattered and were being chased, others stood and answered the questions of an officer quickly passing through. I was at a distance at that moment, and I saw my partner replying, and then the officer moved away from him. My partner smiled over at me. But instead of walking in the opposite direction, he followed that officer, who was headed toward the other brothers. They did not pass the test. Just before he got into the INS van, I went to him: He didn't want to be here without his brothers.

What those brothers would bring with them every day was *jamaica, a* bright red drink made from dried hibiscus flower, which they didn't oversweeten as others might have. They brought it in a beat-up five-gallon plastic jug, full, iced, and many times a day, I'd open my mouth under that little spigot. It was hot work in the desert. Before then I'd never heard of or tasted this drink. I loved it, and not just because it was always cold. It seemed to have made me love the job, because once it wasn't around, either, I was glad when I was done with it.

Blue Eyes, Brown Eyes: A Pocho Tours Mexico

Lots of times I was bored with TV before midnight, so I took the pliers to it—both the knobs were off because they'd broken, and though I could twist the metal shaft of the on off and volume with my finger and thumb, it was easier pinching it with pliers. At night, streetlight outside and not so many cars or motorcycles, I might suddenly get scared. Nothing specific to be afraid of, nothing except me and maybe being alone and being young. I didn't expect or even fear a thief or a murderer or a pervert crawling through a window to get me, but something animal, more or less, substantial enough, hiding somewhere, staring out from the dark. I couldn't calm myself until I went to every room and put light into the space. Looking behind the furniture. Under beds. I opened the closet doors and pushed things around. I'd have a knife in my right hand, a kitchen knife with a blade twice as long as my hand and almost as wide. Once I cleared the area, and my head, I did make sure the front and back doors were locked, and then I could go back to a red couch that was near the TV and I would be safe. That couch was scratchy where it wasn't worn smooth, but it didn't matter. My mom would be out on a date, and instead of the bed I'd be on the red couch with a blanket and pillow, and I'd stare up at the wavy grains in the wood ceiling and remember what I'd heard here or there or what she said or what he said, or visualize or imagine what I'd do if and where I'd go when, and what I was doing there, and how I got here—the long route of it, what I did know and what I didn't. And there was always a girl. There was a particular girl I knew, though she was much older, and she didn't know me. Sometimes it was her. In Archie comics, my favorite, she looked a little like Veronica. Except she was darker, and no makeup, and not those kind of tight dresses. And she didn't come from the United States but from Mexico. Which is where my mom's family was from—from Xalapa and Puebla and Mexico City— except maybe they came from Spain first. My lineage was supposed to be both, all those places, but it was confused and blurred together.

I was born and raised *pocho*—Americanized—and I didn't know much more about Mexico than most: It was where the people who were cooks, custodians, and construction workers were from, *la gente* who ironed and sewed and served food, who weren't afraid of the daylight sun or the nighttime dark. It was Trio Los Panchos and Vicki Carr and Vicente Fernandez ballads, *tacos y frijoles* and *chile picante* and *con queso,* it was *familias* in parks on the weekend, cooking, and at Mass on Sunday, pretty little daughter in white chiffon dress and glossy black plastic shoes and blue ribbons in the hair, it was a mom with a long *trenza* wearing a flowery pink dress that reached the knees, clutching her baby's hand, a dad behind them with big silver belt buckle, blue jeans, and a western shirt with snap buttons, reptile boots, and straw cowboy hat, looking both sweet and strong.

Mexico was a story to me, one that I knew not like a Mexican novela but like an American comic book: adventure, love, honor, pride, betrayal, *güero y moreno.* It was a bright poster in a Mexican restaurant up the street, from East L.A. to El Paso, and north and south and east and west of those: Bearded *conquistadores* in hot, heavy, mythical armor who sailed tall, wood-planked ships, staring from a sandy beach. *Indios* in linen thongs and leather sandals whose hairless chests pumped *pura vergüenza,* both cultural and racial. Slaves and *doncellas.* Magicians and seers. Gold and feathered headdresses traded for glass beads and shards. Hallucinogenic pyramids and misting volcanoes, hot wet blood and molten lava leaking from them like spit or semen. Cannonballs and spears and swords and shields. The first horses neighing and snorting, and the first big dogs, tongues panting. Kings named Moctezuma and Cuauhtémoc who ruled from an island city with roads and highways of water. Jungle. Heat. Rain. Eagles and cactuses and snakes. A sun who was God.

You have to scratch hard, almost unto a frown. Take a rasp to the imagination and then push the calf into the boot, hard onto the shovel of consciousness, and let it clink against those rocks of desert soil, and pile little and big scoops near the dry hole. In the European West, what you're supposed to dig up is Freudian—an id that is blood-soaked instinct and wild impulse, the machine of love and hate which creates the juice that is genital hormone and pheromone, the party, good sex, danger, crime, and its polar opposite, a superego that is the finicky gourmet of civility and gilded culture, common decency and useful manners, guilt repressed and in tabloids, conscience and reason. But for us there's another suppressed, subconscious drama of duality— Cortés and Malinche, a man and a woman, the Indian and the Spaniard, miscegenous father and mother, the heated and on-the-side mixing, both cultures high and low, both cultures of shame and pride, a sexual energy that is both natural and unforgivable, both a result of dominance that is weak and wrong and submission that is strong and brave, and their reverse; and then there is the blood draining from a convulsing uterus and a stabbed or cut-out heart, and the light skin and the dark skin, and the male and the female, a blue mind's eye and a brown mind's eye, both good, both bad.

Call it Veracruz, not Villa Rica de la Vera Cruz, a humid port of foggy drizzle and coarse sand, the land above its shore as green as mold, as wet as mildew. The hotel has a stinky smell of cheap disinfectant blowing through its air-conditioning ducts. The woman beside me, a *conquistadora* of another sex and land and time, with the Castilian *bola en la boca,* doesn't like the odor. Does Mexico smell like this? Spain does not smell like this. There are too many suitcases, and way too many expectations inside them. No, this is not Spain, I hear in my head, responding, sniffing, suddenly worried about the journey. Until finally in a room, higher up than in the original itinerary, red-tiled floors and a whitewashed *terraza* at eye-level to the bronze dome of the cathedral and the blanched municipal steeple, pigeons, and the blue gulf on the horizon, black ships with long-boom cranes and two tunnels through their guts. As night falls, there on the *zócalo,* the Plaza de Armas, near the yellow and red umbrellas alongside the row of restaurants that front it, where the marimbas range, it's *una noche de danzón.* Fanning themselves, so many are lined up to watch, and to dance as well, but the contestants are on the stage. A handsome *güera,* just a few pounds over her ideal figure, what she was in her twenties but not now, in her late thirties, is in her most beautiful red dress, a white fan, white shoes, a white sash around her waist, and a white flower in her beautiful dark brown hair and she sways, spins, steps, twirls with *el suave,* dark and handsome—his is a white *guayabera* and pants and shoes, his narrow-brimmed fedora hat, white, too, tilted just right—and together they waltz, gentle, calm, sweet, as sensual and aroused as a long, middle-aged love.

   In the morning when you're sitting with *un café lechero,* as you wait to ping-ping your glass for more hot milk and hot coffee,

because this isn't what you're here for, you will have to shake
your head no and show disinterest in so many good people selling shirts, nuts, CDs and tapes, *flores,* dresses, watches, cheese,
cigarettes, *relojes,* toy cars, wood sculptures, fans, more watches—
no to the soft-talking men playing accordions and guitars and no
to the fast-talking women promising to tell your fortune—and
lottery tickets, gum, wooden hairpins and bookmarks and snakes.
Or *por la tarde* on the *malecón,* walking the coastal docks, they are
primordial images from broken and confused dreams or memo-
ries—hefty *conchas* and *caracoles* that you can blow foghorn-loud,
rattlesnake belts and Indian sandals, *Virgenes de Guadalupe* and
Jesucristos in miniature altars of sand and shells that dangle electrical cords, glittery mermaids made out of blond-haired Barbie
dolls, turtles and gators and jaguars, sharks, sea horses, starfish, blow-
fish, squid. Smell the *vainilla* and *tamarindo* and milk and sugar candy
and *puros* of tobacco from the mountains of San Andres de Tuxtla,
and eat juicy mango on a long skewer, cut in peels like an arti-
choke, and sliced coconut, skinned and chopped above a wheel-
barrow of them, shaken up in a plastic bag *con limón y sal y chile.* Sit
by a big fan, button pushed in on high, at La Michoacana for *aquas
frescas* and *paletas: horchata, mango, melon, nancha, jamaica, naranja,
piña, fresa, limón, coco, chocolate, vainilla, nueces.*

In nearby Boca del Rio, at night, you choose to drink Co-
rona or Sol or a *vodka tónico* while you're smoking forbidden
Cuban cigars, those addictive Montecristos, and eat fresh grilled
snapper (Excuse me, but please take the head off so that eye isn't
staring back. The waiter laughs, *¡A su servicio, señor!*). The moon-
light moistens the columns and plastic chairs and broken benches
around the little square at the center of town. Not far away, baby-
blue balloons are hooped as both wedding wreath and tunnel on
a stage that will bring newlyweds to the tall tiered cake. Families
and friends, in a polite whispering, clutter the tables of the unlit
street, blocked off on this tranquil night, not a sound in space

except a marimba group another block down. They are beside the water, and, like a phony postcard, little boats bob in the lapping sea.

Shortly after Cortés first anchored nearby, the rocky island where the Totonacas were living, across from the Malecón, was named San Juan de Ulúa. Soon began its buildup into a thick-walled fortress to guard against pirates and foreign attackers, and then after that it became the home of the most infamous Spanish torture chambers known to man—echoing caves that took on names like *el infierno,* where a man chained and bound would live an endless night, only pitch blackness in his eyesight, driving him both insane and blind; or *la gloria,* where a shackled man could watch a needle of light, enough to cause simple insanity; where a set of humid prison cells leaked rainwater, and where it dripped onto a prisoner's skull clamped against the wall, mosquitoes and flies buzzing, malaria and maggots, and rats biting his toes. It is here that Cortés first became known to the Aztecs, where the emissaries of and messengers for Moctezuma boarded his ship to present gifts to him as Quetzalcoatl, where he shot cannons to show them and their king his ungodly powers.

But Cortés didn't get out of his ship onto Ulúa, did he? Or did he—as a man on that island told you as though it were certain as he was, first stand in his armor where the Burger King is now? That's not the beach described or named in the history books: On 23 *abril* 1519, on *viernes santo,* Good Friday, it is said that he landed on *la playa de* Chalchihuecan, the beach of *la Diosa Color Esmeralda.* Not a historical site anybody you ask will know about or any guidebook will lead you to, and you'll have given up finding where it was and might be when you're driving, fast, north in a rented red VW Bug, *sin clima,* you see an almost hidden sign (which *is* green), pointing east onto a unpaved road. There is a *lonchería* right at the corner, tall logos above its straw roof, Superior, Bohemias, Coca-

Cola. Hand-lettered words outside its patio walls detail the cuisine—*cocteles, pescado y antojitos, caldo de camarón*—and sodas and bottled waters are lined up on a colorful plastic tablecloth, beer in a cooler that isn't cold. King Pinotl, who was the one to welcome Cortés to his land, whose people accompanied him on the conquest of the Aztecs, is a dark, kind, and generous *indio* in a V-neck T-shirt and cotton pants, and he embraces you and the *castellana* you are with as he did Cortés. He runs the stand with his wife, who rocks herself in her chair, knitting in the shade. A family beach, he says. Not so many people go there.

This is not like in the south of Spain, and no she really does not want to go down to that shore. So much black stuff in it! It's a spacious cul-de-sac of beach, a lush arc around it of tall trees. You can see the wooden ships anchored off the shore, and then Cortés is rowed in and he disembarks, and he will trade in that hot shining armor (its glaring brilliance reflecting in the sunlight, what made it so convincing that he was the returned god Quetzalcoatl) for the *mantas de jacales* of these Indians, which is so much cooler. The water is at low tide, and its high tide is marked by a thick, mucky belt of debris, of plastic, labels washed off white and clear and green bottles, hollowed stalks and rusting cans. Close enough, she turns and rushes back, her hands keeping her highlighted hair from tangling up too much in the wind, back up to the tree line—no, she will not feel the Gulf water with her toes, and now the dirty sand is sticking between her pretty red nail-polished toes and Italian sandals—and over to the horse near the tree. Look at it, it is the first horse in the Americas. Full-grown, it is small, and calmer than one in Texas. Relaxed, it's carrying a clean Mexican saddle on its back, unadorned leather flaps and stirrups, seat and horn. She baby-talks the horse in English, petting his nose.

Many signs and guides lead you inland to Antigua, the oldest Spanish settlement in Mexico, its first seat of power here, where Malinche was baptized as the first *amerindia* Christian, where Cortés made his, and their, first home. This must be the first Catholic church, this little one with the thinnest, most modest cross, with the smallest, least intrusive crucified Christ above a *Virgen de Guadalupe* and her altar of roses. Its outside walls and bell tower seem curiously arabesque and not colonial—but why don't you want to take a picture of me ever? So I frame. Her architecture and its, both so physically beautiful, curvy and rounded, both competing to be the center of attention, both deserving it. The little children in white clothes and black hair ask for pesos, and you give them each two. A saddled burro droops on the sidewalk under the green shade beside the haggard Hotel Malinche.

Xalapa, where I was told my specific ancestors began, could be my home. A colonial town, capital of Veracruz state, surrounded by villages of Indian culture that is now called Mexican. It is a short ride from Veracruz city to Xalapa, past many lean-to markets that could be props for visual artists—the hanging vines of ripe *plátano* and grape, the stacks of mango and guava and coconut. Look at the one that is end-to-end giant pods of watermelon! The white-mottled green wholes against the juicy red of those halved and wedged—colors of the Mexican flag. Only a few miles from the coast, you will feel the cool of Xalapa's mountain surroundings, you will see books new and used for sale on the streets—writers from every country, on every subject—and you will be able to watch young, barefoot women dancers flailing in a voodoo hippie dance, while shirtless young men beat handmade drums and cowbells outside a bank. Hear traffic around the center of the city, the whistles of potbellied policemen signaling. Smell coffee being roasted and brewed, the beans from the fields in nearby Coatepec. The streets are on the hills of Xalapa, steep as those in San Francisco, and the narrow sidewalks accommodate them with yards of cement poured so high they're like balconies in front of the homes that front them. Look at the intricate carving in the handsome, oversize wooden doors at almost every entrance, the light-stained and varnished excess of trim around windows. The color of Xalapa is corn yellow and it takes a six-inch border of royal blue—you see it everywhere. As you walk, you will find these colors even on the clay pots and vases for sale that the shy women are painting on their laps, ones just finished, drying on old newspaper on the table in front of them. Walking up and down these streets, if your muscles hurt later, buy and rub on *grasa de coyote,* Mexican Ben-Gayo.

Just before noon, the prettiest lady whose face reminds you of your mom—a dark shorty who's a little heavy, but who cares?—in a white surgical cap and chef's apron arrives with straw baskets to the corner beside the hotel Mesón de Alférez. She sets up a table and opens an umbrella, and people crowd around her. Inside the basket are tacos, three for five pesos, or enchiladas, two pesos each. Tacos are not what you expect in the States. They are fried hard, closed up, different kinds of meat inside, and refried beans are spread on top, and crumbled cheese and a hot sauce if you want (not too hot in Xalapa—even though this is where the word for the *chile* we call "jalapeño" comes from). She pulls out the enchiladas the same way: from a clear plastic bag inside another plastic grocery-store sack inside the straw basket. She peels the number of them ordered from a stuck-together lump and stacks them on strips of wax paper. These aren't fried as crispy as the tacos, and cheese can be rolled inside with the meat, and they are exactly what the word translates, "in *chile,*" and so the tortillas are reddened. You eat both with your fingers, and they're not heated up in a microwave. It is a popular lunch spot, and a crowd layers around her, from important government suits and ties to taxi drivers with holes in their shoes, people who come to eat her food, and not only because it is so cheap.

So you're a *pocho,* right? she asks me in Spanish.

Claro, I affirm. *Mitad taco, mitad hamburguesa.* Half taco, half hamburger.

She laughs at me.

Es que vivo en Tejas, I tell her.

Tejas, she repeats.

Pues sí, the land that they took, I say.

She smiles. And you are with *esa guapa gringa, verdad?* She raises her eyebrows and wiggles her eyes at me, that way people do when they are pleased for you and teasing, too, talking about the bad that is so good.

I nod, smiling back.

¿Por qué siempre tienen ojos azules? she wants me to tell her.

I never thought about the reason they always have blue eyes. I don't know how to answer the question.

As you're thinking about where you would want to live if you lived here, you're taking a bus ride, and you pass fields of corn, a muddy river, and the cows, pigs, chickens, and roosters, pass mounds of dirt for brick or plaster, gravel, rock, stacks of cement blocks, stone, and tile, the men in their *sombreros de paja* and pants hanging low, dragging against the heels of their hard shoes, the women in their aproned housedresses that reach their calves, their long black hair, washed in rainwater, woven into a braid, carrying *paraguas* that can be orange or blue or lavender. Stop to look inside the village of Coatepec's *mercado.* These people will jump away if you try to take a photo of them, even if you are only trying to take pictures of the high mound of red *tomates* against the aqua wall, or of the twenty or more sacks of dried *chiles* or *fideos* or beans or cereals or rice, candies, nuts, *hojas de palma, maguey, papaya, epazote, plátano.* A rainy dew begins to drip onto the landscape as the bus climbs, wipers swinging, to the jungle and forest of Xico, which is up the road. There are dark, tall, and wide clouds ready to unload when you arrive—except above the forested volcano, where a surreal mist hangs close around its flat cap, like it both loves it and is afraid. Xico is the source of the romantic fantasy about the beauty of Mexico. It is the international stereotype of the country's village life, the model of the Mexican culture and society that gets reproduced in the hands-on learning areas of America's children's museums: cobbled streets, banners of *papel picado* tied from one side to the other, wooden balconies, decorative wrought iron, the bright paint and tiled roofs, men riding horses, women patting tortillas, boys and girls playing and riding simple bicycles, sleepy dogs sprawled on the street, cats sunning on windowsills, people leaning out their windows, watching nothing, always saying *buenas tardes* when you pass them.

She's come out of a clothing store shaking her head. A small dark man has stopped to watch her cross the street, his eyes transfixed on her exotic, voluptuous beauty—like a feathered, fertile, blue-eyed goddess from that other land.

There is nothing her size, she says. She has on those Italian leather sandals and a skirt bought in Spain and a low-cut black top, and she is pushing her highlighted hair back.

I say, This is Xico, you know?

I wanted a pair of pants.

But this is Xico.

You don't want to live here, do you?

It is a pretty town, I tease.

Or you're taking a crowded bus—frilled tassels below the driver's rearview mirror, as long as the windshield—to Naulinco. A sincere young boy, a handsome eleven- or twelve-year-old, climbs on board with a guitar, his collarless white shirt buttoned to the top so it's snug on his neck, and he stands in the aisle and waits for the bus to start moving and he sings a *corrido* about *los americanos* and the brave men who fought against them at the border and got away, or a love song, a man full of love for his

woman, dreaming only of sleeping in her arms and the year that
was a day. He sings with passion and resonance that is remark-
able for the contrasting dispassion that is in the faraway of his
face, never looking anyone in the eye, and, no applause, the gentle, business-like sweetness that asks for donations and only nods
when one of the few is accepted. Outside the bus's windows there
are bushes of gaudy pink bougainvillea, and bird-of-paradise
whose yellow-tipped blooms are such a brilliant red that they
seem more like sacred Indian ornaments hung near the waxy,
pale leaves. When you get off the bus, you will have to stop at
the plaza in the center of town. Take a look at the long green
pods—green beans pumped and buffed on steroids. Who has ever
seen these before? What are they? *¡Son jinicuiles!* I make them
say it several times, listening. I've never heard of it. *Jinicuiles.* The
boys who have them for sale, piled on the sidewalk on plastic
cloth, smile and laugh at you. The oldest one shows you how to
crack open a husk at its seam. Inside are a dozen round, fuzzy
white seeds, like misshapen pearls, big as walnuts. The white
around the seed is sugary and juicy. You spit out the hard seed
once you've sucked off the tender white, and you throw down
the empty pod when you're done—they are all over the center
of town where these boys sell them. Then you can go on walking these peaceful mountain streets, smelling oiled leather: boots
in every store. You can walk and see maybe fifty *zapaterías,* more
than half the town, and somebody stooped over, hand-stitching
in each one. *Botas exoticas* in the colors *café, miel, y negra.* Skins
that are python, cow, bull, watersnake, eel, rattlesnake, and even
stomach lining, what we call tripe. They are half as expensive as
any boots you've ever bought, and better-looking and -made than
most, and no sales hustle.

   When you talk about homes, you talk to a young man on
the bus ride away sitting on a metal bench beside yours across
the metal aisle, a gentleman named Abelardo. His wife is young,

they have a newborn, and every day, *ida y vuelta,* he sells *yoghurt* in the *centro* to people who have restaurants—he shows it to you in the tied plastic bags and in two hard plastic paint buckets. He is the proud owner of a *ranchito* with five cows. You will see it. There is the big tree in front. You know his is far from the *hacienda,* known now as the Museo de Muebles, that was home for four-teen years to President Antonio López de Santa Anna. Sofas from France, piano from Germany, English clocks, Japanese lanterns, Russian harp, native wood from Tlacotalpan—legs carved with serpents and eagles or into horse's hooves—and any kind of wood—mahogany, oak, cedar, cherry—and design in the beds and bureaus and chairs and tables. Also every kind of precious metal—copper, gold, silver, and bronze. So many rooms, each too exquisitely furnished to be functional, but it's the luxurious colonial archways, the central patio, the tiled *terrazas,* the taste-ful modesty of the estate, that causes such craving envy.

It's this life you are dreaming of when Alberto, the smiling and genial *gerente* of the restaurant you have eaten at more than once now, approaches you both yet again. He naively thinks you are rich. It is surely because you are with *la guapa gringa.* Her Spanish is so perfect, her looks so *italiana!* Oh yes, Spain must be an impressive country, he says, though, no, no, he has never had the opportunity. He clearly thinks you must be rich to be with her. And—he has a house for sale! You should see the view! Oh, how he loves to go out to his *terraza* and water his plants and flowers there! It is small, yes, but suited perfectly to a young couple—he and his wife, Alma, they are not young, but their children—different marriages—are grown. He wants to manage a restaurant in Cozumel, that world tourist area, as soon as the house sells. There people appreciate the very richest food, Alberto says, especially seafood, which, unlike here, is so plentiful. And you know how much the richest food costs, and there is never anything less than the finest preparations! He himself serves us with the highest manner of manners—taking this particular task away from our waiter simply to honor and impress us.

How could a home cost $90,000 in Xalapa? I ask her when he has to leave for a moment.

Pesos, not dollars, she corrects me.

I have the imaginative capacity to envision a two-bedroom, one-bath hacienda.

When he comes back, he has both directions and caramel-sauced dessert crepes with him, and the next morning we have flagged a cab: Murillo Vidal to Paseo de las Palmas to Cafetales to Pedregal de las Animas. Turn near TV Azteca, and on the street that is a *privada* . . . Is that a wealthy neighborhood? I ask the taxi driver. He's an older man, his gray hair a little tousled out of its own independence. The governor lives there, he says dryly, which means it's not the district of the poor. And when we approach it, passing Xalapa's newest, most modern shopping mall, it looks that way: ranch-style houses, mansions, estates—maybe even haciendas. But we go on, making turns, crossing riverlike streams and pondlike puddles that take over after the asphalt has ended. Driving slowly, avoiding puncturing rocks on the narrow road. Asking this one walking if he might know where this particular *privada* is, and then asking that one walking with an open wooden box of tools. He points uphill.

Alberto is angry with the taxi driver because we are late. Disgusted and ashamed of this lowly wage earner. It's easy to find, he snaps, shaking his head. But Alberto is ecstatic to see us. *¡Pasen, pasen!* he says as we pass through a gate. It is a small house. Smaller even than that. And it is gray, as gray as this day is gray, as gray as cinder block. Unpainted cinder block. This hacienda is not painted. Maybe seven thousand, or six, or even less, I whisper. Alma greets us through a crack of the front door, holding back *los perros bravos*. She yells at Beto that he has to take care of them, quickly, and he squeezes through the door. They are German shepherds that seem as big as the first horse we saw on the beach of Chalchihuecan. Alma sweeps us in once they are barking ferociously around the corner, to what she is calling the living room. A sofa and a stuffed chair are arranged curiously—they don't fit the small space. We turn the corner in maybe three paces. And see, inside the mouths of their doggies, their yellowing, salivating incisors. Their claws dig rabidly into the slippery cement floor, and yet somehow they get enough traction and continually leap at us, their necks jerked back at the pull of leash and collar, their eyes on our throats. Alma screams at Beto, who has been straining to hold them back, to take them outside, and he obediently does. Which creates immediate, soft-sell real estate serenity again, and now she can show us the features of the kitchen. They have tiled the counter. They will certainly go ahead and put doors on the cabinets if we buy the house. And replace the faucets. And finish the trim around the windows. And paint. Whatever color we want, we just tell them! They both lead us up the curved, rail-less cement stairs. The upstairs stinks of wet, snarling dogs, too. The so-called large bedroom is big enough only for a *cama matrimonial,* a vanity, a chest of drawers. And there is that *terraza,* on the other side of the sliding door, which they will fix too. To admire *las vistas,* I step outside, and *la guapa* does, too. We both fit if we stand shoulder to shoulder and stay away from the pots whose brown stems seem dead enough. Across the street to the left is an unfinished edifice, not abandoned at all, rusting rebar that limps and sags, wilted, from the two rows of block. To the right is something finished, the oldest house in the neighborhood, a three-story, each lower tier larger than the one above, each level painted another hideous color, and a massive, teetering television antenna centered at its apex. Its architectural influence would seem to be the Gestapo Tower period. It is a friendly neighborhood, Alma reminds us from the indoor side of the sliding glass. One step back and we, too, are inside. Alberto wants to talk about how, if we are interested, to transfer funds. He means ninety thousand American.

A month before he arrived in Veracruz, Cortés navigated his ships into Tabasco. Already on board was a Spaniard named Jeronimo de Aguilar, a priest found weeks earlier in the Yucatán who had survived a crash and lived with the Indians for ten years and wanted desperately to return to Spain (another man, a sailor who had survived along with him, preferred to continue living *"la vida salvaje"*). Aguilar spoke their language, and because of him, Cortés gained intelligence about the ruling Aztecs from the Indians of this region. As they followed the river inland, the Spaniards both conquered and made allies, gave and received gifts—such as twenty *doncellas,* one of whom was named Malintzin—that is Malinche, the mother of mestizo Mexico. Very little is known of her history. What is heard is a conflicting fable, at once the story of a highly intelligent woman who was also a slave, both *puta* traitor and gutsy survivor: sold at least twice, first by her father—maybe a *cacique* from a distant village, though maybe not—and then again by *nahua* tradesman from Xicalanco, and then yet again, until she was passed on to the Spaniards. She lived with Cortés and gave birth to his child, named Martín (a child never legally recognized as his, and doubly disrespected when Cortés's legal wife bore him another son and named him Martín). Malinche eventually married another Spanish soldier, Juan de Jaramillo, who traveled with Cortés.

Don't I have to go see, with my own eyes, where Cortés first met Malinche? Much like the Chalchihuecan beach, it's not easy to figure out the exact location, not a place that any state tourist agency seems to be aware of or any guidebook locates, but on my own I have enough—somewhere on the Río Grijalva. To get there, you have to go to Villahermosa, the capital of Tabasco, Mexico's petroleum state, otherwise made infamous by Graham

Greene's *The Power and the Glory* as the hot, mosquitoed jungle that God cannot tame. Of course you can still fly there (the city came into existence when a landing strip was built for oilmen), but now you can also take one of three classes of bus. The finest, the UNO, brags that its seats recline into beds—*asiento tipo cama*. It's the most expensive ride, but no matter what, it's cheap, lots cheaper than any flight. And it's all night, so no hotel charge either. A deal.

It is a ship ride in the night, bounce and sway, slowing down for the *topes* that seem half a bowling ball big, speeding by the bogged-down trucks with the highway divider lines passing under the middle, inches from trucks and cars going the other direction, the moon, almost full, racing alongside in pursuit, slicing through the blotchy clouds. When the sun dawns yet again, she says she is miserable, sighing—couldn't sleep, such a horrible night. Says she will never do this again, never. It is hot in the bus terminal, it is humid outside, it is more the Villafea, of slobbering men and lewd whistling. Not the expensive cab ride to *très* chic, escalatored Liverpool Mall in search of a tourist bus or agent advice, not the espresso coffee there, not even a visit to a clothing store to look again, for a long time, for *pantalones*. She is sighing. Everywhere a fever of people who don't know, who can't help, who do not. She says, I do not want to do this again. Not the waiter who serves us as though he were a decorated colonel, both too haughty and too obsequious. Not the food that stinks rancid.

Back at the depot, I stop a cabdriver. His name is José, and he says we will drive—a road that disappears during the rains— along the Río Grijalva until we reach the Boca de Chilapas, which is where the road will end. He has no bloody heart of Jesus hanging from a chain on the mirror. No Guadalupe magnet on the dashboard. Not one biblical event recognized on the windshield. No tassels off the headliner. No baby pictures clipped to the ashtray. He doesn't wear dark glasses.

Passing piles of dirt and sandbags, passing the indistinguishable building construction or demolition, passing by the traffic cops and through the acrid scent of roasting tires and plastic— any border-town Mexico, the unromantic ugliness of Mexico, that gray exhaust fume of rattling automobiles and sleaze bars and shrieking *música norteña* or heavy metal. But then the asphalt does end, and a clay dirt, wet, begins to spray José's white cab like cake frosting. And suddenly the light, that light that pours into your eyes, turns green. It is the jungle of *la región de los ríos*. This is where its Indian inhabitants—in Tamulte de las Sabanas and Buena Vista—are against the government and the government is against them. Taxes are too high, José explains, so they don't pay them, and the government offers no services. Dodge the potholes in the reddened road, from one side to another. *Venta de pozol masa, abarrotes y verduras, tortitas de chayote.* Wood burning, meat smoking. *Chozas,* brown jungle houses of dried bamboo and palm, which are beside the everywhere around spindly, olive-green stalks, and leaves so soaked they're too heavy to fan out. Mud houses, block houses, wood houses, all with corrugated tin roofs. Black mama pigs, teats full, cross the road like arthritic retirees. Horses, dogs, chickens, ducks. Roosters strutting. *Vacas* and *becerros* chew the grass meadows of the wide *pantano.* Swarms of white butterflies swirl above yellow and purple flowers. An iguana waddles into the bush. Trees whose wild branches seem snapshot-frozen in a torrential wind, trees like oak, like acacia, like mesquite, trees that are *coco* and *guayabo.*

The red road dies at a metal gate that looks like any ranch gate, beyond it parallel tire ruts that have torn out the grass on toward the horizon. The Grijalva is to the side. It's a wide, fast-moving river, sparkling like polished sterling at one angle, fertile brown at another. To go to the proverbial other side, a two-person wooden *barquita* is tied to the shore. There is an intense buzz of insects, flies that test the human body. There is a hoot that is not an owl's, a coo that is not a *gavillón*. Echoing plops of overripe mangoes dropping onto the juicy soil.

It seems so simple and ordinary on the road back—already seen. Both directions her head has rested against the bench back-seat, dozing, bored, her eyes only half opening at a here or there. But suddenly she sits up and goes into her purse. She pulls out a compact and lipstick. Lifts her Gucci shades to the top of her head, tucking back her hair. She squints into the tiny mirror and makes that putting-on-the-makeup face, touches a pad near her eyes with some powder. She pencils dark cherry around the border of those full, gorgeous lips, and then fills in the pucker with a fashionable burgundy, and rolls them against each other and smacks. Right behind her, I see the very *selva* where *la india* Malinche first and forever was joined with *el español* Cortés. It's why I journeyed here, to colorize my dreaming, images, and story. Done, she rests the Guccis back on her sexy nose and shuts her blue eyes once again and leans back with a resigned, silent sigh—only another few hours here.

Mexico City, the capital of the *mexicas* or Aztecs, was supposed to be an island city of trade canals cut through it, *chinampas,* so spectacular that when Cortés arrived in it, these Europeans, standing at the height of the Templo Mayor, the sacrificial site of the rulers, never could have imagined its luxury and splendor, an *indio* Venice. Like the central pyramid which was flattened by the Spaniards, its stones spread out into what is now that massive *zócalo* and into the walls of the great cathedral, the ruins of what canals are left are like gutters. And if you never went to Xochimilco, you might never conceive of what it looked like: on its banks, the *zacate* grass grows tall beneath the *ahuehuete* trees, the oldest in Mexico, and gardens of azalea, *belem,* gardenia, begonia, even *orquídea,* and dogs everywhere watching over it all. The *lanchas* are colored rainbow, red yellow blue, and a curled painted sign, a cartoon of plumage and flags above, labels each uniquely—Maria Fernanda or Carmelita or Daniela or Isabel Cristina. A man pushes you up and down the calm water with a *remo de pino* as you sit at the long, cabana-covered picnic tables and chairs that are the brightest red, drinking beer you bought at the docks, while merchants float up beside you selling *carne y mixiote, maíz* roasted on the cob, or *esquite,* kernels of it in a styrofoam cup seasoned with salt and *chile* and *epazote* and lime. Flowers are sold, as are tacos and candied apples and shelled seeds and nuts and bonzai plants, and jewelry and serapes, blankets and toys. You can buy tequila bottled in the hooved foot of a real cow. Or hire a band floating by who will rope their boat to yours for any number of songs—mariachi, marimba, *norteña, saltiero y acordeón.*

If the Templo Mayor was once the highest point in the king-dom, both in altitude and metaphorically, as the peak of the blood-spilling religion whose gods and priests were unmistakably men, it is on the exact same plot of land where the goddess Tonantzin was once worshiped that the spiritual heart of Mexico now pumps what is a mestizo blood, the place that is the Basilica of the Vir-gin of Guadalupe. It is only a short ride from the *zócalo,* but when you get off at the Cuatro Caminos stop, it is confusing to know which way to go. A young man who had been standing next to you on the subway offers to guide your transfer to the Basilica stop. He is relatively tall, light-skinned enough to be a Chicano from Califas. He wears a white T-shirt and blue jeans and a black *cachucha* with a "World Champion New York Yankees" logo on it. Quiet, obviously too gentle, you have to stand somewhat closer to him so you can hear him. You don't want to ask his name, whether it's Juan or Diego, and so you don't. Seventeen, he is finishing his diploma, and he wants to go on and be a petroleum engineer. Of course, you say, and you nod, yes, and you say, how good, how smart. You walk together, turning here and there through and in streams of people moving, few words, until he leaves right there, nodding to your thanks, gracious beyond his years.

You are pushing forward through a small mob to where the signs direct you when a small woman shoulders up to both of you, her hair as white as bleached sugar. She tells you that you have to put away your camera better, tells her she should carry her purse in front of her, because there are people here who will take them. She says this as you are still walking, and as she is walking, too, and as old as she is, you have to keep up with her and still she is always a half-pace ahead, and because of that you cannot even see her face except as a glance while you step left and you step right. She is dressed like a nun, or a retired school-teacher, or a nurse, or a grandmother—hard black shoes and white socks, a white blouse that is up to her neck, a black skirt and loose black sweater. Her calves are muscular, pale but not white or brown. You are going to the Basilica, aren't you? she asks, moving briskly. She asks where you are from and you tell her. She has family in Laredo, and outside Dallas and in New Mexico, and in Africa, and in India, and in South America, and everywhere in Mexico. She is a *religiosa,* she says, from a family of *religiosos.* You are walking through a narrow passage with vendors on either side selling rosaries and candles and red roses, paper and plastic and real, and, of course, images of the *Virgen de Guadalupe* on any and every kind of box and jar and cup, pot and glass and mirror and chain, in frames of gold and silver and wood. The old woman never looks up. The new Basilica is ahead, and she is willfully leading the way, pushing, not letting you stop, no commercial distraction allowed. So much *basura* wherever you look and on every side, she tells you as you cross through the Basilica's gates. Trash, she repeats, shaking her head. And she keeps on walking so fast, always that little bit ahead—I will show you where, she says—and into the church itself and to the left, to the side of the main altar and an ongoing Mass, until there you are standing with her on a gliding electric platform, and above is Our Lady of Guadalupe, the blue mantel, the gold frame, the real image and not all the replicas and reproductions that you have forever seen. As your eyes lock on it, you are choking up in some unexplainable way, maybe from the shock of this unexpected experience, and you have coasted to the other end, and so you have stepped off to stare at the Virgin, to make sure, and you read: "¿ . . . no estoy yo aquí / soy tu madre. . . ?" Am I not here, am I not your mother? For the first time, the anciana has stopped, too, but at the opening of another hallway over there, so that you can see her old face even if it's at a distance, and she is look-ing back at you, and she seems pleased. You look away and up for only a moment, since you have selfishly stepped onto the gliding platform once more, and when you look back, she has disappeared without you ever thanking her.

El Paso

A few weeks ago, I got a note from a magazine editor in Houston. She'd read something I'd written, liked it, and wondered, as she put it, why anyone with any sense was living in El Paso. . . . A few days ago, I was up in Albuquerque, wandering in and out of bookstores, almost breathless with culture shock. A friend, a native of Roswell, said, "I grew up thinking El Paso was the big city, and you're telling me the only bookstores there are in *malls*?" . . . The phone rings, and it's another friend who's in Los Angeles. "How's life in the pachuco barrios?" he asks, thinking I'm some kind of exile living on the meanest of the Chicano mean streets, which, I'm sure, he imagines to be unpaved dirt, lined with pink brothels and all-night bars and bad-ass cholos and their rucas who lay claim to most of it.

I like to run up and down the bleachers at Austin High School (like? I *do* it), which is almost my backyard. I especially like it when I'm done and I can stretch out on the topmost aluminum bench. Both the Franklins and the Sierra Madres are so much more intimate from this height, and the city, and Juárez—indistinguishable from up here—look so innocent and plain under all the expanse. Below me, coaches, men and women ones, have the stopwatches running. The girls in the middle of the football field are stretching

their legs, and the boys at the opposite end of the track are splay-
ing over low hurdles. There's another field below, and the baseball team is there. I can hear the tang of ball against metal bat. At
the other end of that field, my oldest son is playing soccer with his
team, and I'm on the watch for the two new boys from Hondu-
ras, who, claims the coach, will make them unbeatable. Then I
see my baby boy, four years old, coming over to find me. He goes
through the maze and tangle of the basketball and handball courts
and players, disappears behind the rock wall—*these,* rock walls, are
El Paso—on one side of the tennis courts, then I see him again,
on the mesh-fence side of the courts, then he's through the gate
and onto the track. Nobody objects to him—*that* is El Paso. A girl
he bumps into rubs his head, and he rounds the rim of the outside
lane, where runners and coach practice the baton pass. And there
he is at the bottom of the bleachers looking up at me. Hey!

It's all-America, except El Paso does not belong to the
United States. Don't misunderstand. It doesn't belong to Mexico,
either. Nor does El Paso reside in the Great State of Texas. *We
all know that.* We hear those senators in Austin chuckling when
they decide a nuclear dump forty miles away from us is just *the*
perfect location. Teeheehee, snarksnark. And so we vacation on
the West Coast. The San Diego Zoo. Universal Studios.

And now New Mexico wouldn't have us. Too late. They
don't even want to share water. Get your own river! *Jajajojo*
(they're bilingual there).

El Paso's the best of Mexican culture: moms, dads, brothers,
sisters, babies, the cuñados and suegros, compadres and comadres.
Grandfathers teach Spanish proverbs. Grandmothers walk children to school. Drivers go slow. In those big American cars. Even
in the trucks. In life, too. But these are los estados: hear the rock
music in that car cruising by? See that glow of television against
that wall? Look—Burger King, Mac's, even Taco Bell! Yech. But
lots of places to rent movies (only American-made ones), and
JCPenney, Sears, Pic 'N' Save. Over at the Safeway on the west

side, they sell California wine (the *smaller* bottles), and French coffee beans, and English tea (who buys that?).

A guy comes to my door. He's my age. Mid-thirties. He asks if I could give him some help, he needs to get back across. Formal Spanish. Respectful. A few weeks ago, two teenage girls asked me the same thing. I got the jumper cables. Exactly what? I ask him. Money? Please, he says. I give him two dollars. The boy with him, maybe four, or five, maybe he's six, he clutches a sweater he has on, stretching the fabric, staring at me.

My next-door neighbor sometimes talks to me in English, as if I don't know any Spanish, and sometimes in Spanish, as if I don't know any English. One time his son (I think he is—my neighbor has all these young dudes with "the look" hanging out in front of his house: they wear baggy gray plaid shirts buttoned to the top and baggy black pants) came over to ask if it was all right if he parked a car on the dirt part of our front yard. Just for a little bit while they worked on this other car. They have a few cars parked off the curb next door. Of course I didn't mind.

It gets hot in El Paso. In case you didn't know that. Windy sometimes, too. That blows the pollution away. (Too much pollution: Juárez? Spend a day there. Watch those cars. Think what would happen to *your* brain if you slept in that exhaust. Think about your brain if you had no choice but to own that car. It's another reason you'd move across, too.) But sometimes that wind gets bad. Maybe you heard that. Did you hear about the snow? Sometimes it snows. Kids break out the carrot noses and tomato eyes and throw snowballs. Until their hands get cold. Nobody thinks of gloves around here.

When the poet Denise Levertov came to town, it was decided that a party for her shouldn't be *open* to just *anyone* who might dress any old way. So an invite list to the Paso del Norte Hotel was made; it excluded, omitted the wrong kind. Nobody around here seemed to think that was anything to get too upset about.

Easter Sunday I got to see Jorge de Jesus "El Gleason" at the Plaza Monumental. The guy is nuts. I swear I saw him get gored by that one bull, and I *did* see that bull's hind leg jack his head when he fell under. The cockfight season is back, too. I hear they're having some in . . . better not say where, because it might be an illegal site.

So why do the best people have to leave El Paso? A friend of mine, an ironworker, was foreman on a project. He made $9 an hour. When they got to the end of the job, with a week or so of spot welding to go, the company laid him off and kept the guy they could pay $4.50 an hour. I recently did a job, carpentry, for $6 an hour. Why $6? "I asked around," this guy tells me (he's a nice guy, too), "and I heard I could get a carpenter for from $4 to $6 an hour, and I took the top figure." It was an office remodel. Somebody before me framed it up. Everything was out of plumb. I had to custom-hang three doors. For his interior walls, I used the best redwood tongue and groove available, at a dollar-fifty a foot, about 1,450 feet worth. Just think if I'd cut that wood as lousy as the walls were framed. I needed the money anyway. When I really need it, I go out of town, where I am paid what I'm worth.

I hear the bugle playing "Taps" at night. Fort Bliss. And the train. Pounding the earth. It's dark. Real dark. Lotsa stars. You should get up on my roof and sit for a while (the ladder I borrowed is still there. I just replaced the pads in the swamp cooler). Now *that's* something! The city lit up like the sky.

Can't forget Chico's Tacos on Dyer Street. Extra cheese is fifteen cents. Burgers for a dollar. So what if the buns are a little stale sometimes. The jukebox is always going, and dress any way you want (GI, biker, teenybopper, badass, sexy, fat), and it's open late. I like the menudo from the bakery on Fort. Think we'll go get some tomorrow. I guess I'm hungry.

Vaya con Dios,
Rosendo Juarez

By now you've heard about a new cop show on TV, set here in El Paso, called *Juarez*. I knew a few months ago, when I got a phone call from a Hollywood producer. I learned that ABC and Columbia Television had paid for six episodes. Three were written, three were not. The question put to me: how would I like to write one or two, maybe three if things worked out?

Now, the first thought you have, if you're anything like me, is how it is that Hollywood decides to call anyone. Like, how this Gilb? Has he ever done this stuff? A screenwriting class in L.A., or at some university, and he was recommended? Or he's related to someone? Or has biggie connections?

Once upon a time, I was only a carpenter living in Los Angeles who, unemployed at that moment, liked to read books and write. A few of my stories had been published in the San Francisco area and in New Mexico, but in Lalaland, I was an employed or unemployed carpenter who read the L.A. *Herald* in either case. On Fridays, there was this special weekend section. It had a column called "Required Reading," and it was about any book, usually fiction, that a writer thought was underappreciated or forgotten. A great idea, but the ones selected, in my opinion, were always the usuals (find them at any chain bookstore). So just before I pack my things to move back here to El Paso, I decide to choose what I thought to be fine short-story collections, by fine writers I knew to be unread in the big cities. The editor says no, that the column is written by newspaper staff and there's no money for outsiders. I say I'll just send it, and if she doesn't like the piece, she can throw it away. I write for about two hours, then drop it in the mail.

Three days later, she calls back. She liked it, the book-review editor liked it, the paper will print it, I'll get fifty dollars. Which was the second most money I'd ever gotten through writing, the first being a hundred and fifty, which I received a month before for a short story a Sunday-newspaper magazine was publishing. Which, to this day, is still the most I've been paid for writing. Fifty dollars is currently the third most I've ever received. Still, she apologizes about it being so little.

We talk on the phone a couple of times after that, and one day we decide to meet in Venice, California, where she lives. We drink coffee in one of those cafés you see in lots of TV and film clippage, outside at a table with one of those umbrellas, in an area fenced in but with a good view of the chic and not so chic who share the cliché boardwalk with the rollerskaters, bike pedalers, dog walkers, oglers and ogled, clothed and not so clothed, people with cameras of all shapes and sophistication. We have a nice time, and become friends, sending a postcard now and then, placing a phone call.

This summer, when I went back out from El Paso to find some construction work, she offered me her apartment my first days there while she took a deserved vacation to float on a river. The night before she left, she apologized for being in such a rush and unable to offer something interesting, but the most important item on her to-do list was laundry. And her best friend owned a washer and dryer, which beat going to a Laundromat. I didn't have to go with her, she told me. But it was okay with me, I

didn't mind in the least, couldn't think of anything else in particular I wanted to do. It wasn't like my first visit to L.A., and I
enjoyed her company.

Her best friend's husband was a producer of a TV show that
was going off the air. I watched a hockey play-off or championship game—it didn't mean a lot to me, and I don't know much
about the sport—with him and a friend of his who soon left. I'd
asked him about film rights, because a year earlier, a Hollywood
company had shown some interest in my book thanks to a review
that had appeared; nothing came of it, but I continued to wonder about it, and now he explained to me what kind of money
they probably would have offered if. After that we sat in their
beautiful living room with some artist friends of theirs who'd
dropped in, Europeans, and drank a liqueur (I think) from Germany (I think), which was a first for me and I don't remember
the name of now. For me it was all a pretty unique experience.
Not my usual crowd. It was nice. The next day I passed a copy
of my little book on to him through his wife. As thanks for the
Hollywood info that no one else had been able to give me.

The guy who called me about this new TV show, *Juarez,*
was that man. Simple as that.

So, sure, I was interested. Who wouldn't be? And I was
especially so because I like TV. And I love cop shows. *Dragnet,
The Untouchables, Baretta, Kojak,* even *Quincy.* The stupider they
are, the more I seem to like them—if, that is, they aired a few
years. I do like the better-quality, more recent ones, like *Hill Street
Blues, Magnum, P.I.* Don't like *Miami Vice* much. Even with Eddie
Olmos. Too sincerely cool for me. But whatever. The fact was
that I could make more money on one screenplay than I probably would from two novels. And two weeks (I figured) (confidently) versus one or two years per book, if published by a major
house. Hollywood is often considered a death trap for many
would-be real writers (nonhacks), but I was willing to test my

soul. So it was arranged that I would pick up the script for the pilot episode at the El Paso Film Commission, chamber of commerce complex.

In case you haven't noticed, every show, especially cop ones, has a hook for those of us who have nursed off the boob, to accept that this one doesn't sound so different than that one, even when the story lines are, if not exactly the same, very very similar. So Kojak had a bald head, was ugly, did good with satin ladies. Columbo was a funny-eyed goof. Frantic Quincy wasn't exactly a cop. Cagney and Lacey were women and didn't have jiggling breasts.

Now guess what the hook for *Juarez* is: Juarez—Rosendo Juarez—is a young El Paso detective married to a beautiful woman, Marielena. His brother, Vicente, drives a Porsche convertible, has a fast-looking girlfriend, a questionable means of support. The show opens a hundred miles south of El Paso, in Mexico, at a fenced-in ranch where these two brothers have capes (don't laugh) and, as the script puts it, while "bringing a severe formality to the endeavor," do their toro-toros with a young bull. Onlookers, natch, are pretty impressed. Cut to Interior Shot, Cantina, Night, where you can "almost smell the tequila." Rosendo and Vicente, a touch socked, are at it again, playing matadores. The cape is a young woman's sweater, and she's right over there cheering them on. In (what else?) a black lace bra.

Mexicans. Or Mexican-Americans, Chicanos. That is, *Hispanics* are the hook. Look at it this way—the movie *La Bamba* was a big hit. Los Lobos' music plays on every radio station, singing rediscovered Richie Valens. The demographics are right, since southwestern "Hispanics" are populating so rapidly. And so *Juarez* will make this great Saturday-night show since, as a producer told a newspaper reporter here, "research shows Hispanics watch a lot of television then."

So maybe that ain't so bad. You take what you get, make the best of it, right?

I read on (admittedly, two to five pages a day is all my temperament can take and I'm real glad that a meeting planned for a few days after I pick up the script is postponed, as it turned out, two straight weeks). I overlook the cop parts that I find improbable, like a young thief carrying a gun and, "exploding" through a "window" (not in any houses I've ever lived in; I even call and ask an ex-cop friend, and we laugh), or the silly characterizations of our main heroes, those crocodile sentiments of Marielena holding an empty silk jewelry box that had a grandmother's ring and a necklace her husband gave her Christmas last, or the noble, quiet solemnity of Rosendo as he deals with this situation—it reads to me as though his house has been burned, or his wife raped, or a cross is burning on the front lawn.

HARRISON

How's your wife?

JUAREZ *tenses, looks back.*

JUAREZ

She's fine.

HARRISON *waits for a real answer. Then:*

JUAREZ

It shook her up pretty bad.
You know how women are.

HARRISON *nods sympathetically.*

HARRISON

Tell me about it.

This tragic assault on his home and wife and, no less, his profession. It's TV, after all. And maybe people like this do exist in somebody's neighborhood, in some cop precincts. I figure this stuff is not my business, and I figure the sappier the premise is, the easier it'll be to write down without thinking too much. And honestly, how could I not want to write that scene where our hero goes into the lieutenant's office yelling? So fun! But what I do have to think about is this, uh, *Hispanic* thing. There are certain things I don't think are exactly right. Not just personally, mind you, but factually. Not that there aren't a few things that I could personally disagree with, too. The embattled minority attitude, for example, that our hero is presumed to have, combined with factual misinformation that is summed up in one scene—an unspoken but visual statement that I believe is the theme of the show—early on:

> *Ext. South El Paso—day*
> Juarez cruises through the barrio. Like most unmarked police cars, the one Juarez drives wouldn't be any more obvious if it were gold-plated. The reactions are mixed: sullen defiance or studied disregard. If, as a Hispanic, he's still not fully appreciated in this country, he's even less tolerated here, where his authority, more often than not, is viewed with contempt. It's not an area of the city any cop likes to visit, and no less hostile toward a Hispanic cop than a white.

In some general, sociological way, there's truth in what is said here. It happens to be more and less accurate in different parts of the country. And though a police officer's awareness, even that of twenty-seven-year-old Detective Rosendo Juarez, who is bright and speaks English well, enough to pass the proper exams, might *might* be somewhat focused on not being accepted in the country—this is, remember, a *cop* we're talking about, not even a doctor or lawyer, where other things do often enter in—it's certainly not as true, especially these days, in El Paso as it might be in a city like Los Angeles, where racial battles are much more complicated. El Paso is a Chicano town, and Mexican-Americans are the majority, as everyday as going outdoors. It's also true that when it comes to stories in print and on-screen, I'd rather disagree with this attitude—I prefer to let the real racial problems stay with political activists; to assume, though it's not yet historically true even in this town, that the racial war is over and Chicanos have won the revolution, are or will be the chiefs of police, mayors, governors, doctors, superintendents, teachers, managers, union leaders, workers, immigrants, undocumented aliens, unemployed, undereducated, poor, all good (just, honest, etc.) and bad (unjust, dishonest, etc.), mothers and fathers, daughters and sons, and then to write human stories for others as human beings, not to score points with or to make stabs at and only at Anglo America.

But maybe it's just me, and mine's not this kind of approach. So grant that this other way of looking at it is okay, right even. But still, it's not accurate here in El Paso that a Hispanic cop is "even less tolerated" on the streets. By whom? By these "South" El Pasoans? The truth is that people who dislike cops don't dislike them because of their race but because of their uniform, period, and these "barrio" (always use this word to bring out the dark exotic, to foreignize and isolate) people on the south side are no different.

Yet the implication of this TV episode is otherwise. Juarez's criminal brother, Vicente, is a symbol of, a foil for, this racial sell-out to the white man's, Anglo-American's, authority. An associate of Vicente's in a Mafialike crime organization, Cergio [sic], makes this clear:

CERGIO

Can you remember when you and Vicente played
here? How long ago was that, Rosendo? Twenty

years? I was young, too. I owned the store across the
street. You and your brother would come in for
candy if you had a few pennies, and sometimes even
if you didn't. Do you remember those days? There
was the border at the river, and there was the other
border, just there, across the park [meaning "The
South Side," between Mexico and the Americanized
world]. And we lived in between, almost all of us.

(*pause; then*)

Do you think it's changed so much in twenty years?

A pause. Then;

JUAREZ
I've changed.

CERGIO *nods his agreement. Then, with an odd smile:*

CERGIO
I think maybe I liked the young Rosendo better.
At least then I knew what he wanted, and what
made him happy.

The implication then is simple. Rosendo Juarez, this "Hispanic,"
this Chicano, is an exception in that he's *not* a criminal. And so
this "south-side barrio" seemingly teems with people disapprov-
ing of Juarez, or, as we will see it again later, when he drives
into the "deeper" sections of the neighborhood, "we can sense
and see the hostility, now even more tangible, more threaten-
ing, as the car is recognized for what it is, and the driver [Juarez]
looked upon with a dark anger, usually but not always silent."
    That this does not depict people who really do live in South
El Paso isn't even important, because this is not about just them,
the facts of their neighborhood. This, remember, is a program

for and about "Hispanics." It is the first "dramatic Hispanic television show ever," a producer boasts to an El Paso newspaper.
"We're trying very much not to make this a cop show, but a
people show."

Other things keep sticking in my mind, too. The bullfighting. The whorehouse, the tequila, the black lace bra. That in El
Paso there are cantinas, not bars. The mariachi (meaning "Mexican") music. The excessive use of *kemosabe* language and speeches
to indicate the character is more Mexican, less American. The
word drops: *amigo, m'ijo* (one man to another), *hermano, carnal*
(though in the script it is *carñal;* for me the *ñ* was a more accurate
pronunciation). Or this speech, by Juarez's best buddy on the
force, Bobby Carillo [*sic*], while he has our hero down in a wres-
tling workout: "Now I got everything a good Mexican boy needs.
I got a brown house, a blond wife, a blue pickup, a white pit
bull, and a best friend with a red face."

And I don't think it's just my sense that this story, though
set here in El Paso, could have been set in just about any reputed
"Hispanic" city close enough to the border—San Diego, Tucson,
Phoenix, Laredo. I don't think there's any feel of El Paso, any
awareness of its distinctiveness. I think the premise is that all the
cities are similar in their Mexican-Americanhood, that one place
where these people are is very much like the next place. Since the
producers seem to want it all in one stroke, it's not at all contra-
dictory that the parents of Detective Juarez live a hundred miles
south of the city, on a large ranch in an extremely comfortable
home (happy *familia* heritage), after having grown up in the criminal
slums of the worst part of town (toughening poverty). This "all-
in-one" is even more pronounced when the dead body of the show
is found. It is a fisherman's son from Mazatlán—a picture of him
standing near a marlin is produced—and Juarez learns that the
young man's mother, Beatriz Cammarota [*sic*], is a maid working
in a suburban El Paso neighborhood. It is extremely unlikely

that a woman from Mazatlán would cross the Texas/Mexico part to enter the United States (she would have gone to California). Mexico is not One Country whose people cross this One Border, its people and entry points are not as singular as the word "Mexican." People there don't migrate with the same thought pattern that Americans do to vacation.

Okay, so maybe I'm being too hard on the show, and maybe it's simply an example of the sensationalism that TV probably requires for success. Good drama often uses extreme situations. The intention of the series is certainly not mean or ugly. I mean, Detective Juarez is written as a good man, a believer in law and order, upstanding, decent, noble. And it's true that there are problems like this in the Mexican-American community, in almost every one in the Southwest, in El Paso. There is racial awareness, a sense of isolation from mainstream America. It's possible that this issue, in a dramatic sense, is an important one to consider. And the show will surely be watched religiously by many who will in fact be happy to see Hispanics in a television series. The city of El Paso and the chamber of commerce certainly like the idea of it, as does the local news media, both print and TV. And it *is* about time this area of the country got some attention, that El Paso did, and attention is money, better incomes for its residents, more opportunities, all those paybacks that make for a more comfortable life. This city has a long, proud, and unrecognized history that reaches back to the Spanish explorers and into the history of Mexico, back to the American West, from Apache Indian raids on settlers to Billy the Kid and John Wesley Harding. And it is about time that Mexican-Americans, "Hispanics," are considered a real and regular part of the United States, and television is probably the quickest place for this truth to sink in.

Besides, who am I to criticize? What do I know? How do I know more about what's what than anyone else? It's certainly true, and has been pointed out to me often in my life, that I am not some archetypical Chicano. And even if my name weren't Gilb, if my father weren't Anglo (German descent), if my mother were some traditional exemplar of idyllic Mexican-American culture (divorced on her initiative, and in the fifties). Maybe I don't know what I'm talking about. Shouldn't it come from someone who is more racially pure, more representative?

So who would know? What, for instance, is the necessary ethnic experience? Luis Valdez made Richie Valens's family farmworkers in the movie *La Bamba,* though Valens's mother actually did urban work. Is he saying that citified Mexican-Americans have lost touch with their roots, have blended in too much with commercialized, nondenominational values? Maybe authenticity should be based on descent lines. Not too much *indio,* not too much Spaniard. Or based on language. More Spanish-oriented, less English-speaking; or the opposite, the more English-acquired. Second generation but not third. Poor parents, but maybe this person should be middle-class, educated. So as to have perspective, but not an overly wealthy one. Or maybe it ought to be a unique, model individual, not of any mold at all. Democrat? Or Republican? Or ex–Brown Beret, or Green Beret, or I can think of a poet or two who would have some interesting ideas. From Texas or California?

Yet it's almost a truism that visitors have seen more of the country than natives ever will. So why not an interested Anglo? A sociology professor. Anthropology or history. A journalist. An artist. A photographer. Or Hollywood people. Why not?

All you have to do is think for one second: there is no archetypal "Hispanic." And that's why not. That's what's wrong with this program. That the "hook," the gimmick, is *race.*

Think another second. What if this show were "about" African Americans? What if this were "about" Italian Americans? Jewish Americans? Et cetera.

We do documentaries, sometimes docudramas, on people who are foreign to us. The Japanese. The Russians. The Arabs. Some people in our own country. Native Americans, for instance. We used to do movies with Mexicans in them, ones about being over there on that side of the river. In the thirties and forties and fifties movies and TV had lots of these Mexicans. You probably remember them well enough without my going into them too much. Lots of bad guys, like not-too-funny Frito Bandidos, wearing sequined hats with bad teeth and strong accents, either dirty or dark skin. Good Mexicans, both male and female, spoke with little accent and were light-complected. Bad Mexicans, the whores, spoke with a heavy accent, were dark and usually barefoot, while the good ones wore their hair up in a bun, and . . . well, you know the rest. More recent Hollywood has accepted the Hispanic presence with movies about gang members, ex or soon-to-be ex, which is usually what the plot revolves on. *Boulevard Nights* or *Walk Proud*. Or the illegal alien. One with Jack Nicholson as the star, the other with Charles Bronson. Both as border-patrol guys.

But there has been a shift in the past few years, and though *The Ballad of Gregorio Cortez* got good reviews, it still was not a large commercial success. *La Bamba* has been, though, in both the Mexican-American community and the population at large. I don't want to say that this is because writer-director Luis Valdez doesn't like to write about the people of his own culture, because the story is about them; but it is not the focus, the device on which the story turns. So there can be good guys and bad, and they don't come to *stand for* something that is racial and not human. (Another thing: the reason Valdez *can* make the Valenzuela family farmworkers is because it is his history, as an artist and as a man, not because of some stereotype he likes to use.) Television has moved along, too, away from the Pepino-type characters on *The Real McCoys. Hill Street Blues,*

Miami Vice, and *L.A. Law* have lead characters whose language is Spanish.

The problem with *Juarez* isn't that its characters are racially distinct. It's that *race is the hook.* And once you make your boat out of that, be ready to tread water—it's gonna sink. It's a no-win. (Racism, in contrast, is a valid subject and is often the subject of quality drama. Think of *Zoot Suit* or *A Soldier's Story.*) Let me put it this way: I may not be the expert on Hispanic People, I may not know what constitutes the ideal Mexican-American household, man or woman, but I am, with my mixed blood sloshing around, an expert on racism. I grew up in L.A. hearing it all. Niggers, kikes, Jews, krauts, Japs, chinks, white breads, beaners. And variations thereof. It is true that this pilot episode means well. Detective Juarez and his wife are almost model liberals (she works for a natural-history museum, restoring Indian relics). But it's simply not good enough to "kindly" embrace an ugly stereotype—it is still a bad stereotype. Mexican-Americans are fighting the crime within themselves no more and no less than anyone else (among them all, the broadest), and I for one am tired of this kind of discussion. Look at it this way: it's not better, as a comment on the people, to serve watermelon to an educated black man sitting properly, in a quality suit and tie at a well-set dinner table, and have him eat it in some proper fashion. That is not liberating the stereotype. The problem with *Juarez,* in other words, is that, like the hippie subculture in *Mod Squad,* like the pretty breasts in *Charlie's Angels,* Hollywood thinks it's on to something *hot.*

So. What do I do? What would you do? I mean, imagine Hollywood dangling this potential money in your face. Like some new drug, a cure for a disease you have (always writing for nothing and feeling irresponsible as a father of two boys). Like I said earlier, I was grateful for the meeting postponements, because I had some difficulties sorting through these conflicting emotions. But on one of the phone calls with the producer, I began to tell him some of the problems I saw. He listened, I think painfully (I wonder to this day if I didn't give away, free, too much), and said he didn't think I was right. I tried to explain better. He told me to try to tone it down when I talked to the executive producer, that he didn't think it would be smart to throw too much criticism at this man.

Maybe you're thinking I had already made my decision to not become involved. Not true. Because I thought the project was salvageable. Cut all the bull (and bullfighting), drop the *amigo* chitchat (which sets up larger racial misconceptions), make Juarez a cop in El Paso, not a *Hispanic* cop, maybe even get some other people involved (I had a list made up in my mind of writers, men and women, Chicanos, I could suggest). I mean, this pilot was not written in stone, and maybe it would be a good idea to get a rewrite of the script. I was thinking I could show them ways that would make it less offensive. In any case, I planned to say (with great coin-shaped tears of sadness) that I couldn't write any script on the basis of this pilot, but if it changed, I'd love to write a cop-show script or two or three. I would tell them what I thought, just as I have tried to do now, as politely as possible. I had no intention of bringing a lighter or matches to light anybody's cigar, that's true, but I'm not the kind who won't sit at a table with smokers. Admittedly, I say for honesty's sake, I would not tell them that to my mind, the least I could get out of all this was an article for *Texas Monthly,* if not a short story based on it all: at least I could go watch some of the filming, hang out a few days and eat some of the great buffet. Maybe negotiate into being a carpenter, or a location finder.

The phone rang for me while they were scouring the town for shoot locations. A message was left at my home. They were in a big hurry, would be in town only a few days, and were staying at the Marriott near the airport. Could I come down to the hotel restaurant at seven-forty-five the next morning before they had to go out? The hour was, in my view, a little unusual for what I thought was a business meeting, but that is not why I returned a message saying that it wasn't good for me. I couldn't because I have two boys who go to school, and I take them (I'm at home writing a novel, trying to, being unemployed, waiting, as I must, for the union to call me for a real job up there in Orogrande at the Star Wars project (I state because I'm collecting unemployment compensation)).

I get a call back later that day. The same producer. A nice talk. He's looking at the Tigua Reservation. The guy taking them around town is with the mayor's office. I joke, say he should have asked me to take them around, get a nonelected view of the city. I'm not joking when I say they should stop by my home since they're driving around, since this meeting seems loose anyway, have a beer, spend five minutes, see what we think of each other. He gets my address. Says he'll see.

A Friday night. Another call. How about tomorrow? I'm asked. What time? I ask back. Eightish, he says. Then he specifies a quarter to. Well, I hesitate. We're up, I'm told. It's not that, I say. It's that I coach a soccer team for the YMCA, that my game is at ten, I have to be there at nine-thirty. I tell him. I don't say that before the game, it's Laundromat time. But I can make it. It's just inconvenient. I say, Well, I'll try, but if not, why don't you guys drop in on me? Drop by the soccer game, I suggest, a block down my street, you can't miss it. Okay, he says, and if not, he'll get me next time, when there's more time.

That seemed fine. Everything seemed okay. And so I didn't make it I figured—well, I figured we could make it a normal hour, less inconvenient for me, since it was a loose meeting anyway. Look, one thing did cross my mind. It did seem a little like a back-door entrance. It was a thought I had. But that wasn't why I didn't go, because I wouldn't have allowed myself to jump to that conclusion without more facts.

Time passes. A week, two, three. I hear there is filming going on in town. It's all over the six- and ten-o'clock news. I wonder why I am not invited, but I figure they'll be in town lots of times, there are still many opportunities to talk. Another week later, I call the woman friend in Venice about an L.A. *Times* article I wanted sent to me. We talk about the TV show (we talked one other time when I first got the script), that I must not have been too interested because I'd missed two appointments. Missed two appointments? I was surprised. Curious. Especially curious because "misbehaving" has been a label I've worn for many years. Unrightfully, I say, just as I do in this case. I hadn't even said anything yet, hadn't said no yet. So I say, still in my surprised state (thinking how nicely we had talked on the phone, how everything seemed agreeable, loose). Well, I guess I can still write my article for *Texas Monthly*. And she blows up: why would I do that? I explain. Tell her my intellectual reasoning. She's still pissed. How could I do that to her! To her? I ask. How to her? She had arranged for him to see my book. No, I say, I gave him that book because he'd given me free information. Well, she says, she'd passed on that article I'd written for *The Texas Observer* (a little piece on El Paso, the galleys of which I received while at her Venice apartment those first days, and then I'd left a published version when I stayed a last night before I came back here). Oh, I say, I see. She tells me that she was trying to help me out because I'd told her how much I wanted to get out of the construction business. This is true, but I guess, naively, I hadn't thought of that producer's calling me as any more than business, mutually negotiated interests, not favors. In fact, it could be said that she is no more responsible for me and this man getting together than God is, by which I mean, who caused what? Wasn't I the writer who sent that article on a whim? And who caused me to read the L.A. *Herald*? If you get my drift. I mean, is it supposed to be my fault that I read this TV script before it went on the air and didn't like it? And—this is the important part—didn't think it was right to do this sort of show?

But, she pointed out, her best friend is married to the producer. And that got me. Because she is a very nice person, and I like her very much, wish her happiness. And maybe writing this article and getting it published would hurt her best friend's husband's feelings, or who knows what else, and her best friend would hate her because she knew me and . . .

So that's why it has taken me months before I've gone ahead. I was torn between my writer's desire to tell, which I think is a valuable thing—and in this case to tell something I think should be told—and not wanting to harm a good person's close friendship.

You decide.

The title of this piece? It's the final line in this premier episode, spoken by Aldo, the Mexican Mafialike king, the ultimate bad guy (limo, bodyguards), as he admires our defiant, brave hero. "*Vaya con Dios,* Rosendo Juarez," he says. Lots of Mexican people say, "*Que le vaya bien*" when saying good-bye. Not this. When I read that stilted expression, I thought of a country-western song. The accent over *Dios* is misplaced, so in comes out DEE-os, and at the end, "my darlin" is added on with a long drawl. Can't remember exactly who sings it. But I hope you see what I'm saying.

Wyoming Eats Coyote

I followed the front-page news story of the coyote hunt out here in Wyoming, wondering if the story was as big across the nation as the Casper *Star-Tribune* claimed. Did a CBS camera crew from New York do something for the evening news?

Assuming that you know as much as my friends in El Paso, you don't know anything about it. The story is simple: out in Campbell County, Wyoming, sheep ranchers say that "predators"—cai-yoats, they're called out here—are killing off their livestock, and the ranchers are losing tens of thousands of dollars a year. Their solution was to allow two hundred hunters two days on the seventy-five ranches. The hunter bringing in the biggest coyote would win five hundred dollars, as would the hunter bringing in the most coyotes. The number of foxes a hunter shot would break any ties.

When it was over, it was another big front-page article. Though organizers moved the drop-off point to a private ranch so no strangers could come and take pictures of bloodied, frozen, rigor-mortised coyotes, the *Star-Tribune* printed a couple of color photos of hunters pulling bodies from a sack. Only twenty-four were killed. And twelve foxes. A thirty-three pound coyote was the biggest, and six coyotes plus one fox was the most.

It's the usual story of the West, of settled man versus roaming, undomesticated wildness. I admit I tend to feel sympathy for coyotes, and especially for the fox, which seems to me such a dramatic, beautiful creature. I've seen only one in the wild, and I felt like something good had happened to me when I did. But, much as I may not like it, I can understand the ranchers' point of view, too. It's lambing season right now in Wyoming, and these people make their living raising and protecting their animals. Coyotes, and I guess foxes also, are to them what thieves are to city people.

I'm inadequate to know what's better, what's best, and I have to tell you the truth, I followed a different plot. I live in the Southwest, and I've been hearing about coyotes for a long time. There are all kinds of coyotes, you know. There's the Mexican-border one, that money-grubbing, and often dangerous savior figure who guides many poor people across the dark frontera into los estados. Where I live, and around New Mexico, coyote is a half-breed, half-Anglo, half-Mexican. Coyote is metaphorically important in Native-American culture. A star protagonist in their traditional stories, Coyote is a trickster, a shaman, a fool. It's this culture's coyote that has attracted the blond, blue-eyed New Age Indians. Coyote's magical powers have helped them find their true, primitive, native essence, which is often, if I'm remembering right, usually part Cherokee.

So here I was in Wyoming, visiting, reading about *its* coyote, when, in the sports page, I read a column by the Casper *Star-Tribune*'s Tom Bishop—his bearded, gentle face smiling in his personal newspaper box. That's when their cai-yoat story became a fascination for me, made me go out and read the paper every day, and read carefully, gripped by it. Here's what Tom Bishop wrote: "For those who are handy in the kitchen—and all hunters are—a coyote hunt offers culinary opportunities that seldom are surpassed."

I debated about which recipe to share with you here. The other one had potatoes in it, which I like, and lima beans, which I hate. I chose to give you the Big Coyote Chili Dinner: ¼ lb. coyote suet, finely chopped; 6 lbs. lean coyote meat, coarsely chopped; 1 cup chili powder; 2 tblsp. cumin, ground or crushed; 2 tblsp. Oregano, 2 tblsp. Salt; 2 tblsp. cayenne pepper; 4 cloves garlic, minced; 2 qts. coyote stock; ½ cup cornmeal (*masa harina* can be substituted); ½ cup cold water.

Los Gallos

Not so many months ago, I was watching a ten o'clock Los Angeles news show that comes by way of cable here to El Paso. It opened with your basic snippets of international and national events of the day, their video stories provided by a network service. The anchor team of the program did well to show the appropriate concern and interest in front of each news piece, but it took no media expert to notice how much professionalism and showbiz were masking big yawns. This was not so with the next story on the local scene. All of a sudden a human face stared from the screen. It was concerned, it was shocked, and its station had been there with a camera and correspondent: out in the land of gangs and lowriders, the sheriff's department had busted up a cockfight. Standing in front of a door whose paint was peeling away in large chunks, the plaster building around it some odd color, the correspondent told us of the events as he'd learned of them. There was no way to be sure how long this had been going on, he told us, but the sheriff had arrested a lair of participants. The screen turned to a videotape shot moments before. A line of men was walking out that door, shielding their faces as they stepped into a paddy wagon, their clothes and hair so dark and unfashionable they came across as though shot in black and white, as though to emphasize the barbarity and primitivism of the event. Back at the studio, the anchor team returned with a subdued, moralistic pause, then went on to their routine of upbeat and heartfelt items, weather, and civilized sports.

As a matter of fact, cockfights *are* possibly the oldest surviving sporting event we have. They can be traced back to Persia, India, and Malaysia, thousands of years before Christ. The Greeks almost deified the fighting cock, and it's believed that the fights were part of the "mysteries" so well attended by most of Greece's famous wise men. The Romans took them even more seriously and were probably the first to organize and stage the fights in miniature stadiums. All the great commanders of Rome were active enthusiasts—it's said that Julius Caesar was a champion breeder and that Mark Antony was warned about Caesar's political rise on the basis of wins. In the Europe that followed Rome, kings were often told of another kingdom's brood before considering battle. Historians recorded that a Danish king no longer had to fear the Germans, since they had devoted themselves to dancing and drinking instead of cockfighting.

The first attempts to outlaw the sport began in England, where a law was finally passed in 1849. Though some of the organizers objected to cockfighting on grounds of cruelty, the majority feared the human element—what kind of people would attend these events? How could gambling, drinking, and bloodletting inspire anything less than the most base savagery? These same attitudes prevailed in the United States when game was brought over by the earliest colonists, though apparently those arguments did not dissuade George Washington, an avid breeder, or Thomas Jefferson. Andrew Jackson did little to improve the status of "chicken fighters" when he pitted roosters at the White House. Even the fact that Abraham Lincoln got the nickname "Honest Abe" because of his reputed fairness as a referee at cockfights has done little to improve the respectability of the sport in this country, where it is illegal in almost every state and even some counties where the state government permits it.

Yet cockfighting does endure, particularly here in the Southwest, where it's a blend of traditions from the U.S. and Mexico (and where it is illegal, though accepted, and often publicly advertised and attended), and the reason *los gallos,* the fights, thrive is not because "cockers" or *galleros* are bloodthirsty boozers who'd gamble away their children and maybe even tie knives on them to see how they'd fight it out if given the chance. The reason is that it *is* a sport, though not one for all.

I went to my first cockfight about seven years ago with my friend Danny. We drove a short way out of the city to a pit in Chaparral, New Mexico, a still-legal one then run by a cocker named Chicago Rod, to watch the birds owned by Danny's older cousin Ralph. At the time, Danny was helping out because Ralph, though a wheelchair basketball star since Vietnam, had some trouble handling the roosters in the pit. As things went on, Ralph moved to a place where he couldn't keep his chickens, so Danny inherited Ralph's brood and knowledge, both of which had been part of their family since childhood.

Danny lives out in a relatively new housing development on the edges of El Paso's lower-valley city limits with his wife and four young children. A veteran of the navy, he's been a laborer on the Southern Pacific Railroad for the past six years, mostly on the graveyard shift. Tall and muscular, he is not one who enjoys the usual workingman's pastimes. He doesn't watch much TV, and doesn't really care who wins what football, basketball, or baseball game. He is the type, however, who would probably be good at any of those sports if he put his mind to it. As you pull into his driveway, you see that what Danny does do as a hobby isn't something only El Paso detective J. J. Armes could figure out. The sound of a rooster is as familiar and unmistakable as the wind is in this part of Texas.

Danny has been getting ready to enter an upcoming derby that a game club planned, and he's in his backyard putting his feed together. The mix is high in protein and oil—along with soaked oats and barley are lay pellets, milo, Canadian peas, calf mena, whole corn, and popcorn, and all of it is coated with fish oil. Breeders will often point out how expensive the sport is; no matter what a champion breeder might earn, it's spare change compared to the overall costs, and this feed is the first obvious evidence. But it's necessary to breed and maintain strong, fat-free birds.

The roosters are kept in homemade chicken-wire pens—about three feet high, wide, and deep—that line the perimeter of the backyard. Several of the cocks share their home with a hen, and baby chickens chirp around a larger coop in a corner under a willow tree. Danny tells me about the breeding and in-breeding of each bird, rattling off names like Kelso, Hatch, and Claret, McLean Hatch and Sweater McGinnis. They're all known by colors, too, like Reds and Grays and Blacks, Whites and Brownreds. Each breed is known for some fighting trait. A Hatch, for instance, is a power bird, and a Kelso has speed. These are the qualities a cock breeder looks for to start a brood, along with an innate and bred-in cutting ability and leap, which are absolutely essential to winning a fight in the pit. But probably the most important characteristic is a cock's gameness. It's this above all that distinguishes a particular bird from its well-known breed, what makes one cocker known for *his* birds and not for the stock. Gameness is simply the bird's eagerness to fight. It's the look in his eyes, his strut, his crow. Cocks, their advocates will frequently remind you, are natural fighters. They are territorial and possessive and, left to themselves, will fight to the death as instinctively as jackrabbits will run from trouble. Much like a champion boxer, a champion broodcock wants to win at all costs and is fearless in doing so. He wants to throw his spurs into his opponent, wants to pluck at him with his beak. Even when injured and tired, this cock will not quit. In a long fight, he's the cock that will still want the win, the one that will leap back from death.

This day Danny and I were going out to a farm near Tornillo to visit a friend of his, where Danny could spar the roosters he was considering for the derby a week later. The five birds were packed up in some boxes used to carry water-softener equipment. Of course, if he wanted to, Danny could order special cases, made of two-hundred-pound waxed corrugated board, with nice handles on top, for thirty-five dollars a dozen. All these things are available and advertised each month in *The Gamecock,* a magazine published out of Arkansas that is a combination *Sports Illustrated* and, say, *Southwest Farm Press* for cockers. I'd venture to say that there isn't a cockfighter around this part of the country who doesn't have a subscription to the magazine. Every thing a breeder and cockfighter needs is advertised in it, from birds to vitamins to scales to souvenir caps and T-shirts. In it are articles about the best way to raise the best cocks, according to one writer, and the best way to raise the best cocks according to another. These are regular columns, letters to the editor, information pieces about derbies from game clubs all over the South and Southwest, pictures of smiling derby winners holding up their trophies. All the things, in other words, that sports lovers thrive on. Danny uses *The Gamecock* to purchase goods whose quality he can't get anywhere around here, but as far as the carrying boxes go, we can load them in the van with ones he's poked holes into that have to be carried from the bottom.

Nino, who asked me not to use his real name, is plowing his field with a John Deere as we drive up. Expecting us, he stops immediately and leads us onto a dirt farm road to his home, which is a larger, modern trailer. There are pecan trees nearby and a grove of them maybe fifty yards farther on his neighbor's property. Nino has been growing cotton and alfalfa for fifteen years. He has a horse and a grain-fed bull in a fenced area by his trailer. He's also a musician and plays, along with his wife, in a band at a bar on the other side of town. Nino's real love, though, is fighting cocks, and out behind his trailer there must be some fifty pens, all neatly spaced and kept as clean as new cars.

A cockhouse is sort of a rooster locker room. Cocks are brought in from pens, as were some of Nino's, or from carrying boxes, as were Danny's, and put in smaller pens stacked like dresser drawers as high as cabinets, which they also open like. Nino's cockhouse is an old adobe building that came with his land, and his pens are two kinds: welded iron and heavy mesh; plywood and chicken wire. Nino works with his cocks, here in the light of a bare lightbulb that dangles from an exposed joist, every day for two to three hours after working his fields. He trains his. Sometimes he chases them, and makes them fly to an old mattress he has on a workbench three feet up. This helps their leaping and stamina. Or he has them climb for a few feet up a steep ramp, carpeted with burlap, to strengthen and extend their reach. It's this commitment that probably explains the several first-place trophies topped by golden roosters which Nino displays in his living room.

After the roosters are put in the cockhouse pens, they are taken out individually and weighed on some baker scales. The birds weigh from four to six pounds, and their weight is written down to the last ounce, as are the pens they are taken from. After that, Danny and Nino decide which ones to match up for the sparring. The difference between sparring and actual fighting is the same as in boxing—a few rounds to juice the reflexes and keep in shape, both mentally and physically. It also gives a cock owner the opportunity to test his bird without having to lose him. The fight is with muffs, which are small—about a half inch in diameter—stitched leather balls with flaps on either side that wrap around each leg of a cock and over his natural spur. The bird's spur grows, and when the cuticlelike growth is too long, it is cut off with a spur saw, which resembles a miniature coping saw, and the muff is held on by a rubber band attached to the leather. Danny and Nino spar several birds this day in a circular pit bounded by bales of hay behind Nino's cockhouse. They spend much of the time in between talking the details about each cock that only cockfighters can and do.

A week later, we drive out of town to a game club (whose name and location its owner requested I not identify) offering a four-cock derby. The club looks like a ranch in many respects, set as it is not far from some mountains and with plenty of unplowed land where horses, one of which can be seen in a stable, can be ridden. But what would be stables on a ranch are filled here with cock pens, and it's hard to guess how many there are within the confines enclosed by the wood fence and ash trees. There are many cockhouses built into the barnlike building where the cocks will be pitted. They are reserved in advance, by phone. Though we've arrived early, already there are lots of cars and trucks and people here, from Arizona, New Mexico, and Texas, and all the cockhouses are booked up. Many of Danny's relatives have arrived, like Ralph and Tito and Jimmy, and some of them, like Danny, have brought along their kids. This is what probably strikes you first, that there are children running around playing, that the wives and girlfriends have come, making the atmosphere more gentle and family-oriented.

While at Nino's, Danny made a decision not to enter the derby but to instead hack his cocks here at the game club; at the derby are some of the best cockers from the Southwest, and he wasn't confident his birds could win the event. A derby is a club-sponsored tournament. In this case, a four-cock derby, each entrant has four cocks he wants to fight. Each cocker pays a hundred dollars to do this and then draws a number. The fights are then matched by those numbers. The amount of prize money depends on the number of entrants. At this one, more than thirty are announced, so the winner—or winners, if there's a tie—who takes the most of four—will come home with some three thousand dollars. A hack is a fight between two birds for money, normally a sum big enough, say at least a hundred dollars for both breeders to be interested beyond simple pride.

Danny has chosen to hack his cock against one belonging to a bearded blond guy from Arizona. Once the birds have been weighed and the men have agreed which roosters they will pit, ones of close to equal weight, Danny and his opponent go to their cockhouses to fit the gaffs on the bird's spurs. Gaffs come in different lengths, from 1¼" to 2¾", and carry names such as jagger, regulation, half bayonet, and full bayonet. These names represent their curves, but what they all have in common is the long, narrow rod of polished steel with a sharp and deadly point. Cockfighters also use knives, called slashers, and they are attached much the same way though only on one leg, but today it's gaffs. Danny, like all cockers, keeps his in a small wooden box with all the other materials. First some soft white mole tape is wrapped around the area of the bird's leg next to his cut spur, then that's wrapped with strips of black tape. The gaff, like the muff, is tied onto a leather slip that fits over the rooster's leg and over that stump of spur. Though some use dental floss, waxed nylon tie string usually secures the gaff to the leg. The tying is done methodically, tight enough to grip the leg for maximum strength and hold during a fight, and loose enough so the bird feels comfortable and undistracted. This period is probably the most solemn, personal moment for the breeder. There is little said between the owner, who is wrapping, and the person holding the bird. The quiet of the cockhouse must remind the owner that as soon as they walk out of there, this bird will either go to the pit and die or come back a champion. When the bird has won more than one or two already, you can imagine the range of feelings that his breeder must have about pitting him again.

As with any sporting event, it costs money to go to these cockfights, and at this game club is a sign posted in a window with the rates and a person behind that window who will collect the money. For first-timers, there's a once-only fee of twelve dollars, which makes the person a member of the game club and of a national organization, the United Gamefowl Breeders Association, Inc. Then there's a six-dollar ticket for the day, and two dollars more if you want a reserved seat. Children and seniors cost two dollars, small enough children are free. The inside of the building is put together by lots of 2-bys. 2 × 12's deck the floor, and the grandstand area is nailed together with 2 × 8's and 2 × 10's painted gray, on either end of the pit and stacked three tiers high. The reserved section is rows of old red theater chairs that face the fights and the derby scoreboard on the wall behind. The scoreboard tells everyone which cock belongs to whom, which opponent is up, and whether the fight is won or lost. Not far away from the scoreboard is a weigh room, with two scales. Beside that another door leads to the drag pit, used if a fight—which must continue until a decision is made—is going on so long that people have totally lost interest. Above the room are three professionally painted signs hung level and tight: NO DRINK-ING, NO GAMBLING, NO PROFANITY PLEASE. This game club maintains two pits side by side, each one about twenty feet in diameter. They are bounded by a foot-high wall, and on the three sides overlooking the seating area, a heavy-gauge mesh rises four feet so that a cock can't fly out among the people watching. The ground cover of the pit is a moist red-brown dirt.

Danny and the bearded guy are to be the first fight of the day, and about fifty people have taken a place to see. Danny's bird is a Red, and so is the Arizona bird. Both cockers are in the pit letting their birds loosen up. Danny takes his—though some cockers do give their roosters a name, most serious ones have and have had too many birds for that—and drops him a few inches from the ground so the bird will extend his wings, reach with his legs, in general make his blood move a little faster. Then a referee, chosen by the pit owner, tells the men to get ready. They grab their birds, one hand stroking the back and ribs as you would any other animal, while the other hand holds the rooster from underneath. They each squat down near a line scratched by the referee into the pit dirt with a stick; the lines are exactly eight feet apart. The cocks, who have just "billed," a beaks-alone tease fight in their handlers' arms, stare into each other's eyes, ready to pit.

The birds are uncommonly beautiful, much more so than one thinks of a rooster. Their size has something to do with this. A rooster is large, a physical presence often overlooked beside the much larger animals that moo and neigh and baa in the barn-yard. The bird is also extraordinarily colorful, as much as the parrot and macaw, though more earth-toned. His featherless face and wattle are crimson. In the case of these Reds, the hackles are a yellow rust; the saddle or back feathers are a mix of green, brown, and white; and the breast and wing feathers are blue-green. The tail is deep olive, and the plumage hangs haphazardly, exotically, if a rooster may be allowed such a word after so many thousands of years of domestication. The feathers' silken sheen is a payment on the roosters' expensive diet.

The referee calls, "Pit!" and the birds are set loose. Their hackles have bloomed, each leaps high into the other, though Danny's bird gets so high he goes over the bird from Arizona. They come right back at each other. Much of the action is a blur, but the flutter and click of steel keeps the eyes on what they can see. The activity of the earliest pittings is the quickest and most lively, and this includes the crowd's. Though the sign read NO GAMBLING, people have been calling for bets. "Ten over here!"

and he'll point his arm in the direction of Danny's side. Somebody will take that bet, and the cockers will make a mental note, especially if either takes more than one bet, which is frequent enough. Lots of bets go back and forth, from five to fifty dollars, though the higher they are, the less often they're matched. Very seldom will someone try to welch on a bet, and when it does happen, that person will not be at the pit again. When the birds get tied up by their gaffs, the referee calls, "Handle." Neither bird seems to be injured, but it looks as though the bearded guy is working the gaffed leg of Danny's bird away from the breast of his.

The referee clocks twenty seconds after the handle. This is how it must be done according to the Wortham Rules, the Modern Tournament and Derby Rules followed by established game clubs, and cockers accept and use them just as participants in every other sport demand and abide by their rules. The birds are coddled and petted while they wait for the next call; their handlers do everything they can to keep them alert. The referee tells them to get ready and starts counting, "Seventeen, eighteen, nineteen," and then the birds are back at the line and flying into each other.

When the Arizona cock hits Danny's clearly, the crowd senses the inevitable. In the twenty-second period after a handle call, Danny cleans the bird's wound with water and tries to keep him fight-ready. The rooster comes out well in the next two pittings because he is a live one, very game, and he does some damage but not enough: it's obvious that he is weakening faster than the Arizona cock. Since Danny's bird will probably not be able to make an easy kill, his only hope now is to stay alive and win a decision, since his opponent is injured, too, and will eventually tire out. Now Danny and the bearded guy are asking the referee for counts. By the rules, the last bird to strike gets a count of ten. If the other bird does nothing in return, the one with the count gets one ten-count, a mark heeled into the dirt by the referee, and then there's a twenty-second handle. After three tens, there's a twenty-count, and if a cock won't fight back after that, the other is declared the winner. If the injured cock fights at any time during the count, the tens start over. After a few more pittings, the count has been going back and forth. About the fifteenth time, it's easy to see that the fight is almost over. Danny's rooster can barely stand, and when he falls, he does not try to break the other bird back. The Arizona bird finally wins, and money exchanges hands with shucks and grins.

There are several more hacks after this one, but at precisely one P.M., the derby is to begin, and the crowd has increased to seventy-five or more, a nearly even mix of every ethnic background that populates the Southwest. The owner of the pit, who wears a blue cowboy hat, makes some announcements before the tournament, then introduces men and women in the audience who are presidents and vice presidents and recording secretaries of game clubs in other states. The applause is polite and friendly, and some of them say a few kind words in return. There's continuously a fight in each pit once the derby gets going. Though a fight is occasionally over in three or four pittings, the usual is many more than that, and the crowd, particularly those with no bets on the line, often loses interest. The drinking rule in the building is self-enforced, though every so often, someone will drink a beer quietly. Rowdiness is not allowed, and the ever-present women and children seem to keep any would-be from losing sight of that. For the restless and hungry, there are the normal distractions. Behind the ticket window is a kitchen, and above the stove is a stenciled sign listing what's for sale: hot dogs, corn dogs, cheeseburgers, hamburgers, burritos, candy, chips, sweet rolls, coffee, soda. Outside there's a picnic atmosphere. Kids are running around, women are making sandwiches, men are drinking beer and laughing. Danny, for instance, has brought tortillas, ham, cheese, and jalapeños, and in another cooler are some iced Carta Blancas and Fanta sodas he brought over the day before from Juárez and the side door of Danny's van is open most of the day for all or any to help themselves.

You notice right away that the crowd is not big on synthetics. It's cotton, wool, and leather here, boots and cowboy hats with feathers, caps with names of equipment companies, western-cut shirts, and jeans; cigars are in a couple of mouths, and the faces and hands are the color and texture of people who make their lives, who do their *work,* in soil, in wind, and in sun. People often talk about the way things used to be in this part of the country, how the West once was. These are the grandchildren and great-grandchildren of those days, the Old West and the present still together in a sport that binds them. These are people who don't live in big industrial cities and don't want to and probably never have even considered doing so, people who don't follow the civilized games played on Astroturf or varnished floors, who aren't near a big-city newspaper that does. As it was for their descendants, that enclosed circle of earth is where the real action is, and there's nothing unnatural about seeing those feathers accumulate around the perimeter of the pit, nothing that isn't already a face of life. I'm sure many would describe their own way as like a fighting cock's, though undoubtedly they'd prefer that a wager on them be a winning one.

My friend Danny, by the way, lost one more of his roosters in a hack later that day, and realized some moments after this that it was because his birds, who usually performed better, needed some water. He won two after that, and evened his money losses, though, as he reminded me, he lost two good birds. One thing I know about Danny—winner or loser, if he'd been one of those arrested out there in Los Angeles, he'd have stared right into that high-tech camera unashamed.

Living al Chuco

I am not going to tell you about the Rio Grande. I realize it's what most of you think of when you think of El Paso. You think of the Border Patrol cruising, dust trailing their off-road vehicles as they chase indocumentados who are looking for work framing houses or cleaning them once they've been occupied. I'm not going to tell you about Juárez in the day or in the night, about its danger or lack of, or which mercado is best for what, or which bar mixes the strongest margaritas. I'm not going to tell you where to find Rosa's Cantina. I'm not going to tell you about ostrich or snake or alligator boots. Though boots are cool. I like boots. I wear boots. But I ain't gonna talk about them.

First off, it's not the river at all. Those of us who live here rarely acknowledge the river you know and see in romanticized movie clips and glossy photos. We talk about the mountains. The Franklins, the bottom vertebrae of the Rockies, are what we see every day, what we drive around and over on workdays and days off. As imposing as the sky, they're outside with us, and the barbecue, on día de las madres and Memorial Day and all the others we pay attention to here. They're there when we pull the weeds— gotta have gloves because of nasty espinas. The mountains are here when we pull the car over the curb, tires across the rough topography of our dirt yards, and we've dragged the hose and soapy bucket over, or new parts and old wrenches. . . . Which reminds me—since the police, on the complaint of some old-bag neighbor who thinks parked cars are a major problem with the neighborhood, have been nagging me about having my '62 Chevy next to my house. Does it run? a lawyer friend asks me. What's that got to do with it? I tell her. It's a '62 Chevy! A '62 Chevy is art! Which reminds me of other things that piss me off about El Paso. Like the newspapers. They really do suck. You feel like reading, you buy a paper from Juárez. No offense, El Paso newspapers, but face it, you guys are drinking the water too much (I forever hear this story about some huge quantity of natural lithium in our water supply). Or music. Man, it's painful to talk about music around here in Chuco. The station I'm recording this in, no offense, but you've made me hate jazz. Your idea of jazz reminds me of, well, Newt Gingrich. It's that bad for me now. This is a university, and your radio station is supposed to inspire the imagination, not deaden it! Whenever I go out of town, drive at least three hundred miles, other newspapers all read heavy like *The New York Times,* and contentedness for me has become hours listening to a radio station. I've lived here so long I've become a cheap date.

It ain't about gangs here. You know what? I'm tired of hearing about cholos. It's about quinceañeras and weddings and birthday parties. It's about Frank Castillo, who's pitching for the Cubs, and Butch Henry, who's pitching for the Expos, about Antonio Davis blocking a shot for the Pacers, and everybody wants Tim Hardaway back on the all-star team. It's about Little League diamonds, Ponder Park, where my boy hit a grand slam last night and struck out ten. "Echela al guante, m'ijo, al guante! . . . Don't swing at the piñatas! . . . ¡Se van los elotes, calientitos, se van los elotes!" Okay, so that last one was about the man who sells the corn getting ready to leave. He sells it on the cob, or in a cup, with both butter and chile.

So let me tell you a couple of other things I love about living in El Paso. Like when Jonathan Herrera and Daniel Pantoja come over to play Nintendo with my son Ricardo, and they get Cokes and Flaming Hot Cheetos. Or hearing my son Tony laughing on the phone with his partner Alex Gavina. Or just the other day, when I went to the hospital where my compa, el mero poeta loco don Ricardo Sánchez, lay, one hundred pounds less in body only, fighting off cancer. His voice is a whisper. His wife, Teresa, has been by his bed for him since they came home, and she asks him if he wouldn't want his feet rubbed. He nods. She peels off the socks. When I tell him that I saw a book of his in the window of a Taos bookstore, his eyes swagger like nothing's wrong, everything's right for him and toda la raza. Staring into death, they are El Paso's simplicity.

Or the light when the blurry sun looks balanced at the last edge of the day. Everything is so sharp, like you hadn't even realized you were nearsighted, or clear, like you've washed off the bug splats from the windshield after a long desert drive. It's white, almost blue it's so white, white like a washed and bleached cotton shirt, and a warm wind blows, puffing it out just so as you're crossing an empty street, the streets of El Paso so serene in the sensuous breeze and magic light, the city so quiet, as peaceful as the pregnant young mami, in cutoffs and sandals, long black hair, holding the hand of her firstborn as they walk, slow, along a sidewalk on Copia Street that looks the same as it did when, not so long ago, she held her own mom's hand.

II
CORTÉS AND MALINCHE

Mi Mommy

I was holding her hand at a train depot. I can still feel my arm in the air, limp and soft with trust. It must have been Union Station, Los Angeles, and I don't know where we were going or why. I was thrilled. I was small, probably just walking, and looking up at her I swear I knew then that she was beautiful. She was wearing a hat, one of those brimless hats that women wore in the fifties that matched the rest of the outfit. Almost all my other early images of her are from the department stores we would go to together—she's trying clothes on, everybody paying so much attention to her; or standing at a cosmetic counter, my mommy and the women around talking so fast and unashamed, giggling, the silver and gold and glass tubes, the jars and sprays, the smallest brushes, the colored powders. On that trip to I don't know where or why, the train depot was in the black and white of a dream, its indoors the faraway of the outdoors, its expanse as dusty as a memory. There was a rose in the hat, I'm sure. It wasn't a real red rose, though, only a decorative one, with something lacy white around it.

I saw her, mi mommy, on her knees crawling toward an altar. I was scared. What was wrong? Why was she doing this? It was big, this church, but all I saw was her. I wanted to cry. Maybe

I did cry. I'm still scared when I remember. I didn't look around, I squinted and closed my eyes, too, only Mommy crawling, stained-glass light, an echo of quiet that hurt my ears. Was I crying?

I think it was La Cienega. It was a Spanish name, and the other stores where she modeled—downtown or on Wilshire Boulevard, department stores like the Broadway or Robinson's— didn't have Spanish names. The store did not seem very large. Just elegant. Racks of women's clothes with beads and jewels, collars and sleeves, strings and straps and bows, low in the front, low in the back. I went into the dressing room, where all the models were changing from one thing into another for the show that day. I watched them for so long, breathed the cool mist of perfume as they hurried through the step-throughs and pull-offs of dress and undress—the zippers and snaps, the gritty static or smooth wisp of on and off. Skin that was legs and arms, and round hips that cut into small waists, bras, even a breast, and panties that showed that dark mystery hair. The piccolo of woman voices. I was such a good boy, they said. I was so cute, they told me. I would be such a handsome man, and they touched me. I remember the warmth of their touch, not in the region of a man, but all over, as in a favorite blanket, my fingers scissored onto its nylon end seam to go to sleep, my thumb in my mouth, sucking. Even then I knew it was woman, the attraction and allure, what I loved, my mommy and her friends, her best friend, the woman from Puerto Rico she could whisper to in Spanish. I was lucky, and I felt safe because my mommy liked me there. But it was this day I remember, because on the other side of the dressing room door, across the main floor, there was an old man in a uniform tinting a display window that faced the street. There were mannequins behind him, and he let me go through a half-door to sit between him and them. He brushed on the tint, and I looked out at the people and cars passing by on the other side of the window. It was so much fun to be in there, the glass becoming a yellow brown, that biting, tart odor. I would run from him back to the dressing room, from one scent to the other, back and forth, the fumes subliminal and intoxicating as I ran from the old man with the paintbrush and can in the room no one got to sit in to the beautiful women in their underwear.

She loved to go to Hollywood Park, and we went to the last race because admission was free. I loved to go, too, and not just because of the horses, the earth shuddering under me from the time they left the gate and pounded across the finish line. I liked to collect the bet stubs like baseball cards, the losers thrown down, a trail of litter that began in the parking lot until it carpeted the grandstands. I collected fives and tens, win, place, or show. Then I got into the twenty- and fifty-dollar bets. It was hardest to find the ones to win. Wandering the track was like walking on a beach looking for unbroken shells. Sometimes we would go down to the general-admission area, at the track level, and sometimes we would walk right over to the nicer area, where there were chairs and tables and drinks, and a number of times we'd be invited to sit in the private, glass-enclosed clubhouse. A man would offer to buy us drinks, and I would get a Roy Rogers, grenadine and Coke. She gave me the green olives on toothpicks from her drink to eat. The man who bought the drinks for us might say something at a distance first, and then approach. Mostly she just told a waiter, or the man himself, thank you so much, so polite, generously happy about the drinks, but that would be it, and there we'd be, she and I at the races. I was her date. I was her man. Those men, in their suits and their blazers, snugged or loosened ties, stinking in their colognes, snapping bills off silver money clips, they were obvious, stupid, easy even for me to figure out. She might light a cigarette. There were times she smoked and times she didn't. She didn't smoke, though, for the taste. It was a look she wanted. I'd complain that I couldn't find betting stubs. She'd tell me to look around where we were sitting, so I'd go search the top of the starched tablecloths, in the ashtrays, hunting the big losers. One time I found four hundred-dollar tickets to win, creased the long way.

She was seeing this one man. Years later, I would learn that she'd been seeing him for some time, even before she and my father had divorced, which was soon after I was born. His voice was loud by design, like a horn is loud. She would ask me, Do you like him? He took us to baseball games. The Tigers and Angels and Yankees, the Dodgers and Giants and Pirates. He let me hang around after the games and get autographs. He would take us to some games early so we could watch batting practice. The year Roger Maris hit 61 home runs, I caught one of his BP homers. He was a big man, a fireman, and sometimes we'd visit him at his station. I was too scared to slide down the pole. It was too fat, too thick. I played handball alone in the white room beside the red trucks. He wasn't a bad man, but I didn't like him very much. I couldn't explain why, except that he was so loud when he talked, and even though he would buy me ice cream any time I wanted it, he was no fun. And so I would answer her. No, I would say.

We were in the kitchen. I was sitting in one of those heavy metal chairs with glossy vinyl covering—we had two of them—and my mom got mad at me. I was used to this. She had a job now that she was older, in a dental office, and things like this happened because she was tired when she came home. But this time he was there. They were always going out, and I was left home alone with our knobless television and a TV dinner, sometimes two because I was getting taller, flexing muscles I could see in my arms. He'd only come inside our house once in a while, and this time she must have told me to go away, to get out of the kitchen. In that loud voice he told me to do what she said. I sat there. Then he was louder, really yelling. I sat there. And so he grabbed me and I held onto the metal rails under the chair and he picked it up along with me. I'm not leaving! I told him. You don't tell me! He was furious, and my mom was yelling now, too, and she told him to leave me alone and he stopped, dropping the chair and me in it, and then I stood up and I went into the bedroom and I was crying, waiting for her to come. She hit me sometimes, and when she got there that's what I was expecting. Instead, she held me and she was smiling. She was proud of me. She said, You're such a man already.

At school, the kids said things. I knew it. I was bigger than them and more athletic, and angry all the time and it wasn't like they were going to say anything much to my face. My mom was a Mexican, and my mom was divorced, and one time a girl told me her mom didn't like mine and didn't like me, either. I didn't hang out with too many kids. At school, I played only with the boys who played sports. There was this one boy—he had his own bedroom and shelves built all around with toys everywhere, every toy, all the best toys, and every ball and glove. He had a basketball, and a hoop on the garage. I would want to play and we did but he was soft, blubbery, and I'd shoot alone for as long as his mom would let me. His mom was always smoking and drinking coffee from a stained white mug and talking on the phone, and one time I came over and she took me into their clean bathroom and got a washcloth and washed my neck and behind my ears, scrubbed so hard it hurt. She was supposed to be a friend of my mom's, but I knew she wasn't, not really, because the couple of times my mom came by for me, only my mom talked.

Sometimes my mom would take me to Food Giant and buy me a chili dog with thinly grated cheese on top that would melt in a minute. When she went out—which was a lot—she would leave me some money and I'd ride a bike down to Thrifty's and buy a half-gallon square of chocolate ice cream. I don't remember what she thought I should eat. She didn't cook, except on my birthday, when she would make chile verde that would stew for hours. She'd buy tamales from a bakery on Whittier Boulevard. Some weekends she would make me scrambled eggs with green chiles that she took out of a can. In the mornings, before she went to work and I went to school, when we went to a coffee shop for breakfast, she'd give me her hash brown potatoes. Even then, at that hour, men would look at her. Even then men would come up to our table, squat so they could talk to her. Introduce themselves. I was starting junior high, I had touched a girl, looked at nudie magazines, and I knew what these men wanted. I was such a good-looking boy, they would tell her. When they guessed at my age, they would miss by years, and then the talk would be about her beauty—how could such a young woman have a son this age? She was too polite to them, and one time I remember this man's eyes, looking at my mom. I wanted us to be alone. I didn't want her to be polite. I was so mad at her. I was so mad then that I think I never got over it.

She'd stopped modeling, and when she and her Puerto Rican friend got together, they talked about the other models getting fat butts and saggy chiches, girdles and falsies. Her Puerto Rican friend was marrying a man who owned the biggest sailboat ever and they were going around the world in it. He'd already done it before. He was so rich he didn't have to work. My mom had to have a job. It made her tired. But it wasn't just that, it wasn't only that she was tired from her job. She was going out on more dates, so she was always busy, either working or out. She talked wistfully about Pancho Gonzalez, the tennis star. Another friend of hers was supposed to be his cousin. She was a woman who talked too fast, too much, and she drank and she laughed wrong. She and my mom both bleached their hair platinum, but this friend's was ugly and cheap-looking. She was a *fea,* short and plump and pimply, but she thought she was as pretty as my mom. She was bad news, I knew, because by then I was smarter than my mom seemed to be. This "cousin" did not help my mom win Pancho Gonzalez, but they got drunk a lot together. My mom's Puerto Rican friend stopped coming around. Maybe she was sailing on the Pacific Ocean, maybe not yet, but she was married, and she was rich, and we weren't.

Though the modeling jobs weren't talked about anymore, weren't around, the pretty clothes were. Bills came in the mail daily. I would answer the phone and a bill collector would ask for her and I would say she wasn't home even if she was. She was working for a dentist who was a Mormon, and she was dating him, and two old biddies started coming to our door and lecturing my mom, and I listened to them with her, for her. I answered their questions because she didn't know the answers. She wanted to become a Mormon, she didn't care how. We went to his house for Thanksgiving, the first Thanksgiving dinner I had ever been to. The dentist's mother had a bun of white and gray hair and a frilly apron, just like one of those grandmothers on TV shows. We had to sit at a long dinner table, longer than any I'd seen on television, crowded with people. It was a feast of full bowls and platters that were passed around, and I ate so much turkey and mashed potatoes that it made me sick the rest of my life, but I didn't think it was because I overate. It was because they didn't like her. Well, I didn't like these people from the start. When my mom and I spoke to each other, because we stayed so close, the others looked at us like we were being secretive, as if we were talking in Spanish, not English. After dinner we took a walk around his neighborhood—it was green with overgrown trees and grass, and there weren't always sidewalks, and the idea was that he would get to know me a little—when my mom said something was wrong, she was bleeding. She assured me it wasn't that kind of bleeding, teased me for not understanding immediately, but he didn't laugh. He didn't like this, didn't want to have to find an open store, and couldn't believe she couldn't know something like this, wouldn't be prepared. She sloughed that off, wanting to be cheerful. She wanted to make him happy. But he didn't laugh. I don't know what happened after that. This was the man I'd been lying to new junior high friends about. Before I met him, she had told me that she was going to marry him. He was a dentist, she'd told me. My dad, I'd tell these guys, snooty, was a dentist. I wanted us to be richer than them. After that day I don't remember ever hearing her talk about him again, and I never asked.

Two or three times my mom had taken me to an old lady's house. It was an old house, with old things, and I had to have polite manners and eat boring food. The woman, she told me, thought I was a bright boy and liked it when I visited her and, my mom said, I might be getting an inheritance from her. The woman was nice, and I didn't think anything bad about her, but this didn't sound right to me. By now my mom didn't always seem too trustworthy. But I didn't know what else to do, so when the old lady died, I went to the funeral parlor with my mom to pay last respects. There were no other people, and still I felt as though we were being watched like thieves. The casket was open, though I didn't look close. It was like a church, with wooden pews, and crosses, and Jesuses, though no Virgins. My mom's knees went onto the padded kneel board, and as they did she made a loud pedo. I don't think I'd ever heard that from her before. She looked at me and I looked at her and we both tried to hold back. The more we did, the worse it hurt, and the stronger was the desire to laugh. She kept kneeling there, her hands folded and her head down like she was polite and praying, but really she was giggling, and she looked over at me, and we both started laughing too hard. There was no inheritance for either of us.

One night, I was watching TV when a man my mom worked for and I think she'd also gone out with, came to the door screaming about her. She was out, a date, I didn't know a where or a who or a when. He was wailing about money, what had she done with his money. He was drunk and howling and cussing. I knew about drunk because sometimes there were bottles in the house, glasses broken sometimes, laughter. I knew who this man at the door was because he'd shot someone. Mom had told me about him before, and I'd heard her tell her friends. He kept beating on the door, and it finally blew open right in front of me just as a cop neighbor I'd called from down the street came running up. A week later she married a man raised somewhere near Lancaster. I'd never heard of him, I'd never met him before. He was the cousin of a woman she'd worked with. He had the stupidest grin, as stupid as his hick name. What I liked about him was that he asked me if there was one thing he could do for me. I said I wanted him to take me to see Washington, D.C., and he grinned that dumb grin and said he would. I actually believed him. He and my mom went to Arizona for a week for their honeymoon, and after that, we moved into his place. He wore a different, clean green uniform every day for his job, and most of the other time, too. There were deer heads and birds and fish on the walls. Maple furniture, a family table with a bunch of matching chairs around it. He had a son who was a taxidermist, and he was proud of him. My mom's new husband was an electrician and a couple of times I worked for him and that's when I heard him tell his working friends he just felt so lucky to be married to such a pretty Mexican gal. A few weeks later she went to and was chosen on the TV show *Let's Make a Deal*. When Monty Hall asked her name, she told him her new name without a flinch. But she didn't win anything big, twenty or forty bucks, and she didn't get to pick a door.

It couldn't have been too long after that she asked me to go to lunch with her. We hadn't gone out together, the two of us, in a long time because she was so busy with a new husband. They were beginning to have arguments, quiet or out loud, about bills and money, and they raced to get the mail first. The lunch was with the loud man she'd dated before. He took us to a restaurant. I don't remember the food or whether I had a good or bad time, only that when he pulled into the driveway of the apartment building where we lived, she jumped out of the car and rushed to the front door, and I was stuck in the backseat and this old boyfriend leaned back to talk to me. He told me he loved my mom and he was sorry and he wished something or other, I don't know. It was a speech, and it seemed as if he might cry or already was crying, but I told him I had to go and got out of his car. Maybe this was why I didn't like him. Big as he was, he was too loud, and yet he would cry. It could've been a coupe Thunderbird, and I didn't even enjoy that. I knew things weren't good between my mom and her husband, that she wasn't happy, and I didn't judge her—I figured out that she'd been sneaking out for these lunches before I went with her—but I stopped being around my mom and her husband as much as possible. I never liked the deer meat or the maple furniture or the Hank Snow music, and I ate with my new neighborhood friends, stayed as late as I could with them, lots of times overnight. For a while after my mom and her husband separated, we lived in an apartment complex on the south side of town, and she would just lie on the couch, half awake, half asleep, depressed. We didn't talk too much. I had a job, and even though I was getting in fights at high school, and she was getting vice-principal calls about suspensions and swats and the rest, she didn't really care, and I didn't think it was such a big deal, either.

She married the loud fireman I hadn't liked, who was almost ten years younger than she was—though nobody ever thought so—and who loved her after all this time, and we moved. He bought her a brand-new house and everything that went in it, and it was as if we were rich, though I didn't feel as though anything was mine. It was all theirs. His and hers. He wasn't around very much. He worked hard at two jobs—he drove a Brink's truck, too—and she had all the money she'd ever dreamed of because he gave her his paychecks as if she were a financial wizard. When we were alone, or when she was joking in front of the women who would visit, her old friends and so many new friends—she was the one who made all the friends because she left her door open and everybody loved her—she would say that he could be boring and dull, that if he wasn't gone most of the time, if she didn't keep him working two jobs . . . Then she'd laugh, and everyone would laugh with her. She always had food, and always a drink. There were jugs of wine, and beer, and other liquor. There was a new blender, the best. He loved to drink with her, too. He loved everything she did, everything she bought, anything she bought, and she bought everything, and he loved her so much. She was the best thing that he could ever imagine happening to him, his life was full of sunlight and colors he'd never seen. I wasn't around much, going back to my old friends in my old high school, going to a new job to have my own money, partying myself now, too, playing with drugs and liquor and girlfriends—I was happy that she wasn't worried anymore. Since she didn't have to do anything but please him, she pleased him. He didn't like "spicy" food, so she learned to cook potatoes and roasts. She babied him when he got home from a job, made him feel like he ran the world. They drank together. They talked to each other and had fun when they drank. When she was around him, she became like him. When he thought he should be serious, he droned philosophically about black people and illegal aliens. My mom was an illegal alien, born out of wed-lock in Mexico, D.F., and baptized at the basilica honoring the *Virgen de Guadalupe*. She often tried to stop him when he went off on a long editorial, but it wasn't always worth it to her, and I began to see that she wasn't only my mom anymore, she was his wife.

My mother was becoming a person I wouldn't want to know, and sometimes in anger, lots of anger at me, especially when I didn't go along with everything she had become, when I was reminding her of the past that she didn't want to remember, she'd get mad. Once I told a neighbor her husband wasn't my real father. I didn't know I wasn't supposed to say this. I was sorry I embarrassed her. I didn't even care about my real father much, only saw him a couple of days a year, but the only times my mother's husbands were "fathers" were when others made that assumption. They were just men to me, part of her life, not mine. Another time, after a year of living in this new house with this new husband, whatever I'd said or done got her so angry she told me she didn't know where I'd come from. She meant it, too, looking at me like I was an utter stranger, a lousy tenant.

I graduated from high school. I moved out. I got a job as a stock boy. I started junior college.

On a Tuesday morning, just before dawn, I jerked myself out of a dream. It was so strong I turned on a light and wrote it down. In the dream, a voice was talking to me, asking me if I wanted to talk to my mom. Why wouldn't I? Because we never did anymore, hadn't really talked in decades. When we did, there was nothing but strain and mutual disapproval, and for several consecutive years, there was nothing at all. I'd moved far away, to El Paso. The voice, not my mom's, was asking me questions from my mom, and I'd started responding to the dream, to the voice, and straight to my mom. It was in the form of an interview, her questions and my answers. I answered the voice, yes, I always loved her. I loved my mommy so much. She had to know I didn't care about whatever was bad that had come between us, that I would remember only how much I loved her. I was always so proud of her. I said I thought she was the best mommy, the most beautiful woman. I loved her so much. I said I understood everything she'd gone through. Of course I didn't think only about the past, our troubles. Of course I forgave her, and I told her I wanted her to forgive me, too. And then I was overcome by a sob that wasn't in my dream but in my physical body and my mouth and my eyes.

Two days later, her husband called me. He was calm and positive. My mom, he said, had been taken to the hospital Tuesday. She was found unconscious. There was a problem with her liver. She was in intensive care, but he was convinced she'd be fine, she'd be home soon. He just thought I should know. I thought this sounded much more serious, so I called the hospital and got a nurse and asked bluntly. She said I was right, it usually was only a matter of time, it could be at any moment, though it could also take days or even a few weeks. I asked about the liver, whether it was the usual reason a liver goes. The nurse asked, Well, was she always the life of the party? I got a plane ticket. I remembered a visit the year earlier, finding an empty vodka bottle—plastic, the cheapest brand you could buy—in the corner of the bedroom I was sleeping in, where she kept a mountain of purses and shoes and wallets. I'd found another bottle, most of it gone, behind a closet door that she left open.

I rented a car and went to the hospital. She was bloated, her hair a tussle—this woman who never missed a hairdresser's appointment—an unappealing white gown tied around her. Tubes needled into her hand and arm, a clear mask was over her mouth and nose. When she saw me, her eyes opened. She had no voice. I talked. Years had passed, she knew little about my life. She knew that I did construction work, thought it was all I did, ever, didn't know anything about the other life I led, the one as a writer. I never told her. I was afraid that she would only be his wife, not my mom, and she wouldn't care in the appropriate way. Or that she would be too relieved, and that all those other years I'd been struggling, when she didn't seem to care, when she disapproved of me, even thought I deserved whatever misery befell me, would be forgotten. I didn't want to give that up so easily. These were the reasons I had told her nothing. But I knew my mom would be proud. I knew she would be so happy for me. I told her that not only was I a writer, but I had one book published and another one just out. I had won prizes. I had been going to New York City and Washington, D.C. I'd gone there more than once, and I never paid. Her eyes smiled so big. I knew she would like this the most. She always wanted to travel the world. Can you believe they were even giving me money? I asked her. She *was* proud of me, and she was as surprised as I was about it. And then I told her why I had to come. I told her about the dream I'd had two nights before, on the first night she'd spent in the hospital. My mom's eyes stopped moving. I said, I talked to you, you were talking to me, we were talking. She nodded, and her whole weakened body squirmed while she was nodding! I wouldn't believe this story if I'd heard it. It was such a telenovela deathbed scene, mother and son, both weeping about a psychic conversation routed hundreds of miles through the smog and traffic and over the mountains and across three deserts, from one dream to another, so that we wouldn't miss telling each other for the last time before she died. She was as stunned as me, as happy as me. You know? She kept nodding, looking at me, crying. Oh, Mom, I said.

Me Macho, You Jane

I've been accused of suffering from involuntary macho spasms most of my life. Usually not to my face. Very few got the huevos for that! Okay, maybe a couple of people have mentioned it. Tell you the truth, I don't know what it is they're talking about. To me it's a lot like my astrological sign. Which is Leo. I remember this party a long long time ago. "A Leo, of course he's a Leo, what else would he be?" My sign had pissed these people off. I was pissed off back. What're you gonna do about it? I snorted, my chin up, the muscles in my hands twitching to knot up, feeling light and quick. I don't remember what I'd done or said, if that was it. Was I too wasted? I didn't belong at that party. Too pseudo-hippie for me (real hippies were too stoned to make accusations). Another one I've often heard is that it's Mexican blood. A hot, spicy colorado. Now you see what I'm getting at? That it's usually a complaint about some behavior, or perceived potential for, these people don't approve of. Sort of like when I'm saying I like cockfights. Not as much as certain friends of mine, but I do. I hear the moaning already. People on low-fat, boneless-chicken-is-okay diets. Somehow roosters fighting is a lot worse than football or boxing. But I've sat in stands with all kinds of people, men and women, at all kinds of sporting events, and it's the same screaming noises to me.

I was raised by my mom. My father lived in the same house as me maybe my first year or two. My first stepfather was when I was thirteen. I was not too fond of this first stepfather. He did not teach me to like manhood. Did my mom teach me to be a macho? She had a mean temper, that's true. And I know I got my temper from her. She was a wild, beautiful woman, though. So I'm telling you the truth, I'm not really sure what being macho is. Except sometimes when I see how some wuss behaves.

Is it risk taking? Danger? Women who take physical risks, look for danger, aren't they being "macho"? Or the threat of violence. Shooting guns. Killing animals. Or men talking about women. Especially a naked woman, real or imagined.

I've come to this office because I need a machine she has offered me the use of for free. Time and place, from a long time ago to now, from L.A. to El Paso and between or a few miles east or north, I will not specify for reasons of security. Though I barely know her, I sense this woman is interested in me. Twitch twitch. Okay, score that remark as macho evidence for the prosecution. I know I'm right, though (go ahead, score that one, too). But I'm not interested in her, haven't been. In fact, I've avoided her a few times because I don't want the trouble. I'd rather we be friends (score that for the other side?). She's into the local power movement, is playing that sport. I imagine how someday she'll run for public office. A Chicana superstar. I'm thinking this as she's talking to me, all these papers strewn everywhere, paper clips and staplers, dirty telephones with long cords all tangled up, posters and bulletin boards, take-out boxes, coffee cups, beer bottles, ashtrays. I'm listening to her quietly, sitting across from her, not really following a story she's telling me about political capital, those who have what and where and how much, and the arguments each has about accumulating more and positioning for it, the difficulties she has as a woman, an attractive woman, elbowing her way in. She is a nice-looking woman, too. At certain angles, she's unquestionably sexy. She's got a husky laugh because she's large-boned, maybe on the heavy side. She's tough, as fearless and aggressive about her opinions as her desires. Her appetite for fun is as big and loud as she is. Big breasts, too. Which all adds up to say that she's not the type I've usually known in a biblical respect. Which is what I'm considering as I'm paying the most superficial attention to what she's saying. Why not? is what I'm thinking. Maybe we get drunk, laugh, maybe we ought to take off our clothes in the dark. For the sake of acting bad, to play, not be romantic. Suddenly she says something that startles me into the flow of her monologue: ". . . doesn't like a woman, a tough bitch like me, onstage getting attention. He's so macho. Like you." She's talking about this politico I don't know personally but can't not know of because he's always news. I ask for an explanation. "You know what I mean," she says. No, I don't. I don't at all. I've never run for any political position. I've never been or even wanted to be anybody's boss. "Yours isn't bad like his," she explains, laughing. Flirting. I don't know *her* well, so how come she decides she knows *me,* knows my "good" or "bad" machismo? In the past I've been nothing less than a gentleman in all respects, and even now, haven't I been sitting there quietly, practically without moving, waiting, listening politely to her about this pedo I could care less about so I can use a machine? I have said or done absolutely zero that would give her any knowledge of who I am or how I behave. Ni una cosa, nothing.

I worked this four-story in Newport Beach, California, a building so close to Pacific Ocean salt water that it pushed against a parking structure sheerwall like an aquarium, above which was a view of uncountable masts of million-dollar yachts and catamarans lining the curving bay's piers. All the other carpenters were Anglo. I'd become the Chicano from Texas. From no less than mythical El Paso: the Rio Grande, adobes, Rosa's Cantina, Tony Lama cowboy boots, Juárez whorehouses. I wasn't just me, in other words. I was an embodiment. I was as wild as the West Texas wind because I was living in a motel room and I didn't want to continue to work for the company once this job ended. I was even planning to leave sooner than that. Once I'd earned enough, I was outta there, thanks, hasta la próxima, and laters. The boys knew this about me because I was still there, the only one still around who'd come out of the union hall. The superintendent called men from the hall when some walls had to be formed up in a hurry for a large cement pour, then a week later, almost two, they were down the road. But he liked my work, and leaving me on was like a long-term employment offer. He kept company men busy all over L.A. and Orange counties. These were guys who talked about which company jobs they'd been at, how many years. It seemed like a good outfit, too, but as complimented as I was, I was there for the money to be made on this job site alone.

I told guys I lived in Texas because I didn't want to live on California freeways and in stucco tract houses. That I had plans to go my own way. I mentioned side jobs I got in El Paso and implied that eventually they would lead to something, or, if not, I just didn't care. No, I did not mention my writing. It wasn't like I had to hide it, since it was not a topic that ever popped up. I didn't and wouldn't want it to anyway, and wouldn't have blinked if it had. With over ten years in the trade at the time, I was a carpenter both to myself and to everyone I worked with, nothing more, nothing less. It's how I wanted it, too. What I inwardly prized about construction (most of the time) was you were judged not by your talk but what you did, on time, right. What I liked about construction was that at the end of the day, when you were joint- and bone-sore, when your feet throbbed, when you required cold beer to numb the pain, you knew you

were tired from really working. You rubbed the yellowed calluses, hard as fingernails on the index finger and thumb of your
hammer hand, picked at feathery splinters in your palms that
seemed to grow hormonally like body hair, wiped away drib-
bling tie-wire cuts you discovered where you hadn't felt them
happen. What I liked was that at the end of the day, you felt like
a man, and at the end of the week, you got your check, and at
the end of a job, you knew you *earned* your money.

Now I'm ready to tell you about The Asshole. The caps are
important in my opinion, descriptive of his transcendent dimension. He's a kid. Looks seventeen, though maybe nineteen. Probably twenty-one, since he could buy beer. He's pudgy, a soft
though unblubbery fat cushioning his belly and wrapping his
arms, where there ought to be at least a little muscle tone (we're
talking about men in the building trades, you know?). He's a third-
or fourth-period apprentice carpenter, meaning in his second year
of four. He rides what sounds like an uncorked Yamaha. He's got
on a black helmet, with a black-tinted visor, and a black leather
jacket. He thinks he is all things bad, and in the morning, he
struts into work with the attitude. He's a biker. He's a champion
football player. He's a sex machine. He's a lots-of-lines doper—
meth and coke, but he's done 'em all and can anytime—and he
gulps white lightning. He's a musician and an asskicker and a killer
if he has to be. His dog is a Doberman, and he's saving for a Harley.
He carries a buck knife, owns a Luger, wants a Magnum.

He doesn't have a toolbox in the lockup, just a hard hat and
bags—hammer, tape, trisquare, pencil (often no pencil)—and so
one of the first specifically irritating things about him is that he
asks to borrow tools the company doesn't supply but that any
carpenter is supposed to carry. A crescent wrench, a cat's paw, a
flat bar, a level, a chisel, screwdrivers, handsaws. At first the loans
were made, like they would have been to anyone who asked.
When he didn't give a tool back for days, once he was asked,

usually it hadn't been lost yet. Usually, though a few times already. Tools getting lost on a job is nothing new, and it's part of the expense. But nobody likes a guy who borrows his shit, and nobody likes anyone who loses his tools. That was just one particular reason the carpenters on the job shook their heads about him.

Mine was different, though. I already couldn't stand him after the first break time I sat down, new on the crew, and he opened his mouth. It wasn't just the boot-high bullshit. It was the whiny, lazy, slow, dumb, loutish American audacity of it. The seeming privilege of it. I didn't like him because he was a punk, and what made my dislike unique was that I was up-front about it. I said so to anyone and most of all to him. Right in his face. "Go away. Go. Away. I do not want you to work anywhere near me. Good-bye." Guys would find this hysterical. The first times he smiled like I was kidding, even though it was clear to anyone with a two-digit IQ I was not, and he bobbed between staying and leaving. The superintendent told him to help here, he whimpered. "I don't care. You do not work here. You work over there, you find anything else to do somewhere else. Away from me. Leave." If he wavered, I was unhesitant. "Now!" I'd yell, to make my meaning less complex.

I had tried to work with him a few times. He was one of those who'd stand there forever if you didn't suggest he do *something,* watching you do everything, all alone, like that was his job description. Okay, I was a journeyman, he was an apprentice, so I'd only shake my head: I'd suggest he lift up the end of this 4 × 6—but that was too heavy for him because it was too wet, or cement-logged, or he'd been out too late, or he hadn't worked out last week. Measure that—he'd stare at the tape, and stare, then give a few numbers, remeasure, and it'd be wrong. I'd even gotten real simple and asked him to get nails, or plywood—that was what laborers did! Or he'd be gone so long I could've forged or glued my own. If he didn't forget, if he came back. He was enthusiastic only when the lunch wagon blew its horn, though he also had bad taste in food. Old wrinkled hot dogs on stale yet wet buns, packaged burritos, Twinkies. He savored these like a gourmet. Quitting time was the only part of the day he was quick. No, I could not understand why he was on the payroll at all. I told him so. And I told him he should learn to take a shower, with soap, and to use deodorant, and to brush his teeth, and to wash his stinking underwear and socks and probably the rest of his clothes once in a while, told him he should hang baking soda from his neck. I was dead serious.

The more insulting I got, the more he began to admire me. Yes, you read that correctly. I'd never heard of such a thing, either, and certainly had never experienced anything so twisted. Would this be unwanted, obsessive macho bonding? I was wild, hooting Texas. I was outlaw Mexican El Paso. To extinguish the chance of having to sit with him at break or lunch, I'd go over with the laborers, all mejicanos, who usually sat a distance away from the English-speaking carpenters. Once or twice I caught him peering at me with the metaphorical equivalent of his mouth wide open, tongue limp on his lower lip (I'd move so my back was to him). I was so exotic! Oh how could *he* become exotic like *me*? I was a Doberman with Great Dane size, or a custom Harley. He did finally come to understand that I was serious about not wanting him near me, not even within my sight. But he came around anyway, like I was an irresistible force, and I'd have to sling more contempt. You wouldn't believe the words I used to send him off. And he'd say and do nothing. He'd disappear, maybe a day or two, maybe come back hours later to talk to another guy, until he thought, I guess, I'd forgotten or forgiven, and then I'd hurl more paeans of loathing. Did the power of them, their threat and fearsomeness and bravado, sting his wimpy psyche until it was testosterone-numb with envy and fascination?

It was like some warped Beauty and the Beast tale. Disgusting. Pathetic. Bizarre. I was not seeking any happy ending. Did I hate the dude? No. I just wanted him to go away, to not be anywhere near me. About his existence I felt an active indifference. That once I was gone, I wouldn't care what his future held, good or bad, and wouldn't care to know. I'd be grateful never to be around the weirdo asshole again, grateful I wouldn't have to be.

When that last day came, I'd already said good-bye to the crew, was about to step off the dust and dirt and paraphernalia of the job site, my hard hat on backward, my tool bags looped over one shoulder, the other shoulder sagging from the weight of my toolbox, when he struts up. And I can tell he's wanting to act like a man. Like one out of a World War II movie or something.

"You're a real good carpenter," he says with a respect verging on I don't want to know. And then he puts out his too-plump, too-soft hand for a handshake.

Graduate seminar, Tucson, Arizona, fall 1992. The subject was books of fiction. I sat at the head of the tables—six tables shoved together to make one in a nondescript room in the halls of the English department. The color of the room was manila, as in folders. It was a one-semester appointment in the creative writing program. I'd assigned a few writers I valued—John Fante, Langston Hughes, Juan Rulfo, Naguib Mahfouz, Cormac McCarthy. An initial list also included Paul Bowles, and I was considering Hubert Selby, Jr. Note the shortage of female names. And I was taking over an established, and preenrolled, seminar from a professor whose course title was "Women Writers and the World of Their Invention." I hadn't been told this small detail when I accepted the employment, and when she sent me her course description, I knew very quickly I was the wrong construction worker for the duty. I had to think and act fast to order books I knew, and

I did consider retitling the course "Men and Their Books." With Selby as a possible (my sincere hesitation was that a movie had been made; I was interested in the linkage of style and story, and movies cheat close reading), all I'd have to do is add Charles Bukowski and the tanks would be gased. So I didn't. I wasn't there yet, and they didn't know me, and I was afraid nobody would laugh. I did have three other books on the list. Ones by Pat Little Dog (Pat Ellis Taylor), J. California Cooper, and Leslie Marmon Silko. Who are women. Since people didn't recognize but one of them, they thought they too were men names and men books.

When I arrived, there was much less laughter than I could've imagined. Upset students, nervous faculty. A sexual-harrassment charge draped everyone like a trench coat, and, I was to learn, hiring me, a male and a man like I was, was met with such disapproval it was as though all I wore was a trench coat. I was asked to add more books by women, so I added two, an anthology of stories about and by bad girls, and a novel by Jean Rhys. I'd already decided to pass on Selby, and I dropped Bowles. It wasn't as if doing this troubled me in the slightest. I wanted to joke and say how I really really liked women. How I'd teach any they wanted me to, and I'd read them, too! But I left my sense of humor out of it. My physical presence did not seem to inspire too much confidence, either. After my first meeting with those in charge, eyes stumbling around like the words were, after I said I had absolutely no discomfort adding and subtracting books for this course, that I even sincerely agreed with the student complaints (they enrolled for a course for and about woman, and this large and loud guy shows up), after that, standing in the busy hall with my first-day escort, I just couldn't hold back one bromita, one small crack. "Where's the men's room? They do allow them here still, don't they?" I thought it was a little funny. My escort pointed, unsure, without smiling.

I sat at the head of the tables, a couple of months in. One student in the class was the program's most bitter—unhappy with the state of Arizona (she was from the East), unhappy with the department's MFA program (evidence: my visiting, substitute presence), unhappy specifically with several professors (her unconventional thesis not being received enthusiastically). Since there was much grumbling going on with many students, I didn't know whether this was simply a common by-product of all writing programs, or all graduate schools, or not. I'd read none of her creative work, but she was bright, and most of all she was hardworking, a trait that went a long way with me.

The book assigned that week was by Rick DeMarinis, a writer whose work I admire as much as I like him. An extremely rare combination. Though DeMarinis is highly regarded among fiction writers, I teased the students, warning them that he lived in El Paso and was my friend. The book, *The Burning Women of Far Cry,* is a comic coming-of-age novel set in Montana. The women are smart and sexually wild and they drink, the men scam and pine for women and drink.

Usually this student was quiet and needed prodding to speak. This evening she opened the seminar. She picked up DeMarinis's novel by a corner and held it in the air. Picked up the novel like it wasn't a book, with a thumb and finger, at the farthest corner. Like it was soiled. Smelled. Like her fingers would be smeared by it. Holding the very least of it possible. She turned her eyes away like it didn't deserve their contact. Picked up the novel, eyes averted, held her arm out toward the center of the tables, dropped it, and said, "I can't believe we're expected to read a book like this in a graduate-level seminar." Her tone was contemptuous, defiant, fearlessly in the right.

Her complaint? The portrayal of women. Especially the excessive depiction of their glorious breasts.

To be honest, I hadn't especially noticed the breasts in the novel. And I'd still say that they do not dominate any character description, are not part of even a motif. What interested me in the story was the broken family, the stepfathers, the jobs. What consumed me was the commanding, simple beauty of DeMarinis's prose. Yet the student seemed to have a good, quality argument. I could see how tasteless, how male-fetished the subject might be. So if talking about women's breasts is an inappropriate fixation, how much should be attributed to the writer's character and how much to the character's? Is it breasts in general? I'd have to confess that I like women's breasts. I keep this mostly to myself, but is it wrong to admit it openly? When I hear guys talk about them (about tits, to put it bluntly) with other guys, I think so. Is that generalizing? I don't like all women's breasts, or only breasts, not even mainly, just as I don't like all women. Or is it size? Criticize the consistent description of size? When we criticize, do we criticize the writer for willful obsession, or for what is written unaware? Which are his character's flaws, which are his, and how ought they be controlled or not? All of these, and many angles I'm sure I haven't thought of, all of these great topics for discussion in a graduate creative-writing seminar.

I say that now. Because when the book plopped on the table, as the room went silent, so did I. I lost sentence consciousness. There was, indeed, only one word left in me, yet inchoate, spiritually forming, physically germinating: *kill*.

As there are differences between men and women, there are differences between men and men. They are bulk and muscle, and they begin to be sensed at an early age. Eventually one boy will recognize another's, and we get in fights to test boundaries. As young men, we act more or less on bulking and muscling, or not, to a level of satisfaction and resignation. We learn who we are going to be physically smaller than. We accept the larger and smaller distinctions among us. In a dispute with another man, we silently scale each other. At the construction sites where I've so far spent most of my adult work hours, which is where lots of *those* guys go after high school, arguments are too often not subtle. When there's verbal screaming, a real nonverbal howl kicks. Whereas in a world of ideas, at universities, words are king. Arguments are supposed to be bulky and muscular, not the person advancing them. Even ad hominem attacks are too physical in nature. It is the very condition that I love about a university environment. It is a paradise where brutishness is the bottom, where civility and manners are high tools of learning.

No *guy* would have dared to do what that student did. Unless he thought he could kick my ass. When male students look me in the eye, and I look back, we've opened a discussion. We have either decided mutually to accept the rules of the idea world, or we have scaled. *And* we have scaled. Because we always scale each other, no matter what. There is no other possibility. He would never have spoken to me thus without being afraid or being ready. But this didn't even occur to the student. She felt right, plain and simple, and self-righteous outrage and behavior never led to anyone smacking her in the fucking face, which parallel activity on a construction site would lead to almost assuredly. Men don't hit women. The rudeness of dropping the book, my friend's book, a book I assigned for a course with only good intentions, that insult to me, *at* me—a male student would have known the wordless realm he tossed it into.

So what did I do? Nothing. We had none of the potential conversations I spoke of above. I think I tried to maintain some professorial decorum. I don't remember if I achieved any. I have no memory of what anyone else said. Stunted conversations, or was that my attention? I do remember telling myself that I was being paid. This was a mental game I learned from miserable construction jobs. I dismissed the class very early. I remember

my rage and disgust, seeing around a hot desert light glaring in
my eyes as the sun was setting. I remember it as my last class,
even though I sat at the head of those tables a few more times.

Several years earlier, I'd taken up coaching because I couldn't
stand it anymore. Coaches were either overpraising baby-sitters
or Nazis. I picked up a seven-to-eight-year-old team that included
my youngest boy, but I was too late to get an eleven-to-twelve
group. Meaning my oldest son, Tony, had to find a team, and
quick. Which turned out to be one coached by a man I knew
because I'd coached his son several times. I will tell you this
honestly. His son was not so good an athlete. To put it more
ungenerously, he sucked. He was a kind boy with a good and
gentle heart who didn't like sports. He may not have been able
to say so in words, but his body wrote clear sentences. It was his
dad who wanted sports for him.

There were a few reasons I didn't like this coach very much.
Most had to do with his being an overbearing Christian. A new
Christian. One of those who didn't understand that someone else
could have a belief that was as well considered as his. If he wasn't
loud, which he was sometimes, his sanctimonious moralism was
always screaming. He'd been a foster parent, and now his job,
an admirable one, too, was as a houseparent for a larger group
of boys at a home. He thought they should behave like they
were sixty-year-old men grateful for any conversation. Line up
politely and be quiet. Listen to him. Listen when he's talking!
It was like school, day and night, and the main lesson was that
lessons were to be learned. No time for art or music or any parallel
waste of time. Almost all the boys were Chicanos. They spoke
Spanish, and their English was strongly accented, often broken.
He didn't like that. Not at all. He'd shake his head. What *is it*
you're trying to say? he'd snap, intolerant, as if stupidity were an
accent or a mispronounced word. He didn't think there was

anything valuable enough about Mexican culture that wasn't already better in the U.S.A.

His son was to be their example. In all things. I'd coached lots of these boys, just as I had his son. I liked his son, and I liked the boys. And the boys, including his, liked me and our teams because we had fun when we played and we mostly won, and if we lost, no big deal. All of which was why this man didn't like me. He didn't say so. It was a sense I had is all. An instinct. I was inferior, he was sure of it. Something about me. And so, I swore he didn't think these boys ought to like me. I swore he took up coaching because he didn't want someone like me, and my influence, around his boys and his lessons. He didn't want to let it be said that I was a better coach.

These were my oldest son's peak years for basketball, and he had quickly become the star of the team, unquestionably the best player. I loved that. I was proud of my Toño. I loved it for him, and I loved him for it, and I loved it because I didn't like the coach. Underneath, I felt I was a better dad and coach and man because my son played basketball better than his. I was proud in larger ways, too. Because of how the coach thought, because my son was a Chicano.

They were winning this game quickly. When Tony got the ball, he scored. It wasn't like he was hogging it, wasn't like he was trying to hot-dog. That was never his style. When he got the ball, he tried to get it to others, but they wouldn't shoot it, or they missed, or they sent it back to him. He shot and usually made it. The other kids didn't mind. They liked the winning part a lot.

And they were winning easy, and big, when the coach shouted. For several games previous, he'd been yapping at his son for not taking charge, for not shooting, not rebounding, for standing around doing nothing. He was mad on that deeper level, too, as disappointed as I was proud. Then I heard him go after

Tony. It was about not putting it up so much, about having the ball too much. The coach was wrong. In principle, as an idea, he was right, but not in this circumstance. It definitely wouldn't have been true if it were his son, is what I'd say. His logic and principles and understanding would have altered then. There was a kid like Tony on everybody's team, and most boys were closer to his son. But in truth, it wasn't about either boy. No, I'd say. It was about me. It was about me and him. That's what I'd say.

It was when the coach barked at Tony again, told him he had to sit down, that I leaped out of my chair across the court. Something uncontrollable gripped me. Stronger than anger. Pride. Respect. Fairness. Not that I was working around those concepts clearly. "Motherfucker, you leave him alone!"

My hot voice echoed off the hardwood floors and high ceiling of the gym, bounced louder and more rude off east and west walls—a proverbial echo, unobstructed, magnified by cool, whispering autumn air. I couldn't believe it had come out of me, since moments before, I'd been sitting there, watching little kids playing ball in a game I sincerely didn't find slightly important. Tony didn't, either. He didn't even care that he was being yelled at.

The coach glared at me, appalled. Worse yet, I caught something else, too. An I-told-you-so smirk. Now he had confirmed that I was from the crass, violent, low-class, vulgur, gang-ridden, unfit-to-lead culture he so clearly wasn't. I'd justified him and his self-righteous fundamentalism. But I was shamed equally about being an American, the ugliest kind. Abuelitas, sitting gracious and gentle near me, with Sunday shawls over their shoulders, watching their sweet nietecitos playing and being nothing but young and sweet, leaned forward, stunned, disgusted, as if I'd hocked one onto the foot of the *Virgin de Guadalupe*. Two little girls got off their seats to step out onto the court and look at the face of the goon. Their innocent mouths were open, and even their eyes wanted to keep their distance. If I could've left, I would have. It was that I was in a corner and the door was at the other end, and I couldn't.

Spasms. Twitches. Juice. Blood. Alignment of moon and stars and sun and planets. Hormones. Sex or violence. Meat. Or manners. Nobility or a lack of. What you're embarrassed about, what you're proud of.

Here's a list: I like women. I like women better than men. I think some people deserve to get their asses kicked. I don't go to bullfights. Well, I've been to a couple, but only because they're in Juárez and it's something to do. My current drink is tequila and grapefruit juice, or vodka and tonic with two squeezes of lemon. I don't drink beer very often, and I love baseball and basketball and don't care for football much. You don't like that, screw you. I love my family. I love walking the streets, or up a mountain, or a desert trail, alone. I eat beef. And serrano chiles.

L.A. Navidad

That December was a mist against the skin at six-fifteen A.M., a slimy dew that burned away only hours after the sun rose. I switched on the wipers; squealing, a few streaks. It was almost too cold to have the car window down on the drive to the job site. I wore a sweatshirt until, an hour with the hammer and nail bags, concrete mud and rock, I was warm enough, and then the gray winter shadow of moisture in the air became another of afternoon smog. Winter wasn't cold but an absence of hot, a T-shirt. Winter in Los Angeles is grayer than in spring and summer and fall.

It was Saturday, a half-day of OT, tools back in the lockup, and before I headed home, I drank a few of the beers with the crew next to the superintendent's shack by the excavation pit, a city block big, off 2nd and Beaudry. It would be called a clear day in Los Angeles, the sky would be called blue. Three months earlier we'd moved into a two-bedroom apartment in East Hollywood. We'd left the last apartment, which was cheaper, because of a little legal disagreement with the landlord. I'd had this job—a thirty-story poured-in-place—for two months, and if I didn't get laid off, it would last a year or more. As depicted by an artist on a billboard next to the site, it was the first of a projected four highrises to go up against the Harbor Freeway.

Once I got home, I wasn't even able to think of a shower before Becky slammed through the door.

"Come on!" she told me. "We have to go now!" She was holding the baby, Ricardo, in her arms.

"What?"

"He called me a stupid Mexican." As black as her hair was, her eyes glared even blacker. "I am so mad!"

"What?"

"This man. When I was pulling out, he didn't like something I did, and so he screamed at me. 'You stupid fucking Mexican! Why don't you learn to drive?' I almost had a accident driving back. You just had to be here, I had to get you."

She was furious. She did have this primordial temper—ancient, pre-Columbian. When we had fights, we really had fights. I imagined them as telenovela metaphors of the conquest, a spilling of Indian and Spanish blood.

"He's not getting away with it," she said. "I wish I were a man. He thinks he can say that to me, I can't believe he thinks he can get away with saying that to me."

"So where's Toño?" I asked. He was five.

"He's waiting for us in the car."

I shook my head as a kind of sigh of resignation: there was no backing off. It had been years since she'd made any demand like this. The first time, not long after we met, she escorted me to a telephone booth, where she'd been waiting so patiently, where some rude guy refused to get off the phone. She told me once, Why have a boyfriend who's big if he can't do what I always wish I could?

It wasn't a long drive, a few blocks away, off Vermont and Santa Monica.

"He might not be there by now," I suggested. I was still having to work myself up some, getting mad, too, but I had converted, decided she was right. Seemed like we were getting a lot of this stuff lately. Like whenever we walked into the store owned by those Armenians around the corner, they'd watch us— all Mexicans were thieves, you know.

"He went into the restaurant. I saw."

"But you probably only know him by the car he drives."

"I'll recognize him."

We parked in the mini-mall lot. It was where the nearest Laundromat was, where a bakery that sold the best buñuelos and pan dulce was. She led our family into the House of Pancakes, ignored the sign about letting the hostess do the seating, and up the first aisle, Ricardo pressed against her shoulder with one arm, holding Toño's hand with her free one, until she stopped.

"Him," she said.

It was a booth by the window, a parking-lot view. I centered myself on the open side of the Formica table, directly across from the salt and pepper, the suger and diet creamers, and the flavored syrups. He was seated at my left, my age give or take, a much older man across from him. Stunned, the two of them had absolutely nothing to say, even though their mouths seemed to be reacting.

"You remember her?" I said. "You called her a stupid fucking Mexican." I was dirty, concrete dust all over me. My hands were callused and chapped, a weave of wood splinters and tie-wire scratches and scabs. "You remember when you called her that, don't you?" My voice was not soft, even in normal conversation. "You were in your car. You were thinking you were a big man."

"This is not the right place for this," the old man said to me. He looked very scared.

"I'm not talking to you," I said.

"Dad," my guy said. He look worried beneath my gaze. No, he was definitely not in a very good position, even if he was inclined to respond physically. "Please, Dad."

I was examining his face. His teeth, his nose. I angled just enough toward him, my shoulders squared, my work boots planted. I was right-handed, he was seated on the left.

"What do you want?" he asked.

"What do I want?" I took seconds. Becky was smiling, fierce pleasure, at the guy. Toño had pulled her hand a step behind her and, as though nothing unusual was taking place, was staring innocently at something else. I turned my head that direction and saw the waitress standing maybe five feet away, at her chin a tray with plates of eggs and pancakes, a hamburger and fries. She'd been caught midstep, her lips fixed into a zero of alarm.

"I want you to fucking apologize is what I want you to do! I want you to *apologize* to my wife."

His brain was lagging behind the shock.

"You think I'm fucking around? You think I'm not *serious*?"

"He didn't mean it," his dad said. "It wasn't anything. This isn't right."

"Not *right*?" That was loud.

"Dad," the guy said.

"You *are* going to apologize!" I was too loud. I was mad, really angry.

"I'm sorry," he said in a quiet voice, almost inaudibly. He was speaking to his left hand, which was squeezing his right thumb.

I didn't quibble about quality. "Okay. So you *remember* this next time. You remember."

I led the way out, moving fast because I was worked up but also because I expected to see a cop's uniform and I wanted to avoid that. The restaurant's baby blue and orange decor seemed freshly painted, as cheery as plastic flowers. There wasn't so much as a tang of a fork against a plate. All the eyes were wide and unblinking on us as we circled around that waitress, around the hostess now standing next to her sign, and through the double glass doors and back out into the parking lot.

I was still mad. Mad about everything, mad at her. "So what the hell were you doing here, anyway?" I was backing the car up, and it was the first thing I'd said since the restaurant.

Now Becky was scared of me, too, and her voice turned fragile. "I wanted to buy a Christmas tree," she said. At the corner, a lot had been formed, fenced in by fraying twine. XMAS TREES, $19.95 AND UP. "I didn't know which one you'd like, and I couldn't decide."

The Donkey Show

It must have been about five years ago when I told Bill Wittliff—who owns the photos that comprise the volume *Boystown,* published by his Aperture Books—that I had seen the collection of Nuevo Laredo whorehouse photos he had archived in the library at the Southwest Texas State University (there are many more than what was selected for the book). We laughed about them. He said, "You should write an introduction when I publish the book."

What I remember thinking right then, the precise thought, which hasn't left me since, was why? Why would I? Based on what would I be considered qualified? It was curious. We didn't talk about anything but my flipping through the photos. What I remember seeing in them then, what I remember telling him and laughing about, was the men I knew, a couple we both knew I saw in those photographs—I mean look-alikes, not the real people: Look! It's Crumley! Look, isn't that Billy Ripley? And there's one I swear is George Bush! I had a running partner in El Paso, a major chingón drunk, Jacobo, who was from San Antonio, which isn't that far away from this border boystown—that's him! It was fun to imagine teasing him about how he'd become archived, it was all stupid funny to think of all these photographs this way. But why did Bill Wittliff suggest that I write something obviously appreciative? I liked him, but I'd have bet he knew less about me than I did about him.

When I looked at the photos then, and the ones chosen for the book, I'm still inclined to focus my eyes on the men: so many guys drinking Cartas have rockabilly sideburns, and those toothless dudes with TV-commercial grins, and the blubbery slobs suckling or groping a breast like they're diapered babies. Check out the shirts these boys got on—checkered, flowered, about any make of gaudy, clothes you still find plentiful at about any local thrift store. There's what looks like a pair of just-bathed and groomed born-agains, smiling like it's Sunday brunch, and there's what looks like your favorite high school teacher, you know, the intellectual one. And there's a sheriff, deputizing a woman with a badge in a very special place, and you notice that even standing next to her, he thinks he's above it all.

But that's not what you're supposed to be seeing, not what these photos are supposed to be about. No, if you pay attention to this book, you start picking up on it—or I do, dummy me missing the obvious: it's the putas, you're supposed to be looking at the putas. Although it is kind of confusing. Back when I was first told about these photos, the story I got was the one Bill Wittliff relates in his essay, that they were found in "a little pile of negatives all stuck together." These are what a whorehouse photographer takes to sell back as mementos for a couple of bucks. Wittliff treated this like "found art": art not conscious of being art, such as an old, discarded sign dangling from a post, whose purpose was advertising, but given the passing time, it now has the look of art. In his essay, Wittliff explains that after he bought a first stack of negatives, he made a deal to buy all of the photos these photographers took. And clearly these photographers' focus changed, or their understanding. They thought they were taking "art" pictures, glam/carny shots of the women who make a living in this woeful business. They believed they were being rewarded for their art and photojournalism skills.

Yeah, you're supposed to look at and think about Mexican *whores*. This book is about them. Beautiful and not at all, placid, strong, crude. Exposed. Not as bad as you think. Or worse. Oh so willing. Oh look, there's one reproduced big. She's been beat up. And another of a young prostitute, maybe twelve, sad on a bed. Not all's fun there, you know.

These are "art" photos from the real border.

You ever see photos at a morgue? Naked bodies. Doctors sawing and slicing. There's some found art for you. Reality. Death. Another of the oldest shows, one that isn't ever going away.

I didn't want to care about this book. I like Bill Wittliff, I like the movie *Lonesome Dove*. I wanted to have some "arty," distant, worldly point of view, too.

But instead it made me realize how I'd been trained to have shame. This puta world is what so many Americans talk about when they talk about Mexico. And it's this "conversation" that makes so many of us feel like our blood is less than dirty. And this kind of book only renews this shame for a next generation—a book not for Mexicans or Mexican-Americans, this is certainly not one that is going to be collected in such a household. It's what Mexican-Americans have to be taught, that this is a fundamental American perception of Mexican heritage and culture.

All I could think was what *is* this endless fascination for Mexican whores? Why do these guys obsess over this so much? If it were in their own poor neighborhood, if it were their poor junkie alcholic aunts and cousins, would they be so intrigued?

And that's when a "found art" thing kicked in for me. This book, the entirety of its black-and-white photos—grainy, cheap, mundanely composed—is the unconscious, the subliminal: a dream, a fantasy, a phobia. These are the images of their Mexican border fetish, and it is depicted with such unawareness, with such a comfortable arrogance of historical power, it can seem to them, almost charmingly, like art.

The Border Trilogy
by Cormac McCarthy

My mom, a lively, attractive Mexican woman, married two times
(and I'm not numbering the almosts) after she and my father—a
marine sergeant in World War II—separated and divorced. With
lots of suitors, my mom chose them. She was their trophy and
they were proud, which she knew and used to her advantage.
She didn't have to work anymore, and she made life a party. They
gave us a good place to live, furnished—I remember both times
I got a new mattress. They were hardworking men, consumed
by their jobs, male-only professions. One time, during a move,
she decided to show me a photo. It was the love of her life, a
handsome guy, probably Mexican or Mexican-American (she
called him Spanish, the euphemism of the time), young, at most
twenty-one. Black pants, a white shirt, and holding a guitar. I'm
sure they were polished black shoes. He was smiling, and he
looked happy. He was as poor as me, she said, as if that explained
why he wasn't a husband before my dad.

I mention this because I've thought of Cormac McCarthy as
I would a stepfather—or, rather, the men of his novels. They're
the fully realized versions of the men my mom might choose, the
kind I've had to pay attention to as well. They smoke cigarettes,
Camels and boxed Marlboros, they drink but not to get drunk—

or only in an understandable crisis. They work dirty and stinky when they work. Being unfaithful is as far away as a college degree. They're believers in these personal religions that we all really know deep down. Laconic or nonverbal, you know they mean it, mean nothing but manly good, that they want what they do to stand for what they say. In other words, they're like John Wayne in his Old West movies—*Rio Bravo, She Wore a Yellow Ribbon, Fort Apache,* all still high on my favorites list. I even wanted to believe in *The Alamo* because the Duke was in it. When I thought of how I was supposed to be as a man, of course I adopted John Wayne as the model. Likewise, now, when I think of how writers are supposed to be, I think of Cormac McCarthy: don't say anything, don't be flattered by praise or disrupted by criticism, don't read anything they write about you, just do your work, because that's the thing. Which is just about everything I can't seem to do and wish I could.

I have mixed-up feelings about my stepfathers and almosts. They were men who needed an exotic, sensuous, wild, south-of-the-border experience, and the love or loving of a beautiful Mexican woman was wish fulfillment, the envied romance for I'm-a-man status, the gold medal of conquest machismo. It's the going-to-Tahiti story of the rugged West—a beautiful Mexican woman stood as real romantic adventure for them, a story that all the other guys would listen to and think about. They were very proud to speak a little of that Spanish language.

I read McCarthy's Gothic *The Orchard Keeper* when it was given to me many years ago by an El Paso bookstore owner who wanted me to know the writer who'd moved to town. I tried, unsuccessfully, to read *Outer Dark.* I liked the more playful *Suttree.* But *Blood Meridian,* my God, that was a book to study a couple of pages a day. It felt translated from something, maybe Greek: Homeric in both historical scope and literary convention, it was an aorta slash of prose, finely elegiac and gaudily ornate, sumptuous, its blood-and-viscera subject chapping the southwestern-desert frontier, riding hard, surviving implausibly from one end of the West to the other. It's a Comanche massacre of a book, oddly inspiring in the beauty and bounty of its gore, impossible not to compare to great tomes. I can't claim to divine an understanding of its bitter meaning, of the metaphorical human truths those characters, the Kid and the Judge, stood for, but, my mouth open in awe as I read, I didn't really care.

All the Pretty Horses, the first volume in McCarthy's Border Trilogy, did not shift the swath of territory of *Blood Meridian* but did its tone, with a sweet, sad story line: John Grady Cole, the sixteen-year-old boy who loves horses, raised bilingual because of the maid Luisa and Abuela (her grandmother), disappointed that his mother won't give or sell him the family ranch in San Angelo, rides his horse south, toward the border, with his friend Lacey Rawlins. They stop for good old ham and beans and biscuits on their way across the floodplain and along fence lines and through pasturelands, shooting and gutting rabbits and building campfires and drinking coffee black. They pick up a younger boy, Jimmy Blevins, who's more trouble than they can account for as they hit the river—crossing the Rio Grande, that baptismal breach, on the other side of which, in sultry and violent Mexico, lay all initiation rites unto manhood for these brave boys, milk-and cow-fattened with the lore of the American West. John Grady falls in love with a girl—and she with him—too rich: a doomed love, one that never could be, was never meant to be.

I had to stop reading when it hit that beautiful Mexican girl riding an Arabian. Put the book away for a long time. I think I told you about my mother. One of the things that one stepfather really liked, decades before it became as popular and well known as ketchup, was that Mexican salsa she could make. In fact, my mom bought it at a store in a can. I saw her pouring it into a bowl once. We both cracked up. At the time, my mom didn't know how to cook so well. That was the marriage that didn't last long.

The Crossing, the story of Billy Parham and his brother, Boyd, is the second installment in the Border Trilogy and a compendium of mythic Westernalia, descriptions of which might be the best ever written: wolves and Indians, bullets, urine for setting traps, squalls of coyotes. Billy feels remorse for crippling one lone wolf ("from another world entire"), her leg maimed in a sprung trap, so he ropes and walks her to Mexico to set free, encountering all sorts of brutal carnivalesque characters, dogfights, rifles out of scabbards (something about that makes those my favorite words—"rifle out of scabbard"—don't you feel and hear the hollow scrape, the steel against leather? Gives me boyhood goose bumps!), until he has to shoot his now pet wolf to save her. Tasting her blood, which tastes like his, he buries her high in the mountains. Going north, he passes more Indians in wickiups and caves, and bad and good Mexicans, and once crossed back, he finds his childhood home abandoned; he and his brother are orphans, their parents viciously slaughtered by an Indian they befriended, so they become "outlaws" on a dangerous hunt across the wild border to steal their own horses. Billy's brother is killed in the adventure, and he feels a responsibility to take the body home. Sharing black coffee at a campsite, in the darkness, a wise and articulate Yaqui Indian with hardened decency, Quijada, talking of a Mexican *corrido* (ballad) about a *güerito,* explains its meaning—sounding to me a little bit like a definition of McCarthy's literary romanticism:

> The corrido tells all and it tells nothing. . . . It tells what it wishes to tell. It tells what makes the story run. . . . It does not owe its allegiance to the truths of history but to the truths of men. It tells the tale of that solitary man who is all men.

Quijada, musing philosophically, still believes that the brother should be left behind: "I think the dead have no nationality." Billy, almost following the marine credo, will not abandon him there in Mexico. "But their kin do," he tells Quijada. Alone in life now, Billy has grown up, and he is going home with his well-earned maturity and masculinity—taking, no doubt, that souvenir *corrido* with him.

Cities of the Plain, McCarthy's final volume in the trilogy, puts John Grady Cole and Billy Parham together, three years older, working a cattle ranch north of El Paso and south of Alamogordo. They're stomping mud from their boots and shaking off a little monsoon rain and hanging hats on wood pegs. They go whore-housing in Juárez and do some whiskey shooting (which should be one word, too), backing that up with some cold beer. In the morning, in the bunkhouse, after they down some coffee, black, after they eat the ranch cook Socorro' s eggs with *pico de gallo,* after they "pass the salsa yonder," they mount their horses and round up stray calves, crossing paths with coyotes. ("What do you reckon he's doin out here in the middle of the day?" "He probably wonders the same about you.") They're in and out of the tack room (which is so very cool). They see deer and talk jackrabbits and owls and mountain lions and rope wild dogs, saving the pups of one of them. They break horses. John Grady, the lead in this volume, is especially stubborn about one that's thrown him. She's a fine horse. He knows horses as he knows himself as we know metaphors.

I think you can train a rooster to do what you want. But you wont have him. There's a way to train a horse where when you get done you've got the horse. On his own ground. A good horse will figure things out on his own. You can see what's in his heart. He wont do one thing while you're watchin him and another when you aint. He's all of a piece. When you've got a horse to that place you cant hardly get him to do somethin he knows is wrong. He'll fight you over it. And if you mistreat him it just about kills him. A good horse has justice in his heart.

John Grady Cole has fallen in love with a Juárez whore who works at the White Lake. She's sweet and she's beautiful. Innocent. She's young, seventeen or even younger, stolen away from her home in Chiapas. She has grand mal epileptic seizures. And her name is Magdalena. (Since I never have nor will in the future, please let me write that again: And her name is Magdalena.) John Grady wants and intends to marry her. To visit her and propose, he gets an advance from his boss, Mac. To buy her freedom, he sells that horse. He restores an old shack at the other end of the ranch to make their marital home. But Eduardo, her boss, her pimp, loves her, too, and he is not very interested in selling her or letting her get away. A doomed love. John Grady has a knife scar across his cheek from his days in prison back in *All the Pretty Horses*, when he fought a *pachuco cuchillero* (one of the many badass words I loved saying out loud, imaging any setting I'd be in: See that dude over there? A *cuchillero*. Imagine it better: a *zacateco cuchillero*). (McCarthy's use—a lot, too—of untranslated Spanish is always good. It has never been considered equally exotic or decorative or literary for Chicano writers to do anything similar, but, ironically, only irritating. I think that's because of the English-only fear, which is not a worry in the work of McCarthy, whose main characters drawl.) John Grady and Eduardo meet for a life-and-death fight, exquisitely rendered. The final chapter of the trilogy closes, philosophically, in El Paso.

I was drawn into this book, and not only because so much of it was set in El Paso and the region around her, in cities and streets I know well. Years ago, the White Lake was one of my favorite bars to take out-of-town visitors, not because its prostitutes were beautiful but because they weren't in the slightest— think of a cook in a hair net at an elementary school cafeteria, who's been there many years, extra pounds per year, assembling Wednesday's enchiladas with rice and beans. I was drawn to the trilogy not only because it is so much fun to imagine, through

literature, every boyhood nature and gun and knife and whiskey
and woman cowboy fantasy ever lived or subliminally conceived.
I was drawn not only because I love John Wayne movies, this
trilogy being the best John Wayne western ever written. It's the
prose. Does anybody know how to do this better? At once complex and simple, erudite and common, inverted and invented, a
prose that is Cormac McCarthy:

> They set off across the open tableland with their ropes pop-
> ping and loud cries, leaning low in the saddle, riding neck
> and neck. In a mile they'd halved the dogs' lead. The dogs
> kept to the mesa and the mesa widened before them. If
> they'd kept to the rim they might have found a place to go
> down again where the horses could not follow but they
> seemed to think they could outrun anything that cared to
> follow and run they did, two of them side by side and the
> third behind, their long dogshadows beside them in the sun
> racing brokenly over the sparse taupe grass of the tableland.

It is this archprose that vaults his work so far above the genre
western and its popular writers, the late Louis L'Amour and the
San Angelo writer touted to be his inheritor, Elmer Kelton,
Texas's favorite.

It's also Mexico, that subterranean appeal it makes on the
American psyche, coming from a source who knows of it well
but is not of it. It's crossing the frontera into that unknowable
land and encountering its inscrutable people, where life is lived
and not settled on—or so the mythology would have it.

> "Dont you think if there's anything left of this life it's down
> there?" "Maybe." "You like it too." "Yeah? I dont even
> know what this life is. I damn sure dont know what Mexico
> is. I think it's in your head. Mexico. I rode a lot of ground

down there. The first ranchera you hear sung you understand the whole country. By the time you've heard a hundred you dont know nothin. You never will."

Mexico, with its mysteries of violence and love. Where an
American boy becomes American man and, once through, after
his passage, rocking on his front-porch chair where few if any
Mexicans or descendants live, has some stories to tell.

I remember the first time the awareness of a uniquely literary
delusion caught me. I'd been rereading Tolstoy. I'd loved Tolstoy,
and, just as I was supposed to, I identified with his main characters, took these trips from one part of Russia to another, maybe
Kiev to Moscow, Germany to France and back, considered these
journeys we all traveled if we pursued art and intelligence and
wisdom. But on the reread, in my thirties, I realized I did not
take these trips, and that the characters actually did, because they
were rich, that if I'd been around these people, I'd be hanging
back at one of those summer or winter homes, picking their cherries. I'd be a minor character, mentioned for the same purpose
as a piano. My metaphorical story would be about staying and
working and would be the length of a poem, not as exciting as
that of the people who lived in the big house, who came and
went, riding, too, in horse-drawn carriages. Before I picked up
McCarthy, I had just reread Gabriel Garcia Márquez's *One
Hundred Years of Solitude,* a story situated farther south of the
Mexican border but with bizarre and exotic happenings, love
and birth and death and sex. I didn't flinch or sigh once. But
it's not a western, and westerns are supposed to have gunfights
and knife fights and tack rooms and such, and I got over it. I
do love John Wayne movies. Did you know that he married a
Mexican woman?

III
THE WRITING LIFE

Un Grito de Tejas

Imagine the writing scene looking like Santa Monica Beach: near the pier, it's another sunny southern California day, not too hot to want to hide in shade, the shore shoulder-to-shoulder bodies, pudgy to muscled, splashing, the waves as ferocious as seven-year-olds. There are many kinds of writers frolicking there, published and not yet published, of all colors, and lots of that skin darkness without sun or tanning lotions. Not so many years ago, when you'd have been half as tall and following your mommy around when she shopped, visiting here was another mouth-open trip to the other land, like Beverly Hills or even the west side of Los Angeles. What you would remember about Santa Monica Beach then was the park on a cliff above the sand, its groomed lawn and peaceful benches, and there above the sand, those people wore stylish white dresses or suits, white shoes and hats. Santa Monica wouldn't have seemed like a beach hang to you back then. You'd go to other beaches, where you were supposed to, or maybe just did.

Let me take you on a drive to the east side of the literary West, starting at that beach. Get on the Santa Monica Freeway and drive past the Robertson and La Cienega exits, past Hoover, Vermont, Normandie, past downtown L.A., into East L.A. But no, do not exit. Just keep driving east, really east, and pretty soon—well, not so pretty soon, but eventually—you will have crossed so much desert Southwest that you'll find yourself in El Paso, the Chicano Ellis Island. Half the people you've ever met in Los have lived in El Paso or Juárez. But keep driving. Like nine more hours. If you were to stay on the Santa Monica Freeway (around here called I-10), it'd take you to San Antonio and the Alamo. Which might also be a good point to start this story, but do what I suggest here anyway, and get off the interstate and take State Highway 290 to Austin, the capital of Texas.

What I want to answer is what it's like to be a Mexican-American writer these days, when our numbers are so many we can go to any beach in Califas, when many now know what you mean when you say Califas, or Nuevo Mejico, even when you pronounce "Arizona" as if it actually has the vowel "i" in it. What I have done is lead you to the western-swing dance of political and arty and tattooed-hipster Texas, every native's second home-town, because so much of the cultural love of the Texas Republic is centered here. If you look back in the American sixties, the most exotic music and spiciest food and mystic wisdom came from India—Ravi Shankar, chicken or vegetarian curry, and all that nirvana meditation. In here-and-now Austin, tacos are like pizza slices in New York City, there's Flaco and Santiago Jimenez squeezing accordians wildly, and dude, if you want wisdom, you read about it in Spanish, you go to the local psychic, and if you don't speak no *español,* you better be fluent in enough Spanglish to get that deep truth.

The downside, as my camarada Mando likes to say: they keep remembering the Alamo to remind us not to forget that we lost the war.

Excuse me for a second, I'm getting a little sleepies now that I'm back here. It's hot, you know, and I theenk I might wanna leettle siesta. A leetle hard for me to concentrate *a veces.* It's sometheeng I been learning *aquí mero en este estado tambien. Ay, gracias,* I feel betters.

Wasn't I telling about Texas letters (I'm not talking about *ñ* or *rr*), how it is here, how it's all *torcido aquí,* like transformed for the times? Twenty years ago, even ten, maybe even five, when the university professors would teach the literature of Texas and the Southwest, even when Don Américo Paredes ("With a Pistol in His Hand") was close enough, at least metaphorically, to be across the hall, you wouldn't see one thing written by a Mexican-American in those courses. That's changed. Now, sometimes, they'll be up to two class lectures on our people's cultural effect (or affect—not sure which word is right) on the state and region.

Especially in Austin, the Chicano people have influenced the literary establishment. Take, particularly, the magazine of the state, *el mero patrón del estado, Texas Monthly.* They say that any writer who wants to be taken seriously here, for a magazine of this reputation to get behind him, has to make it with the editors of this magazine. Even though, by their estimation, it is as important as any periodical in the country, it is stand-alone concerned only with the issues of Texas. Its high standards are much like the old days of South Africa, when other issues weren't darkening that country—it knows what diamonds are, how exquisite and rare, and the focus and concern is as clear as a De Beers. Besides its own writers' craft and income, this mag shows how it cares about us, too: over the years, there have been several stories about one of us who has died, and sometimes one of their writers does a piece on one of our musicians, or a boxer, or our cholo or graffiti trouble, and they do like our food. A feature article a couple of months ago, with color photos, was about where to get our best corn tortillas. In a laudatory recent bio in the alternative Austin weekly, the *Chronicle,* the newest editor in chief is even quoted as saying he has made an outstanding offer to one of our most famous writers, Sandra Cisneros, to send him a story about not loving the myth of the Alamo. An against-the-tide gutsiness that is hard not to admire.

So just imagine the honor it was for someones like me to be asked to contribute! I had another New York book coming out, I'd been given one of those Guggenheims and even had won a couple other of those eastern-award thingies, but that the editor in chief now wanted *me* to give them something! He'd said he read one of those articles I'd published in *The New Yorker,* and he liked it. *¡Ay!*

You know how we are. I had to stop my brains from sizzling with all my schemes of getting some and had to write for higher goals, not just to impress *las rucas masotas.* Which, *tu sabes,* wasn't so easys for me, *si me entiendes.* I like the girls. When I was only a *chavalito,* I, too, thought I would grow up to be a boxer, *el mero mero chingón.* I probably can't help myself. Like they think, I guess I like to fight, you know? Fighting, *hijo de su,* that feels like *ME, vato,* you know? Especially when someone pisses me off. *Pero,* I also have this other drive? And, you know, I guess I decided I like the girls too much. So, *sabes que,* I must have, like, decided I wanted to be a good lover man instead, play my instincts that ways. You know? So, you know, I decided to be a writer. What better ways, *verdad?* You sit alone for long hours typing, and when you get out, *¡hijole!,* all those killer models . . . yeah, *se vale,* it's worth it. Musicians and artists, even *los ricos con los* bucks, they get nothing *como los escritores.*

But this was a special opportunity: to include something from our people in their distinctive pages. It was such a big risk for them, I understood that, and I didn't want to mess up nothing. I even had to not goof around for a while there to get a manuscript to them. And, hard as it was for me not to think of chasing *muchachas* instead, I did it, just like I promised I would, on time. I was proud of it, too. I am such a macho, I even thought it was good!

The editor in chief, he called and said he liked it, but . . . You know how it is when they go "but." He said, like a dentist after an X ray, I should come over and visit the office. All those swats I deserved over my junior and high school years in the vice principal's office, well, as much insight as I have into my flawed character, I still get nervous being sent slips to go to the office. So I said, You couldn't just tell me in writing? (It's what I get away with when I publish in New York City.) He shopped the story around to find someone who could work with me. And finally, in an E-mail note, he explained to me how I should take the advice from this assistant editor he found just for me, and that I should work with him "constructively"—hey, but don't that word sound like from boring high school teacher lady, talking slow, because she thinks you're so much dumber than Emily Brontë? *Quela,* it's probably since I got this jalapeño blood that I couldn't slow up that fighter in me. And then his assistant (who has even been promoted to their head sports writer) had suggestions for me on how to write correctly, like his people, and how what I got puts readers to sleep, and that I gotta wake up (he said my piece "puts them into a dreamlike trance," but since I seem to like *una napita* once in a while, this siesta need in my *sangre,* like wanting the girls too much, I see now maybe he was only trying to be culturally sensitive) (or could be they got like commercials, maybe, and that's how I think they make money to pay for the pretty paper they print on). Well, what happened next I feel even sorrier about. I couldn't show a good attitude. That too-*picoso* boxer in me felt disrespected and insulted. Like I'm thinking they're treating me like I'm so young and inexperienced, or like I'm just a stupid, like English learning. I told you! I yelled. Didn't you say? I yelled. I even screamed how I should be paid for doing *exactly* what I said I would and *exactly* what he said he wanted. My hot-*chile* temper. I dunno what I got in my jeans (or do they mean genes, or both?).

Here they were, doing me a favor, giving me a literary opportunity in this land we lost, and I'm going off like they're . . . well, I won't say that word. I'm sure it is how they treat everybody, and I ruined my opportunity by throwing verbal *chingazos,* believing I shouldn't have to accept being told by these people how to write. I am so obviously spoiled by shoddy New York City standards. I do trick those who aren't from here and know how we are. In the East, they think I'm smart enough already. And what I wrote that *Texas Monthly* couldn't accept, I sold to la *Harper's Magazine.* Those East Coast *fulanos* loved it just as I wrote it, and published it in June 2001 without any editing or advice whatever.

I may never learn, but you still might. What I am telling you is that we are, unlike in the past, being offered never-before opportunities, only you have to watch out and not mess up and look bad for our peoples. We play on the beaches in Santa Monica, and continue to make homes in the sands of the desert Southwest, and even though we're told how we lost the war in Texas, we are making our history proud again, even our own unique literature, and that sooner still, if we let ourselves do our best work—without having to perform as the stereotypes they have taught us is in our blood.

What I Would Have Said
About the State of
Texas Literature

Yes, a publicist at Grove Press had very diligently mailed me a copy of a fax she'd received weeks earlier for the first-ever Texas Book Festival. Yes, it read clearly that I was to be on a panel, in the House Chamber, at ten-thirty A.M., November 16, the first day of the event. The evening before, yes, I took a phone call from the moderator, Rich Oppel, editor of the *Austin American-Statesman,* who told me what he intended to say. I did get there on time without anybody's help. Early, even. About half an hour before I left for the capitol, I'd made notes—word count about several fingers on one hand—on an utterly great idea, straight from the brain, I assure you. My yawning was simply an open expression of confidence.

Afterward somebody asked, Didn't you get the idea when it said "House Chamber"? Hey, man, it sounded like a comfortable room to me. I don't know where *you* grew up. Didn't it occur to you, somebody asked, when you learned that Mrs. Laura Bush, the governor's wife, would be there to introduce this "opening panel" at which you were featured? Yeah, well, it was morning, it was way early, I'm not from Austin, I've never done this gig before, I've been real busy, real busy, and nobody told me, they should've told me a lot more better. These Republicans

are always trying to set us up, you know? Now that I get to think
of it, I'm disappointed in the ex-librarian Mrs. Bush, who is very
kind, very generous, who loves books as much as me, who was
doing something inspired for Texas and its libraries and its literary arts with an extravagant, and successful, fund-raising festival,
despite marrying the man who beat Ann Richards, who is cool
even if she never did put me in such a position to make a fool of
myself, which is also the point, you see?

I'm telling you, it wasn't my fault that only one-syllable words,
one at a time, period, next word, with pauses to help the memory,
exited, distantly related, from my mouth. A couple of days before,
after a public reading in San Antonio, for a good cause, too, where
I had to sign several books for a couple of fans, two give or take,
all of which was extremely exhausting physically and mentally for
me to do two days before this other event, after which, at an ex-
cessively nice—if you'll excuse the expression, *very nice*—house,
there was all this food, and I hadn't eaten dinner yet, and then I sat
with Larry L. King, and got to smoking one of the host's Cubita
cigars, listening and listening, drinking and drinking, spirits, not
just that French wine, laughing too much to remember the serious business that lay ahead of me. Anybody who knows Larry L.
King probably would have been aware of his profligate drinking
and talking. I'd never met him before. He admitted that he's not
even supposed to be smoking cigarettes, and yet he did, and a lot
of them, I'll tell you. Later, William Hauptman and Marion Winik
kept me up late in that river walk hotel, digging at my psyche, I
think, for material which is mine. They knew that in two days, I
was supposed to say something intelligent and dignified and co-
herent (I know I told them repeatedly, and they simply did not
care), and yet they did not relent on working me over, even though,
by then, in less than two days, I had to be prepared. And then the
next night, the night before, back in Austin, it was Marion Winik
once again, using what she got on me against me. There was a

reporter present from *The New York Times,* it was a bar, there was
his wife. Need I say more? This is the state of Texas Literature,
too, you know. And so it's not just my fault.

I'd compare it to that scene in *Journey to the East* by Hermann
Hesse. That's probably not the right book, and there'll be a head-
shaking letter to the editor. Which is also the state of Texas Literature. . . . Hmm. How *did* that go? I've been out for a few nights,
and been real busy, I'm not from here, and it was really a long
time ago when I read Hesse. Here's the scene I'm thinking of from
wherever: a psychic literary night of dimly lit faces, masklike, in a
black Catholic fog, staring at you, deciding whether you're in or
you're out. Compared to being in the literal daylight of Texas,
feeling a little hazy, at the Speaker's podium, the state's most famous
speaker of all, the Hog, in a bigger-than-any-in-Alaska portrait over
your shoulder, in that darkly aging European Renaissance hue of
historical majesty but with "Remember the Alamo!" patriotism.
A fifty-foot ceiling for enchanced, epic echo in the luxurious
cavern of the august chamber. Distant faces staring up at you,
going way way back, too, so impervious to your unadjusted sight
you wish you had a pair of glasses, some prescription shades in
this bright Baptist light, your jury attached to coastered executive chairs at desks with a voting mechanism, that yes/no electronic board behind the other shoulder. A red velvet and polished
brass horseshoe gallery for observers. You never heard the board
lighting up, but every face was very silently not smiling or wink-
ing. When all I'd expected were a couple of tables pushed together, folding chairs, an audience of twenty to thirty.

For the record, here's a set of words I do recall around my
mouth region and microphone range at the time of the incident:
rich, uncles, daddies, and, the, excluded, unpublished, complain-
ers. Lovers never see the beloved's flaws. Américo Paredes is
ignored, Port Arthur used to say Janis Joplin only screamed, the
old boy Texas triumvirate didn't think much of Mexicans who

live near that river, wasn't Dobie a little racist. Weak funding for El Paso schools. How come I've never read a single story by even one, say, black construction worker I've worked with from Houston?

What I would have said is based on what Rich Oppel did say characterized Texas Literature: in a place rooted in soil but unromantically, unsentimentally, because of the natural forces that are constant reminders. Which is empowered by history, which always reinforces or subverts myth or tall tale. That is held by honor, which forces larger-than-life issues of good and bad, right and wrong, and which is driven by a humor that distrusts pomposity and snaps with skepticism for political trends or party affiliation. And, last, which is gripped by a rugged individualism that resists generalizations, even this one.

One thing I have to admit strikes me about this depiction, on the positive side, on first impression, is how it sure does sound like me and my work. That noble implication, particularly.

A second thing, a question, from my rugged, individualistic, skeptical side, is how many books and authors would have to be eliminated if the sentimental and romanticized restrictions alone were enforced? I'd cover a few wagers they're not the ones to get the biggest advances.

But okay, *por fin* (there's another trait, missed, Spanish syllables sound like words, like, my favorite example, the street in downtown Austin, Nueces, is pronounced "new aces"), here's the real great idea I came prepared with when I walked into the House Chamber: that this sure does sound like a description of Ross Perot. Doesn't it? Be honest. It does, right? A mythic, romantic, sentimental Ross Perot for all Texas times, in many Texas settings. Not necessarily such a pretty picture *now*, is it?

I learned from years on construction jobs that there are two lists to describe workers—particularly the apprentices—who are kept at layoff time versus those let go, this being a process usually founded on a simple "intuitive" judgment. While one was thought to be growing into his feet, fiery, hardheaded, the other was clumsy, too difficult to work with, and never learned. One got a winky grin, the other a head-shaking raised eyebrow. A foreman or super chose as if pulling out one or the other explanation sheet for his decision. If you weren't quick, you, too, might go away nodding with understanding, satisfied. Because when you shut your eyes and honestly considered the activities of the two, their behavior was, at best, exactly the same. Those in charge didn't have to be conscious of how or why they kept who they did, and in most circumstances weren't, but the result was the same: of a clean-cut white guy, a Chicano, a black, and a white with scraggly hair, guess which one was the best worker?

I imagine someone living in a separate Texas, remembering an equally long heritage that is almost completely ignored— go to Mexico, see the pyramids at Teotihuacán—or a state history that isn't liked—read *With His Pistol in His Hand*—because it's not so pleasant, some unnatural forces being constant reminders of disempowerment. Imagine that person who is rugged and doesn't accept generalizations, who jumps at that traditional pomposity and arrogance, who's proud of her saga and lineage (just as likely a him, but make it a her, which is also a more difficult fit in traditional Texas), trying to reinforce her past or to subvert the traditional myth that has called her names at the worst, romanticized and sentimentalized her exotic sex or transcendent passivity at the best. Think of her standing there listening to Ross Perot, think of what would happen if she were talking back to Ross Perot. Is she still considered a rugged, individualistic maverick? Or do you hear him harumphing about her "political correctness" and "multiculturalism"? How disrespectful she'd sound *complaining,* how "negative"? How *her* version of pride and history sounds too angry to him. How her *complaining* is revisionist. She's poor. And poor is simply not as fascinating as rich.

Poor does not sell magazines. Poor does not sell movies, TV shows, or books.

I'm telling you that I would have remembered to say all this, too, if those other panelists hadn't distracted me. Bill Broyles, one of them, came with a typed-out essay. That was a very disruptive influence. I was fully prepared with my own extemporaneous exegesis, but he was so well organized and well spoken that I couldn't stop admiring him. Especially jarring and destructive to my memory was, after he talked about Dobie and Webb and Bedicheck and McMurtry, and a whole bunch of names I'm sure are on many University of Texas literature-course lists, was when he talked about all the writers at *Texas Monthly* with whom he'd personally been involved. So comprehensive was he, it caused me to forget my own list of male Texas writers and camaradas neither present in life or conversation at the festival, including Cabeza de Vaca, Américo Paredes, Tomás Rivera, Rolando Hinojosa, John Rechy, Tino Villanueva, Ricardo Sánchez, raúl salinas, Arturo Islas, Max Martínez, Lionel Garcia, not to mention a few of the *tejanas,* like Jovita González, Alicia Gaspar de Alba, Carmen Tafolla, Evangelina Vigil-Piñon, Gloria Anzaldúa, Rosemary Catacalos, and Norma Cantú. And then the other panelist, Naomi Shihab Nye, well, once she started talking *pedo* pleasant and decent, right after I spoke, or muttered, or . . . look, all I'll say is that it was a good thing she wasn't sitting next to me, because I would've given those silky tan braids of hers a couple of real hard yanks. If everything's so great in Texas writing, Naomi, how come you didn't invite me to go out to lunch with you? Huh? I was hungry, and I'd had a bad morning.

So there you have it. You see how it wasn't my fault, mostly. You know what, though? I forgive you all. I'm not saying I'm forgetting. Sorry. But I do find it in my heart to forgive. Let's just do it better next time. You know what I'm saying? We can do better.

From a Letter to
Pat Ellis Taylor

El Paso
January 13, 1989

A couple months ago I discovered and then got bothered about the fact that one of the (if not *the*) most popular English-department courses at the University of Texas was the one that Mr. Dobie started, "The Life and Literature of the Southwest" (translation: "Fiction from and about Texas"), although there is not one writer of Mexican descent represented in that course. That struck me as Mighty Strange, and no less so because two of Texas's most important writers, Rolando Hinojosa and Américo Paredes (the movie *The Ballad of Gregorio Cortez* from his *With His Pistol in His Hand*), are faculty. I guess it struck Rolando so strange that he asked to teach the same course, though his uses an extra adjective in the title—"The Life and Literature of the Hispanic Southwest." As I understand it, a student can't even get two courses of credit for taking both.

Which gets me to a subject you brought up a few months ago, about your writing getting criticized for not striking Deep in the Heart of Texas. Let me tell you what I've learned—that "Texas Literature" is considered, uniquely to this state and from

137

inside it, a *national* literature, one separate from the U.S.A., in the same way French or British literature isn't just called European (New Mexico is the only other state I know of where the same might be said, but I think there are considerable differences). Maybe everyone else knows this, but I didn't. I realized this after I got back from Paisano, reading through a copy of a journal (*Southwestern Historical Quarterly*) whose page after page are reverent and nostalgic embraces of Frank Dobie and Walter Prescott Webb. Out on the Paisano ranch, I read quite a bit by and on Mr. Dobie, but I suppose I must have thought, naively, that interest in him was arcane—I mean, I know people from all over the West, even a few in Texas (though most of them are illegitimates or disavowed from here in El Paso), some are even educated, and I'd say many if not most haven't heard of the man. It occurred to me, in other words, that Texas takes its Texas Literature seriously. Surprise, right? Anyway, I think it was Dobie who established this Republic of Texas attitude—he went over to England as a Texan, not an American.

That's one observation. Another has to do with me saying that you're in a Janis Joplin tradition of writer, which explains why all the young people who like that kind of rock'n'blues like your writing a lot (your book was very popular in those classes I taught). But this fact doesn't bode too well for you with the chambers of (artistic) commerce in this republic. Janis wasn't very popular with them, either. Until she died—now they've got a monument to her there in Port Arthur. Writing tastes could be said to parallel music tastes (or at least that's a way to look at it, to make a point or two), and my impression has been that the trend in the country has gone classical. That is, go to school, be trained by and learn the skills at the proper conservatories from the proper teachers, play in one orchestra after another. In the writing world, that seems to be called "creative writing." Nobody'd deny that these people play skillfully or are talented, nobody'd argue that classical music isn't beautiful and good for the senses, but what about rock'n'roll or jazz? Would Buddy Holly's or Roy Orbison's music be better if they'd "studied" guitar? What about BB King or Bobby Blue Bland or Chuck Berry? Duke Ellington? My feeling is that they played in garages and on porches and in nightclubs and that's why their music is like it is. I'd say that the literary sound in the country is Classical Only, and it's no different here in Texas, though I think around here, it's expected that a little Bob Wills be mixed in some. Anyway, I think the belief is that good-boy and -girl writers should wear the proper literary attire in public, and your writing, Miss Taylor, gets too naked. Good writing has proper manners, and your writing has this bad habit of getting loud sometimes—really, decent lady writing must show more constraint and control of itself, Miss Taylor.

Here I can't remember how I planned to link this to Rolando Hinojosa teaching his own "Literary Tradition" course about native Texas writers like Américo Paredes and Tomás Rivera (and maybe even himself), but I'm thinking about Tex-Mex music, and about how I was thinking these things while I was wandering the lonely halls of UT. I mean, I don't know how a person is supposed to punch it out with that tough-guy cowpoke-type heritage, especially when it's not even wearing a cowboy hat anymore, just a clean white shirt and tie. I sort of saw all my deep thinking there as halfbreed-like and *short* (next to all those tall, lanky siblings of cowboy thoughts)—you know, like that cook in *Lonesome Dove* who knows lots about critters to eat, those snakes and bugs, but doesn't have much say about the Big Drive. Maybe next time I'll have it figured out and let you know.

Yours,
Dagoberto

Eulogy for
Don Ricardo Sánchez

When I heard of Ricardo Sánchez's death, I was at a pay phone on a faraway street in these states. I don't even know how many miles from El Paso, but culturally it was much farther. It was three days later already, and at that moment other friends were on their way to a rosary. As saddened by the news as I was, I felt worse. I felt irresponsible. I'd seen him in the hospital two days before his death and told him how healthy he looked—he did, too, especially compared to when he first came home—and I'd promised to drop in on him the Friday before I left, and I didn't.

That feeling of not doing enough, or not being there, that was at the essence of knowing Ricardo. He had such a ferocious appetite, a hunger that made demands on him and everyone around. He wanted attention, wanted what he had to say to be heard. *Really* heard. Heard and disseminated and admired and respected. He was insatiable, persistent, and, like some fundamentalist preacher, unwaveringly certain about his scripture and calling.

So how could it have been surprising that it was a cancer of the stomach? Or that it had reached into his liver, where that vivid blood of his was produced?

He'd often come over to my place and get a lecturing rage going about someone or something, some perceived insult, some real untruth. He'd be talking his pedo like it was direct from the eternal, which, stunningly, it often seemed. Ricardo preached high standards that were noble and righteous, but sometimes his conclusions were laced with conspiracies he saw as attempts to overshadow him and his contributions. I thought of this as a problem of space: he didn't think there was enough room for everyone. It was like a reflex he had. If one person or idea was being given room, another was being locked up, and the only option was confrontation and attack, which, naturally, he had to win. We all have imperfections. One of his was that he couldn't see too many in himself, particularly while in the heat and fury of his outrage. I learned that when this time—for fifteen to twenty minutes, you were required to listen and *only* listen—was up, there'd be this spent pause. That was when I'd take my opportunity. "You're so full of shit, Ricardo, you know that?" We'd both crack up. Ricardo's friends were those who could laugh with, and at, him. Ricardo's friends were those who would bear this twenty-minute tirade calmly, understanding that it was as much Ricardo's burden to have it.

One of his favorite rants was about phony pachucismo, the glorification of cholos. He'd done too much prison time in California and Texas. He knew what *bad* was and where it lead. "Is that what they want their kids to grow up to be, carnal? Do they want them to go to Berkeley or Soledad?" Ricardo used his poetry like a bludgeon, and when the young saw and heard him, books and poetry weren't effeminate passions of goodie-goodies and weaklings. A teacher I know at Roosevelt School in the Segundo Barrio still talks about how changed his students were after a visit Ricardo made. In our community, where literacy is still so low, where being a man is still thought of as requiring physical toughness and mental badness, Ricardo's presence, as well as his contrasting past, proved that intelligence and learning could be manly and courageous—not attributes of people who have less presence and force, but more.

He was an asset too unused and unrecognized by El Paso, and it did hurt him. He wanted his hometown to know how good he'd done. That he was the only person who'd ever gone from a high school GED to a PhD (a fact explaining his complicated autograph—Dr. Ricardo Sánchez, GED, PhD). That he was the first pinto, ex-con, to have ever been tenured as a full professor. That his body of work had been prestigously archived at Stanford University. He wanted all this to be in the news, in people's conversations. He was insulted that a local writers' hall of fame ignored him for so many years (he is being included this year), that he wasn't, as El Paso's most reknowned literary native, one of its first inductees. His anger about his hometown caused him to have odd overreactions. One time we were together at a copy store. There was a bulletin board where business people had stapled cards—typing services, résumés. Ricardo pulled out one of his professional cards from Washington State University, which said he was a professor, and stapled it up there: he desperately wanted El Paso to know what this Chicano from el barrio del diablo—from whom they never expected anything— had accomplished. He wanted to tell all those who tried to ignore him to screw themselves every way he could, and at the same time, he wanted the people, the barrio, to be honored and inspired by his achievement.

By constantly wanting to prove that he'd transcended the neighborhood he was so proud to have grown up in, he proved how much he still lived there. His way of survival there, and later in the joint, caused many, who'd never visited either, lots of discomfort about his brusque style. He was still the Brown Beret pachuco admired when he was wanted and needed in the early seventies for the literary bravado that kicked the doors open, but who didn't suit the polite—he'd say co-opted—wine-and-cheese parties of the eighties and nineties.

Smaller, unrecorded events I carry with me: we were at The Tap, a downtown bar, one early evening when drinks came to our table. The waitress pointed to a man at the bar. He wore a white cotton shirt with no tie, slacks—not exactly white-collar but not blue-collar, either. Mejicano, Chicano, both. Ricardo didn't know him, but the man knew Ricardo. When Ricardo was most disgusted with the contemporary Chicano writer-poets, he would boast to me that for all their attention and acclaim with middle-class academia, he was the only one who could and would walk into any bar in any barrio and someone would know who he was and buy him a drink because he was from the neighborhood and didn't have to pretend he was. Here was evidence, and instead of saying to me, like, ¿no te dije?, he was genuinely humbled. He immediately wrote the man a poem on a napkin as thanks, and he never mentioned it again.

And then there were these moments of his family. He was so proud of his daughter and sons, so proud of his wife, Teresa. Teresa was the love of his life, and the two of them loved their children. His own feeling was so strong that you realized it was simply an unspoken assumption, unlike so much he had to prove, to argue for. This was another Ricardo Sánchez you had to discover when you visited him, when you ate tacos with him on Tyler Street, when the table was pulled out so you could fit in the small kitchen. But it was especially there at the end, watching the family around him, touching him, rubbing his feet and thighs, sitting, talking. It was Teresa being there every moment. It was love like I've never seen or imagined. Enviable, blessed.

A few months ago, I was in a discussion about poetry with some Texans considered influential in these literary matters. They were saying it was only what was on the page that counted. I didn't agree and I still don't. Ricardo Sánchez wasn't about the word alone; he was inseparable from the page. I know that this was exactly how he thought, too, that a poet wasn't just a person who wrote down some words for print, but one who lived a life, who stood up and read it right to your face. And that's how he was unto the very end—uncompromising, fearless, and, in a word, brave.

I miss you already, carnal. Like a real older brother. Your voice, your wisdom. Nos vemos. Nos watchamos.

Notes on Lit from the Americas

What I most admire about Rolando Hinojosa's work is its honesty of region. Real characters, real South Texas, where he's really from. Years ago, seven or eight, I knocked on his door at the University of Texas. His office is inhabited and much used; besides the papers and books leaning and stacked and stuffed any which way, on top of a file cabinet, he had one of those midget refrigerators. For his lunch, he explained. Austin is notoriously sweltering most of the year. He didn't mention how cold it kept those long-neck Mexican beers. There was more than one for each of us. As I recall, he stashed a bottle opener in the top drawer of his gray institution-issued desk. So, Rolando, I asked, who's your favorite Chicano writer? He did not hesitate a moment. He wheeled and pivoted that office chair toward a gray bookcase at his back and, like someone who placed every book in an exact spot, went right for one: Heinrich Böll. Which is the other thing about Rolando I like, his humor and play. Rolando was the very first Chicano writer I'd read. About 1975. Though listening to César Chávez, though watching actos by Luis Valdez, I still thought serious fiction was either European or beat—Camus, Dostoevsky, et al., or Kerouac et al. *Estampas del Valle* shocked me. Ordinary people from the neighborhood, talking right on the printed page!

★   ★   ★

I read too much bad lit and I get tired of it. Yes, I do often think it's me, my nasty temperament. But maybe even because of—or as proof of—that temperament, I also think it isn't me at all. So much of the fiction I come across is what I'd call tract, rigor-mortised by some transparent issue, about as inconspicuous as a banner. Not to say I disagree with the issue. But good writing and good intentions are not the same. Lots confuse having strong ideas, which are important socially and culturally and politically, with strong writing. I don't agree with many of the ideas of Rich-ard Rodriguez, but his prose is superior. Bad writing? I think I must mean didactic. As in, so much for me to teach, so much for them to learn! O yawn yawn. Or do I simply mean didactic in a paternalistic/maternalistic, or a know-it-all (modest or immodest, though immodest is much worse), or just a school-goal way. Me, I don't particularly like it when it *is* considered children's lit.

Write from the gut and soul. Spill it. Write from *las alturas* and from *hoyos* (avoid cheap, italicized, affected use of Spanish words). Don't offer excuses, explanations, apologies, *apologias* (the Latin). Remember Danny Santiago? His *theme,* his gimmick and hook, was being Chicano. Explaining. i.e., apologia lit. In other words, don't write for Them. Don't respond to their issues (if they ask about the gang problems in your community, ask them what they're doing about their biker and pedophile problems). Try to please God or the Virgin and not others (well, Others). But pri-vately. As in silent prayer. They know you are flesh, know your tears of joy and pain. You will quit your day job; if you're a writer, you'll be fired often enough, anyway. If you want to be The Leader of the People, if you want to be a Saint, if you want to be The Guru, please don't pretend to be first of all a writer. Unless you're dead. As in, don't write for public acclaim. Unless you need the money. Be honest about that is all. Good luck, by the way. Don't be neat. Too neat, anyway. Don't try for an "A"— maybe even drop the course. Read books that are not about you and yours. Wasn't Doestoevsky the ultimate Russian writer because Russia was the unavoidable backdrop and setting and scene and circumstance and not the theme of his fiction? Write stories as though it is over and we have won. Unless it's a story about the fight. Like Oscar Zeta Acosta's. Unless I'm wrong about all the above.

Steinbeck

Not being precocious in matters of literature, even to the end of my teenage years when I still thought of "book" more as a verb, long before I'd read a poetic sentence, even I knew of Steinbeck, *The Grapes of Wrath* and *East of Eden*. His name was bigger than these titles, than the movies that were made of the novels. His name was as up there as that of Marilyn Monroe, Sandy Koufax, John F. Kennedy.

Eventually, when books did become active nouns for me, John Steinbeck was in my first stack of them, and it was not a good experience. That's because I'd been drawn to read *Tortilla Flat*. If this were all there was, I would have left it at that, groaning about him as I did this novel. I mean, what's with these sweet, mystically dumb and lazy Mexican "paisanos"? What nonmedieval writer creates lines like: "I swear, what I have is thine. While I have a house, thou hast a house. Give me a drink." But this is how he had these "native" characters of the Monterey Peninsula speak to each other, even as, or especially when, they were drinking red wine by the gallon. Terrible as it was, I'm easier on the novel now: it is simply another of those "exoticized" novels by a writer whose home was near—though on the good side of the tracks—a historically earlier culture that fascinates for its "strangeness." It's what young writers often begin with once they are stricken by the sense of mystery that is around and in them, that isolating awe which drives them to write. It's what bad writers never know how to transcend.

Because what Steinbeck attributed to chromosomes in Mexican-Americans—lazy innocence and drunken happiness— he came to understand as social and political conditions when he matured to write about the people from the Dust Bowl and the Central Valley of California. And that was when he became great, and that was when what he wrote about was what I wanted to read, what I admired and was inspired by. When what he wrote wasn't just about poor Okies rattling across the Southwest into California, or about lonely people living on a ranch, but about how people are, and how they should be and should be treated, and so about me, too, not to mention what I care about, and what I believe in: that the West is not the East, that the West is a land unique, ruggedly beautiful, as are the people from it.

The premier writer of the American West, Steinbeck didn't do Cowboys and Indians. You see hitchhikers and waitresses, truck drivers speeding by cotton and corn fields. You feel wind and it's dusty, and the sun is hot and too bright. There are trains pounding railroad tracks, rivers and creeks and bridges and long stretches of highway. There are lone oak trees in dry, grassy fields, vistas with rolling hills and mountains. Men hunt for wood to camp by a fire at night near gulleys with rocks and boulders. There are working ranches, and horseback riding and shooting rifles don't make the story.

Steinbeck tells us stories of work, the dream of what work can do for people. Lennie and George, in *Of Mice and Men,* are sent to the boss's ranch near Soledad for a job, expecting no more than to earn a living, hard as it comes. What they dream of is a house where they might listen to the rain outside, a couple of acres where they can raise rabbits in winter, have a chicken hutch, leave the thick cream on the milk, grow alfalfa, have a vegetable garden.

Remember when *cause* mattered? When it wasn't passé to care about the working poor? When being rich wasn't in itself the only state of achievement? In *The Grapes of Wrath,* Tom Joad, an ex-con guilty of beating a man, released from prison with four more years of probation, comes back to his Oklahoma home to find his parents, sharecroppers displaced by the cigar-chewing bankers and anonymous corporations whose roaring tractors, rolling like tanks in a war, intend to pacify a land where families once were born and buried.

The story of the Joads, traveling across the West to find work in the dreamland of California, is about disillusioned poor people who begin to organize against the meanest spirit of capitalism. Steinbeck takes on the dangerous and divisive issue of fair and decent labor; he is unafraid to talk about lousy wages and the abuse of workers, unafraid to extol the virtues of union and strikes. He allows Tom Joad, a man who can kill, to become inspired by a no-longer-religious preacher, to be the hero of his novel: "I been thinkin' a hell of a lot, thinkin' about our people livin' like pigs, an' the good lan' layin' fallow, or maybe one fella with a million acres, while a hunderd thousan' good farmers is starvin'. An' I been wonderin' if all our folks got together an' yelled. . . ."

The authorities say Steinbeck is sentimental, his work melodramatic. But if that's so, even if it's only that, I'm sentimental for him now. Because so many people, and so many writers, have left behind or never learned a respect for manual work, for people who carry and use tools for a living and get calluses and chapped hands and dirt under the nails, who bend and stoop, people who work by the hour or the basket, who build and fix things, who dig and plant and pick. The literary world is a powerful suit-and-tie business, and the well-dressed stories that editors look for are too much by writers whose game is played as professionally as Harvard MBAs, whose marketing goals are not meant to cause a reader to step outside the privileged cubicle to see who's sweeping the floor in the hours after they've gone home.

Get Over It,
Good Brown Man

One day, when I felt like I was in a little trouble, I decided to take a job teaching English. I'm allowing this line to be about nothing so that you can shake your head a few times and mutter about the state of education these days and then, done, and curious, I'll have your attention again when I write these next ones. Okay? This profe work takes me twenty-five miles down the dangerous highway above my South Austin rental into the hill country of San Marcos, at the college the undergraduates Lyndon Johnson and Tomás Rivera have made famous, Southwest Texas State University. In one respect, a place far away from the city where I myself began both my childhood and my education, and in another, well, I teach at night. I took my required English classes at night, too. There were older people in those, and since they were dulled by boring all-day work, kids, and spouses, I looked bright. I'd flunked daytime English the first time I took it, and that was at a junior college. Whereas, when I took it at night, I got a "B."

I teach—and by choice, I add boldly as fall '98 ends—the first semester of freshman composition. What I like about it is that, aside from the basic point of the course, which is for students to learn to write a competent college-level essay of about three to five pages in length, the subjects of these papers are wide open and unlimited. Are mine to choose. To invent. I get to learn what other people might think about something I might be thinking about.

So I think of topics. For instance, I think of journey. "Journey." And to offer an example of a journey such as I have in mind, I have them read the Nathaniel Hawthorne short story "Young Goodman Brown." There is much didactic information here. Note, I say, the obvious allegorical quality of the title character's name. It is not so obvious to freshmen. Young, as in, the experience of this character is one of youth. Or innocence, which is to say, before experience. Good man as opposed to bad man. Brown, a common name, an everybody-knows-one name, an everybody-has-this-experience name. Quietly, I will admit to you that I like the "brown" part, too, for its cross-cultural reference. It's a very crude, transtextual (if there is such a word) leap on my part. Very few brown Puritans. Nevertheless, I get a kick out of it. As I say, quietly. I never mention this to the students.

The story is about Brown having to take a walk into the forest one evening. His newlywed wife does not want him to go. His wife is named Faith, and she wears pink ribbons. You get the picture. He must go, he says, and so he does. It is a journey into the darkness, led by a satanic figure who looks very much like Brown himself, somewhat aged, or like his father. As the travel progresses, Brown encounters, one by one, each of his moral educators who were beyond reproach, each on his or her way to that darkest spot in the forest for the event he himself feels so compelled to attend. He stops, he is left alone, he is certain he will resist when a black cloud of voices floats above him, more voices from his Salem village, and therein the one voice he will not believe he is hearing. Will not until he picks up a pink ribbon in the path. A surreal cacophony proceeds as he journeys deeper into the place those Indians live (or, I tell the students, as it might have been in a more current setting, black people, or Mexicans, or Arabs). Brown gets there, and when he wakes up, in a fit—did he have a dream?—and he comes back to the village the next morning, his sweet wife, Faith, running up to him, so happy. But he does not see her in the same way now. He never sees her or anyone else the same way again, and, long life that he had, "they carved no hopeful verse upon his tombstone, for his dying hour was a gloom."

So what happened? I ask the class. Lots of ways to talk about this story, I suggest. He got an itch, he was thinking about some cute chickie not his wife, he went out drinking, started getting that guilt thing, drank more until there it was, he went with the baddie, and when he got back to his wife, well, it was not the same. Or was it a glimmer he caught in *her* eye? Or a little note from someone else she got? Even a long time ago? Is disappointment, disillusion, this process, something we all must go through?

A student, one with tattoos and a tank top and writes well, says, Just a restrictive religion back then. It's ridiculous that they were making such a big deal about going into the forest. It's just a product of the author's time. We don't have these kinds of religious hang-ups anymore.

Another says, So what is it you want us to get out of this? He sits in a chair against the back wall, a cap on. He was whispering to another student while I read the story aloud. He swore, he told me one time, that he would get an "A" from me on a paper one of these times. He says, You want this one to be about going from innocence to experience?

Another sits in a front chair, near me. He is ex-military. Early twenties. He is self-assured and neat. He says, Goodman Brown made too big of a deal out of it. I got over this kind of thing years ago.

Years ago? I ask him.

Yeah. I mean, he shouldn't have raised all these people around him to such heights in the first place. You find out that your father or mother, for instance, aren't so perfect, and you get over it. He made too big a deal out of it. He was bound to crash.

I guess that's easy enough, I say. He should just get over it. He was just being a wuss or something.

I want to go now. It's late enough, time to leave. I'm tired and disappointed. I thought everybody would like talking about this journey, how scary it is, what we do when we go through these events in our lives. Not this class. I feel like a wuss myself, like some soft English professor who dwells on ideas and never sees sunlight.

Maybe for me, that student goes on calmly, it's that I've been studying martial arts since I was young.

Martial arts, I say.

You learn to think differently, to behave differently, he says.

That would be a new approach, I say. The study of literature through martial arts.

I don't know why I'm pissed, but I am, and I hold him up outside the class, no karate, no kung fu. So this kind of experience, this journey he took, you'll never suffer from one, never be sucked up with doubt and fear and guilt? That can never happen, not even for a few hours, like when you're sick or something?

Not me, he says. But it's not just martial-arts training. I study Zen, too.

This Writer's Life

So far my writing life comes almost entirely out of the cause and effect of my experiences—as opposed to my beliefs or ideas, as in description, not prescription—and I say this not to assert a strength but to admit my weakness. It's that I don't think I have a good enough imagination. I feel handicapped by what I require when I sit down to write something. I can't make it up out of nowhere, feel almost ridiculous trying. I don't like this. I don't. For me, it's because of the details—a needling itch, a melodious sob, the sweetest nibble, or the most disgusting scent. I can't pretend to be a banker or an architect (their pencils), not a butcher or cowboy (their calluses). I can't imagine going to Saskatchewan or Alabama, can't write about following a path up the Himalayas or rowing down the Danube. I can't write as a woman. I can't write gay. I have never been a junkie or in a band. I don't know how it is to run for an elected position.

Here's the refrain I have used as my defense: experience teaches by surprise. It's what I would say about the how and what I do as a writer, what drives my work. It's in adventure, physical excitement, that stories arrive and even offer themselves—this being out there, not having to push the brain to think of things or characters or incidents, but finding them, discovering, that is, being caught up in and smacked by the unexpected, by the mystery. Living. And it's with this real surprise, this wonder and shock and fascination, that I myself become absorbed and, through an assembly of words, each like a chunk of tile that I place, that I try to relate something of the experience, something true. By "true" I mean what is in fiction and nonfiction and poetry. That's another thing I would say. That reality isn't as "true" as literature. When I call something I read "good," one of the reasons—besides its crafted beauty—is that it's true.

I did a reading not so long ago, and at the Q&A, I was asked why it was that I seemed to write only about what my questioner called losers, why my characters didn't ever seem, well, to be rich. If you've read the above paragraphs, I think you can figure out my reply. I'm holding out on this and refuse to criticize myself for imaginative weakness. Though many writers have and do pretend to write from a poor or working-class point of view, I will try out rich and comfortable as an experience, would not attempt to write about it any other way, and then, yes, I believe I would be capable of relating to a reader the literary surprises of wealth.

Did you notice that above, second paragraph, I used the metaphor of tile setting? And, of course, the discussion of money in the previous graph. I'm thinking of the jobs (how I think of a person making money) writers hold to be writers. I was in the construction trade for sixteen years, but for whimsical reasons that are too long a story, I've just come off a remodel job (first construction work I've done in years), and I was tiling a bathroom. Gray Italian tile from Home Depot, a dark blue grout. Pretty. It was me and a longtime friend from El Paso, Sammy Montez, and we were in the upstairs of this large New England house. What had been an attic was now two bedrooms and a bathroom. We were clocking in very long hours, and, well, certain things seem customary to us. Like, where's the beer? You

know, a few free ones from the owner of the downstairs refrigerator. I told Sammy, looking for some distant and large and funny
explanation, that it must be cultural. I was joking around, but he
nodded, convinced. The people we know in El Paso, a Mexican-American community, we'd be doing something like this,
it'd be beer, tacos, lots of eat and drink coming up the stairs every
once in a while. An almost obligatory offering to the guys working, out of generosity and worry about our stamina and well-
being—and also to keep us there till the finish, especially after a
few twelve-hour days. But out there in the East, we stack what
we bought in the refrigerator, and people drink our beer!

I've been out of that construction work three years. I took
a job as a creative-writing teacher. I wanted to write more, and
it seemed like a good gig, and anyone I've ever known would
tell me how it beats construction work. But I did worry about
what the experience would turn me into—when I write, I feel I
have to *be* in the world I write in, and I feared how I would sound
on the page and in my head if the people around me, no longer
fellow workers but students, were calling me Professor. I worried that . . . sorry, I'll stop there. I, too, get tired of the interior
battles with my demons. The truth is, I needed any job real bad,
so I was not this contemplative. It was there, I took it. And I had
accumulated all these friends, a couple very good friends, who
had gone to these creative-writing schools to learn to be writers
(I hadn't) and who didn't write out of their experiences but simply
made up characters and stories, as I believed not only couldn't
be done but shouldn't be. And they were fine writers I envied
and admired. About ten years before, the first time I taught creative writing (as a visiting writer), I told the students about writing out of their own real experience. You know, my above
refrain. How I didn't want that other. I was all self-righteous and
even pugnacious about it, feeling right, like I couldn't be wrong
and wasn't. Then Larry McMurtry came to visit, and somebody

asked him what he did, and he said he just closed himself in a room with a typewriter and he made it all up. So, I told the class afterward, there's also that way to do it. So now, I figure, I am old enough to change, too. What I want is to be more open, to allow that people can write from all kinds of points of view if the writing is good and the writer smart. I want to widen my narrow, limited thinking. Though I'm the teacher, I am the one who wants to learn.

A few months ago, I interviewed for a job at the University of Arizona, the school that has probably the most money in the poor Southwest. I thought of going to Tucson because it's in the center of my region, equidistant from Los Angeles and El Paso and Albuquerque, and I miss home. The creative-writing program is considered one of the best in the country. Part of the interview process is to teach a class. Which means reading stories in a graduate MFA workshop, then leading a group discussion. Well written in every respect by the best student in the program, the story I was given was about four middle-class to rich Anglo men in their twenties, their talk a cool dialect between surfer and hip-hop, drinking and drugging, crossing the border for some proverbial on-the-other-side fun. At some point, two of these stoned and tequilaed characters go to the proverbial whorehouse and, in the same room, I guess using twin beds, each have sex with a puta. They watch each other, and whatever one does to his, flips or sides, the other does. Because, as they watch each other, the story's sensitive underlayer is meant to teach us, the two are having a sexual-identity crisis. They really want sex with each other, and it's so difficult to admit.

I'll admit this: I am tired of this oh-so-usual story of Mexico as a tourist hole for Americans, a place to splash and spill fluids. I'm tired of Mexico being where American Boy goes across the dangerous, exotic frontier to come back A Man—the whores are cheap, and even the pretty girls will swoon for him. This is my family you're talking about. My mother's mother, my mother, the mother of my children. Does it simply not occur to anyone? But you know what, it *should* at the major school of the Southwest. In the heart of what, before the Treaty of Guadalupe Hidalgo, was once Mexico, what for many is still Occupied Mexico. The people outside the walls of that campus, those dark people who drive the loud garbage trucks and wax the campus linoleum and keep the quad grass groomed, the people all around the campus and this Southwest region are of Mexican descent. It is a Homeland for Mexican-American people. Do I have to point out that the names of these states are of Spanish language origin?

What I do is let the students talk first. There were sixteen very smart people in the class, though none Chicano or Hispanic. (There was one, a Chicana, in the creative-writing program, and I did meet her.) Except for me, nobody mentioned a syllable of what I've said here, not even a woman offended as a woman. Let me put it another way. Imagine someone from, say, El Paso, writing about "Milwakee." Imagine someone from El Paso turning in a well-written story and spelling Milwaukee the way I have here. As the story went around the room for discussion, how many people would it take before someone told that El Paso writer the correct spelling of the city? Well, in the story we read, these characters went to "Tiajuana." Tijuana is a rather well-known California border town. Not one of these smart students brought it up that this Mexican city is not spelled Aunt Juana, even if it is mispronounced that way all the time.

Experience teaches you by surprise. A former construction worker, I can read these stories of lullaby rides down the Danube, of cross-dressing bankers, and I can sit there and talk to those who wrote them about composition and character development and dialogue without shaking my head. I'm getting better. I'm not there yet, obviously. I'm sorry. I am trying. Honest.

If You Were A Carpenter

For many years I lived and wrote in a solitude that wasn't just the usual, necessary quiet of every writer—the desk, the chair, the sealed-off room. I earned money in an inarticulate world that stretched out electrical cords in the morning, humped construction material, ripped and banged and drilled, that in the late afternoon wrapped those cords up again, collected tools, drank beer, and talked . . . but never about books. Outside the room I closed myself in to write was the city of El Paso, three hundred miles from everything, far from much of what most take for granted. Like bookstores.

Which probably explains a lot of why my recent book tour seemed like an adventure to a new continent and a different time. Suddenly I was being accosted by these inhabitants, "readers," I always wanted to exist but I conceived of more as fictional characters, not human beings. Sometimes these very people would approach me and ask questions. One was, How did you become a writer? They didn't mean it like it might sound, as in rhetorically, with a sarcastic overemphasis on "you." I promise, they were curious in a complimentary way. And I couldn't easily explain the phenomenon either. I told them I suspected a disease.

Now that I'm back in my El Paso solitude, I want to offer evidence of my insight: you might remember hearing in the news about President Clinton's Miami summit with the leaders of the thirty-two nations of North and South America. What you didn't hear about was a presummit weekend gathering, a month earlier, in Washington, D.C., and Annapolis, Maryland, of artists, journalists, and scholars from the two continents. Among the thirty or so invited were Maria Elena Cruz Varela, the Cuban poet who spent two years in Castro's prison, Sergio Ramírez, current leader of the Sandinistas in the Nicaraguan National Assembly, and Father Gustavo Gutierrez, the Peruvian priest and liberation theologist. Also included were the essayist Richard Rodriguez, the sociologist Seymour Lipset, the novelist Elena Castedo, the right-wing jazz critic Stanley Crouch, and Todd Gitlin and Paul Berman, representing the American left. And, also, me.

Our first evening we were all invited to Al and Tipper Gore's vice-presidential residence, the Admiralty House. It was pomp and circumstance of categorical distance from my El Paso life. As is my manner—my disease—I could not focus in on the appropriate specifics. Like conversation. As others are getting to know one another, combining bites of hors d'oeuvres off silver platters and banter with ambassadors, I'm staring at the furniture or the picture frames or the casings around the doors and windows, the base and crown moldings. Mr. Gore eventually directed us to a circle of chairs before we entered the dining room, and though I was sure he was discussing this new moment in the Americas, the new opportunities that a group such as ours coming together symobolized, I wasn't hearing a word. Instead I was watching how he articulated, his mannerisms as they contrasted against a window behind him. I was looking at his shoes (a black cowboy boot and an air cast that looked more like a hiking shoe), and I was looking at how the others were hearing him, their twitches and scratches. I'd noticed that the circles had divided into semis that were not North and South. On one side, bland bureaucratic suits, dark blue and gray, dull white. On the other, artistic colors and patterns. Yellow and red and orange and elegant black. At dinnertime, when were asked to interpret the event, while others seemed to have outlines with, like, roman numerals, all I could say was that I felt like I was at a wedding.

Another question that came up on the book tour was, Do you think all of this attention, the new world you're being introduced to, will affect your work?

I always said no, I have too much material. But privately, the answer was just as much yes. I dwelled on it. Since I'd bought the house my writer room is in over a year ago, an old front door had been hanging there, ugly and getting uglier, without even a threshold, waiting for me to replace it. So I drove my pickup to the builder's store. I haggled a $350 door down to $80 (it was the last one, and it had two bolt holes at the top for its display). Got out my level and square and tape and skilsaw, pencil and chisel, drill and holesaws. I stained and varnished it. Not to sound too immodest, I'm pleased to say the answer really is no, it has not affected my work. I've even decided to keep my tools out and add a room. A new office.

Northeast Direct

I'm on board Amtrak's number 175 to Penn Station. I've traveled by train a couple of times in the past year, but last time, I discovered that each car had one electrical outlet. Besides lots of room, besides that comforting, rolling motion, it's what I think about now when I think about the train. My Powerbook has a weak battery, and I can plug in and type as long as I want.

The car is empty. Maybe three of us new passengers, while two previously seated. So I do feel a little awkward taking the seat right behind a guy who I saw hustle on several minutes before I did. He'd already reclined his aisle seat, thrown his daybag and warm coat on the seat by the window. He was settled. I'm sure he was more than wondering why, with so many empty seats all around, I had to go and sit directly behind him. But I felt something, too. Why did *he* have to pick a seat a row in front of the electrical outlet? And if he grumbled when I bumped the back of his seat to get by, I grumbled because I had to squeeze past to get over to the window seat behind him.

I'm over it quickly because I've got my machine on and I'm working. And he seems to be into his world, too. He's taken out a daily planner, and he's checking a few things. I see this because, his seat reclined, I'm given a wedge view of his face. I see his left eye and the profile of his nose when he turns toward his window. When the conductor comes by for our tickets, the man asks if there's a phone, then gets up to use it. I get immersed and barely notice his return.

I pause, my eyes have floated up. He's holding a thick new book. I'm sort of looking it over with him. The way the cover feels, the way the chapters are set out. It seems like an attractively produced history book, and I bet he just bought it. He puts it down, then reaches over to the seat in front of me and brings up another.

The other book is the paperback of my novel! I *cannot* believe it! He stares at the cover for a moment, then he opens it. He's reading the acknowledgments page! When he's done, he turns back to the title page, then puts the book down. He gets up and goes to the forward car where the conductor said he'd find a phone.

How improbable *is* this? I mean, my novel is definitely not a Danielle Steel, not a John Grisham. If it is this much shy of miraculous that I would be on a train with someone who had heard of my books at all, how much more miraculous that, because of an electrical outlet on a train, I'd be sitting inches from a person who just purchased the book and is opening it before my eyes? And look at it this way—of the possible combinations of seating arrangements in the train car, how many could give me this angle? And what if he hadn't leaned his seat back?

I know what you're thinking. That I should lean over and say, Hey man, you will *never* guess who's sitting behind you! No, that's not me. I don't want to do that. I won't. I want him to be my anonymous reader. How many opportunities does a writer have to learn a truthful reaction, really truthful, to his writing? How absorbed will he be? Will he smile at parts, groan at others? How about his facial expressions? Will his eyes light up or go dull?

As he's walking back, he's staring at me a little too strongly, but he can't know who I am. I'm feeling, naturally enough, self-conscious. He can't possibly know he's in the eyes of the author himself—to think it would be even *more* ridiculous than that it's true. It could be the bright yellow shirt I have on, which is more of a banner, a United Farm Workers T-shirt celebrating César Chávez. It reads, cada trabajador es un organizador. People are always looking at it and I practically can't wear it because they do. But he's not paying attention to my shirt. It's that I'm the dude sitting behind him, typing into his ear, breathing on his neck while we're on this empty train, with so much room, so many seats, with so much possible spacing. I think he probably doesn't like me. He's probably got names for me.

He sits down. He's picked up the book! He's gone to page 1 and he's *reading*! Somehow I just can't believe it, and I'm typing frantically about him and this phenomenon. He's a big guy, six-two. Wire glasses, blue, unplayful eyes. Grayish hair—indicating he's most likely not an undergrad—beneath a Brown University cap, which indicates he's probably not a professor. Grad student in English? Or he's into reading about the Southwest? Or maybe the cover has drawn him to the purchase. He's turned to page 2! He's going! I have this huge smile as I'm typing. Isn't it so amazing? Bottom page 2, and yes, his eyes shift to page 3!

Suddenly he stops there. He gets up again. To go to the phone, is my bet. I'm taking the opportunity. I'm dying to know the name of the bookstore he's gone to, and I kind of arch upward, over the back of the seat in front of me, to see a glossy store bag, when just as suddenly he's on his way back and eyeing me again. I squirm under the psychic weight of these circumstances, though also from the guilty fact that I'm being so nosy. I pretend I am stretching, looking this way and that, rotating my neck—such uncomfortable seats, wouldn't you say?

He's reading the novel *again*. Page 4, page 5, page 6! A woman walks by, and he doesn't even glance up, isn't even curious whether she is attractive or not. He's so engrossed! He's *totally* reading now. No, wait. He stops, eyes to the window where it's New England, beautifully composed and framed by this snowy winter. Those tall, boxy two- and three-story board-and-batten houses painted colonial gray and colonial blue, two windows per floor, hip and gable roof, nubs of chimney poking up. Oh no, he's putting the book down. Closes it, mixes it into his other belongings on the seat next to him. It's because he's moving. He must hear my manic typing, and he feels crowded, so he's picking up his stuff and going up an aisle. What an astute, serious, intelligent reader I have to feel so cramped! My reader wants to read in silence, be alone with his book and the thoughts generated by it and his reaction to it, and he doesn't like some dude behind him jamming up his reading time and space with this muttering keyboard sound—it makes me *smile,* thinking how much more keen my reader's psychic synapses are to be responding to what his conscious mind cannot know is occurring. It must be a raging psychic heat, a dizzying psychic pheromone. When he has settled comfortably into his new seat, he pulls the novel back up. He's reading again! Reading and reading! When that young woman passes through on her return, no, again, he does not look up. He's dedicated, fully concentrating. He's really reading, one page after another.

New England: white snow, silver water, leafless branches and limbs. Lumber- and boat- and junkyards. The bare behind of industry, its dirty underwear, so beautifully disguised by winter.

My reader has fallen asleep. We haven't been on the train an hour, and my writing has made him succumb to a nap? Nah, I don't find it a bad thing. Not in the slightest. It's really a compliment. How many books do you fall asleep with? The conductor wakes him up, though. He's sorry, but he found that daily planner on the seat behind the man and wanted to make sure it belonged to him. My reader goes right back to sleep. He's dead asleep now. A goner. I pass him on my way to buy myself a drink, and he's got his left thumb locked inside the book, his index finger caressing the spine, pinching. You see, my reader does not want to lose his place.

We both wake up at New Haven. Probably getting a little carried away, I thought he might get off here—walking the book into Yale. He reopens it. He's at the beginning of chapter two. He does read slow. He's lazy? I say he's thoughtful, a careful, considerate reader, complementing precisely the manner in which I wrote the novel. It's not meant to be read quickly. He's absolutely correct to read it the way he does.

Forty-five minutes outside Penn Station, many passengers have boarded, cutting off my reader and me. He's still up there reading, but with the passage of time, and our physical distance blunted by a clutter of other minds sitting between and around us, the shock and mystery have lessened in me. I have adjusted, accepted it. By now I am behaving as though it is ordinary that a stranger two aisles away is reading my work. Like every other miracle that happens in life, I am taking the event for granted already, letting it fade into the everyday of people filling trains, going home from work, going. He is reading the novel, and I am certain, by the steady force and duration of his commitment, that he fully intends to read unto the end. He and I both can look around, inside the car and out the window, and then we go back, him to the book, me to the computer keyboard, no longer writing about this.

So when the moment comes, ask what, how? Tap him on the shoulder, say, Excuse me, but you know, I couldn't help but notice that book you're reading, and it's such an amazing coincidence, it is *so* amazing how this can happen, but I was just talking

with a friend about that very novel this morning—change that—
I was talking to two friends, and one thought it was just great,
while the other—change that—and one thought it was just great,
and I wondered what you felt about it, and how did you hear of
it, anyway?

After the conductor announces Penn Station, we stand and
get our coats on and, the train still swaying, move down the aisle
and toward the door with our bags. I'm waiting right behind him.
Could easily tap him on the shoulder. But nobody else is talking. No one, not a word. So I can't either, especially when I'd
be making fake conversation. Train stops, door opens, people in
front of him move forward, and a woman steps between me and
him with her large, too-heavy-for-her suitcase. He's shot out
ahead of me quickly, up an escalator, several more people between us. When I reach the main floor of the station, get beneath
the flapping electronic board that posts trains and times and de-
parture tracks, I have caught up with him. He has stopped to get
his bearings. Just as I am at his shoulder, he takes off in the same
direction I'm going.

So we're walking briskly side by side in cold Penn Station.
You know what? He doesn't want to talk. I am sure he has no
desire to speak with me. Would definitely not want to have that
conversation I'd planned. No time for me to fumble around and
maybe, eventually, tell him how I am the writer. This is New
York City, no less. He's in a hurry. He'd grimace and shake his
head, brush me off. He already thinks I am one of those irritating people you encounter on a trip, the one always at the edge
of your sight you can never seem to shake. And so as I begin a
ride up the escalator toward the taxi line, I watch him go straight
ahead, both of us covered with anonymity like New England
snow.

Dream Comes True*

A week after the good news I got laid off for mysterious reasons,
honored thus by the company for my loyal service, and, because
I made a little bit of a scene leaving, a certain subject for conversation for at least a few days at a few dinner tables, maybe even a
thought or two in a hot bathtub or under a shower and for certain in the memory of all around me who talked to me and
worked with me. And then two weeks before I get my airplane
ticket, I go to the grievance court to find out, though it was me
who'd been there in the dirt hole from the start, that it was nothing personal, it was a reduction of the workforce, and there is a
man, my own local's business agent, who sits with the steward
who's saying this, and oh he's not taking sides, even though he's
lying and I'm like shocked because I wouldn't have even guessed
that the steward, my job site representative, would be there and
of course nobody told me how the process was supposed to work
and how could I know until I'd already lost? I'd walked into that
arbitrator building and read the brass plate inlaid near the entrance

---

* What follows comes out of a notebook. It was a typewritten journal entry,
the writing no-look-back. However, for it to appear in this book, some sentences were edited to simplify and clarify what would have been too sloppy and
confusing. Otherwise, it is as it appears—commas, periods, and the rest.

and it said for the dignity and security of the working man. I don't know what it can mean, I guess I'm too dumb, but I need money, we're getting close to that edge again, I'm getting close to that again, but still I ended up taking more chances, staying home and typing, not wanting to go back out there, working words guiltily, never enough to compensate being not employed maybe I'm unemployable, it would seem always being honored like this, and there's even people daring to flip me off when I give them shit about their stupid ass driving, and my boys crying playing fighting wanting, and though there's no grass outside, and I'm going to San Francisco.

I'd been trying to get a bag of weed for three weeks without any success, looking in drawers and smoking age-old half joints until I finally I get some from the upstairs neighbor, a big bag of ancient homegrown harsh and not so good but I needed a buzz just to calm down some, to take some vacation since soon I'd have to go back out there, and he gave it to me because he didn't smoke it anymore. Me either mostly.

I was already wearing my new pants. I worried only little about the Olympic traffic. Ricky goes buh! buh! when we see a bus. Tony and I scream the opening notes to the Chips theme for any cop bike or car but do the whole tune practically when we really see a highway patrol bike. It's his favorite TV show. Ricky does a daa-daa to any motorcycle, and Tony goes Ricky thinks all motorcycles are chips, like isn't he naive? Tony's gonna lose at least one of his bottom front teeth, and that's what I'm thinking about when I'm getting out of our car at the Bonaventure Hotel, the tooth fairy. I'm going to San Francisco, yes I've got my tickets got a couple stories I can read. Jesuschrist I'm going to San Francisco as a writer! What the fuck am I doing? Is this what you do, is this how they did it? Jesuschrist my son's losing his baby teeth, I gotta go back to work next week. Don't let that tooth fairy cheat you, man. You tell 'em there's other tooth fairies. The night before he sat on my lap late, watching the Olympics, thinking about tooth fairies and rest of his life teeth, flicking the one around with his tongue. Today all these ABC-TV buses are here at the Bonaventure where I'm being dropped off, across the street there's a building I worked at and Tony says, There's your job site. What if one of those guys heard of this or I saw somebody still working at it?

On the airport bus I'm seeing my hometown city, the ringing of the national anthem still very much in my mind. I know the Olympic torch passed this street too and it all means more Ronald Reagan America. It was a long ride as a kid down Imperial Highway. The first time I saw that webbed building that is a restaurant, that is LAX, and my bicycle hadn't been stolen yet. How irresponsible am I unemployed even though I'm going to San Francisco thinking I'm staying for maybe three nights, borrowing money so we can pay the rent? I'm imagining strange San Francisco literary nights, maybe some strange woman, even though these are the eighties and I don't have a job and I've got two babies and my life's nothing like Kerouac's. Jack Kerouac San Francisco. Jack Kerouac was a bodhisattva who said he was like the flame of a common man writing, the light and energy of that, equal opportunity. Fuck I'm going to San Francisco and they're paying for the ticket!

It is a dream and it is happening. Sir, who are your favorite writers? What are your influences? Uh, I dunno. No, it wasn't him, but okay, maybe it was him, and I used to read this, and that . . . damn, look, there must be a mistake, I'm telling the ticket counter woman. I'm supposed to go there today, not August 08, today. Well sir you'll have to go . . . I pull out a letter to confirm that I'm not dreaming this shit up, and she gets a man over who pecks into the computer keyboard, and then I'm on an empty airplane and I take a window view of the line-up of LA airplanes. We're in an Olympics slowdown and then there's low visibility in San Francisco but there it is the coast the Pacific Ocean. a canaled orchard of a city of tract houses. I order two Bloody Marys and shut my eyes, open them for Juan Rulfo, a story in a book and above clouds, in clouds, then a jetty under us, we're landing. I should shine my boots, and I do take a piss before I get off. Maybe it is cold in San Francisco but I don't care. I've got my Olympic Games Los Angeles T-shirt on because I don't wanna dirty my new Mark Hopkins hotel shirt and then I hear the phone pages on load speakers, mispronunciations of Dagoberto, until I'm with the woman named Susan. In the parking structure, looking up the pan ceilings, at the columns and their capitals, I say this is what I do for a living, but it's like she's too nervous and distracted, maybe because she's borrowing money from me to pay, she's got no cash. I have my litany of questions to go through, like did I win by default, why would they think mine? Like, when am I going to be deluged by book publishers, how many people publish books out of this? Twelve, thirteen years ago already since I came here the first time. Berkeley was where a guy I went to high school with told me, a month after he'd gotten back, about his personal rape and pillage Vietnam. I don't say how Berkeley was a fantasyland to me, the Paris of my mind, like where they kept the secret vault of so much intelligence I embarrassingly don't have. What is this year of my life, this year of rats roaches, pricks dogs snobs, evictions breakdowns freakouts headaches headaches headaches that pain, money money rent laid off quit waiting for work unemployment USA! USA! I'd swim my laps at the Y, only a half mile, push my little weights near monsters. I'm writing, I've been writing, all the sudden I can write again, I know again what I want to say and the day before the love of my literary life Wendy Lesser in that blue ink print says she's gonna take another story. . . . In front of me, Susan's uncomfortable. I was kinda hoping to laugh loud, talk about like drugs in the past when we're passing I think it's the Oakland Bay Bridge. I wanted to talk about

getting us a drink before we started anything, but when she thinks
it's funny when I say I dunno I might stay one day or two or
three, I'm starting to feel the weirds, I'm starting to get that look
at me and I'm thinking I better cool down, but like always I
wanna say you're the nervous one I'm the one that'll go anywhere you want and I'm not worrying about what you might
say or do. I point out highrise buildings. I say look at that building. I say look at those cranes.

Susan points me to the men's room without my suggest-
ing it. I guess I can change my shirt I say, and she says yes. Maybe
she's nervous because we're so behind schedule because of my
late flight and because it took almost a half hour for her to refind
her car. I put on my Zody's dress shirt in front of the mirror
and I splash on the Old Spice, sniff the pits and button the shirt.
Pretty fancy. The place is too. Here is where a job I might want
might be. Everything's new and modern. There wouldn't be
one screamer foreman. I'm given a quicky tour and I fumble for
the coffee and sit, talking to some guy, but let's go, and I hop up
and Susan's back—here's a list of the past winners. I recognize a
couple names, like Al Young and Philip Levine, names I know
have books, but there's also a lot of other names of who knows.
Oh well. I know I never would have been hired here either. I'm
starting to talk. A guy, Jim, says to me he wished he didn't have
a job that required a tie, so I start cranking about construction
lay-offs and all the jobs I've been through. I meet the other winner, who's moving to LA, her boyfriend's gonna be an actor, then
I'm talking to another woman who reminds me of somebody.
Outside we're waiting for a taxi. I answer, say yeah, published
in and I mention one I was never paid for or informed of. Writers are always getting ripped off somehow, some way, someone
says. Next answer: No, I haven't been writing so long, the first
awful thing I ever wrote was when I was twenty-eight and I was
so arrogant I thought everyone was nuts to not think it was the

best ever. Even this one woman, a poet who had a book and who liked me who I asked to read this, she was excited to, but later said I really don't think it's good, I thought you could do better. But I'm so fucking arrogant and stoned on Colombian back then that I'm thinking what does she know? I kept a page of it, just to remember. It was awful. I don't remember her name. Someone says, you should find out her name and send her a note.

The taxi driver says that LA isn't a taxi town. I'm pointing out yes construction workers are different. How that guy's got a union carpenter sticker on his hardhat. I've been thinking that once upon a time I'd seen this hotel we're going to, the Mark Hopkins, but I'm beginning to see this San Francisco, the look of the people, the casual wealth, the smart look on faces, even on bicyclists, the unsleaziness, and no, I've never seen this hotel before. There's a doorman. It's old wealth, none of that LA flash and cash, just calmly rich, subdued, ancient money. I'm following them up stairs. What I remember now, as I write this, is soft carpet under, glittering light, a certain elegant quiet, this huge painting on the stairways: an obviously very rich lady, a wavy white collar, the neck of a stiff gown, her lips puckered, her eyes certain and directed, her blond hair tight on her scalp, a hard little bun of it on top of that. I'm thinking when I see this that I feel like I've walked into some very other world—that's obvious, of course, but what I mean is well the contrast, the streets of my life Imperial and Western and Long Beach Blvd and Vermont and Washington and Atlantic and Rosecrans and Tweedy and Whittier and now Sunset and Hollywood. This last week in LA, in a heat wave, it's all still inside my head and body so that the only thing I can compare this San Francisco to is book pictures and images on TV. But I'm wearing my Zody's $9.99 dress shirt, my Tony Lama's, and JCPenney's pants. I told the girl when I bought those how I worked there once for over a year—it was two years—as a stock boy, that was my first years of junior college, and even there, those bosses at Penney's then, I was thrown that smug, you're too worthless to amount to anything look by the suit and tie department managers, like they'd never gone to junior colleges, weren't like me. I'm sort of spinning you see, and the reason I'm stuck on this Penney's thing is that an old friend who I met working there moved to Berkeley, took Uno, my cat Chica's kitten.

I'm in a fantasy, not in a hotel, it just looks like the Mark Hopkins, maybe the richest hotel my mind can imagine, more than it can imagine. There's little round tables in the first room with white tablecloths. Another large table at my right, wine bottles chilling in silver bowls tinkling with crushed ice. A Mexican waiter, red vest, a linen towel slung over his arm, I'd swear, is that possible? My memory could easily be wrong, but if he didn't he should have. He asks si el señor quisiera vino blanco o rojo? I say como no, hombre, dame dos vasos horita o la botella mejor. I don't know if he wants to smile or he doesn't want to smile but I do know he's pleased it's me who's the Literary Award winner. Settle down, I'm thinking. That's not Roberto or Hector. White wine's fine, I say in English, also not wanting to get into that trip. He gives it to me, but I'm so nervous all I wanna do is slug it, I can't possibly hold the glass steady, be still, stand there, but I'm being introduced to Professor Hart, UC Berkeley English, can you believe that?! I gotta tell him. Tell him how I'm the guy who failed my first English comp class, then went to another junior college where the requirements were easier at night so I could pass, and I took the one other but after that those two required ones I could never take an English course again and here he's from Berkeley, giving me a literary prize! He's distinguished, smart and like British precise with words but casual, and relaxed, and he says, well obviously you don't need them now.

I'm led to a table. The professor introduces me to the Mrs. Jackson of the prize and her daughter. Oh man, what am I here for? She asks that, yes, but she means something else, something nice. I get a refill of my wine. What do you write? Short stories right now. Oh. I believe these awards have been given to some very good writers, she explains. I say, I just happened to see a couple of weeks ago that Raymond Carver got the award. He writes short stories. He's considered one of the country's leading writers at the moment. Real big. I'll have to look him up, she and the daughter state in unison, genuinely interested.

Now I'm standing. I'm talking to Herb Gold. He's that handsome, liberal San Francisco look. A fine suit and tie that would go to all these occasions and look just right. We're talking about my conspiracy theory: That it's "Creative Writing" and did he see Rust Hill's essay in Esquire? See, I say, there it is, there's the proof that if you don't have like introductions. He doesn't know anything else, Herb Gold says. I like this guy. He wasn't mentioned in that issue as an important writer. Even the book review editor in the LA Herald wrote an article about this magazine issue and said how come Herb Gold, for instance, wasn't asked what he was doing? That was the first time I knew that he was a big time writer, heard of him at all once I'd been told I'd won the prize. He and I are talking, like writers, you know, and he's being nice, but I'm gone. I'm not really in the room and at some point or another standing nearby is this woman, who's a reporter from the SF Tribune. I'm hearing myself say something, that I'm a halfie and that that has always made things different for me, I've swung in and out of worlds, feel more like I'm an American writer from Los Angeles, and that as far as this Danny Santiago thing goes, I have to confess that I enjoyed the book once I got over wondering if it were a gay coming out story because of the first and fourth chapters. I enjoyed it, thought it was mostly pretty funny stuff, and what really impressed me was that the writer was 73 years old, that was impressive, white dude or not. The problem is that it seems like another culture rip off and that's the history of Chicanos, always being used for the advantage and money and prestige of white America.

That waiter's come back and is asking me if I want more white or red wine. He's added this other dimension to my mental hysteria. All the shit going on, these people, I'm standing there in my new Penney's pants and Zody's shirt, feeling different cuz of that even, I'm worrying about how to hold these goblets, I'm practically shaking, and this waiter's around. He comes up and asks these things in Spanish. I answer him in Spanish, like talking to him, but I think it's probably weird and don't think it feels right in the situation so I say thanks a lot in English when he pours me even more white.

I'm in love with Wendy Lesser. She's the editor of The Threepenny Review and I tell her I have this terrible urge to kiss her thank you thank you but I won't right there. I'm spewing words now, who the fuck knows what I'm saying, I'm not drunk. I'm just energy high and I'm saying I've been around lots of different people, how my old man ran a plant that washed those tablecloths there and it's where my mother worked and grew up next door and that's how I became the famous writer I am today.

Fortunately Wendy sits next to me in the dining room where we're gonna eat. Somebody's directed me to where I sit—there are name tags or cards with black marks-a-lot lettering and there's one with my name on it. I feel like snuggling up to Wendy, I like her so much. She reminds me of a couple of women I've known distantly from college, brilliant and knife sharp and always knows exactly the right thing for me like she's already wondering what this dish in front of us is too, has already said she'll wait for everyone else to start, particularly I'd guess the Mrs. Jackson who sits directly across from us. It's pineapple applesauce, or anyway pineapple's the taste. Professor Hart's on my right and across from him is the director of the San Francisco Foundation. I suppose I've already been introduced to each person at the table, but even those moments are as clear as dream memory. Professor Hart's brought up this Danny Santiago Dan James thing again, to make conversation, and the director's explaining it to Mrs. Jackson. Professor Hart mentions something about Richard Rodriguez. Sure, I also didn't mind reading him, he's a good writer, but no, that really isn't my experience. English was in my home, it's my mother, she was born in Mexico City, my relatives I guess go back through there and Puebla and Jalapa and Veracruz on her side—that's what I wish I could do with the money, go to Mexico City, knowing to myself I won't and can't. No, I've never been, only a little of Baja and the border towns. I have this second cousin who comes up and keeps telling me to come there. I keep wanting to move to Mexico and he wishes he could move here. Yeah, that book's okay, *Hunger of Memory,* he might be a point of view, it's not mine, and politically it's not very popular. Myself, I just think in ten years all this political conversation will be unimportant because of when they publish more of us. Things are changing so fast. I think it'd be better to ask say Rudy Anaya, Rudolfo Anaya, he's in Albuquerque, the University of New Mexico, he's got published novels, or Ron Arias, he's good too, or like Leroy Quintana even though he writes poetry, they're the ones to ask, or Alurista in San Diego, their views are important ones. I don't say this: I hate talking about this, I just write stories, not one book published yet, I wanna write novels, win Pulitzers for them, make enough money to float around whenever I want, not expensively, just in my car, and I don't wanna get in this other shit because I'm tainted and suspect because in the first place I'm half, and this is my confusion of life of writing, asking me these things dreges up my very own personal Who Am I? And I wish I could explain how I'm already too weird according to most and I don't need anymore problems.

The conversation still going and Mrs. Jackson has this comment to make: Have you ever read *Tortilla Flat* by John Steinbeck?

I think that's the best book ever written about Mexicans. The director's smiling right at me and I think I could crack up out loud, but I just say I liked *Grapes of Wrath* and what's that other one, *Of Mice and Men,* but she's insistent about how maybe *Tortilla Flat* is his best book and I want to like this lady, so old she's harmless as a baby, so I nod smiling, staring at the new food in front of me. Thank God for Wendy and the wisdom of having her sitting next to me. I love women. It's papaya and there's two asparagus and two long armed pieces of fresh shrimp. I'm thinking this isn't the main dish, I'm expecting bloody meat or maybe something real gourmet like hen and I watch Wendy and she's eating the asparagus so then I can eat. I say, hey Wendy, I've got to read something, much as I'd rather not, but I've got something supposed to be light and funny and another a little maybe inappropriate for this setting—actually both aren't appropriate. She asks if I have "Parking Places," which is the one she just accepted for publication. No. How about "The Rat"? That's the unpleasant one I mentioned. I can't believe she'd have thought of it. Yeah, I say, yeah, you're so great! But you know, what about, there's this one line, but before I even say what it is she says just read it. Just like that. That easy. It would've taken me days to think of that. I'd already spent days thinking about *maybe* reading it—the story's Becky's choice too, she told me to read it, and like that Wendy's reminded me that it's my own story I can do with it whatever I want. I'm not reading a sacred document, and even if it was, it's mine anyways. That's how smart she is. I dig in, the food's great.

Pretty soon it's dessert, mousse, probably not Jello Instant Pudding Chocolate flavor. And pretty soon Professor Hart's giving his occasion speech about Mrs. Jackson 's husband and their friendship with Steinbeck and Scott Fitzgerald and all the sudden the room lights up even more. I'm seeing Gatsby wealth, Lorne Greene going to San Francisco with Little Joe, Hoss has to stay outta those fancy hotels because no matter what, he never looks right, he's just too goddamn big and dumb looking. And the professor talks about Mr. Phelan the senator and mayor of San Francisco, maybe he was just a little corrupt, and out come two plaques, one for me, and envelopes with money money, one for me, and I'm not supposed to read first. The other award winner's is about the sixties and early seventies and bare feet and I'm trying to hear but I'm gone, like floating above the room and seeing down on the table cloth Diane Johnson over there. Wendy'd leaned over and whispered to me she was the one who picked me and my stories out. There's maybe twenty people at the table, goblets and silver, the Mark Hopkins Hotel all through the meal, the waiter still dropping things off in Spanish. I wanted another one of those rolls because they were so good but it was such social misery to butter and eat that I said ya no quiero mas pero gracias eh. Would you like to read something? Professor Hart asks what seems suddenly. I say an introductory something about how at my age now, I'd been feeling disappointed that I wasn't at the very least gonna make Cooperstown but this thing didn't look too bad, maybe it's even better, so thank you, and thank you, and then I read "The Rat," the voice in my brain crumbling in nervous fear, my manuscript just laying there on their white tablecloth, my own ears picking up my own voice, the print just like what I'm writing here, there in my face, a bell tolling outside at the darkest part of the story like a musical score, the whole of it something like echoing in the Mark Hopkins Hotel of my mind.

Naturally I can look up when it's over. And I think—maybe this sounds conceited but that's not why I'm mentioning it—I think it has made an impression. Mrs. Jackson looks at her daughter. Her eyes are open. She says, I think we're seeing the next generation of writers, saying that to her daughter but with this other look, maybe like the dude who said he couldn't and didn't read the story when I sent it to him because he had such a strong repulsion to rats. I'm still reeling in my nervousness, but it seemed to me, spinning like I was even, that everybody heard the story I read, they listened. What I mean to say is, well, that maybe I am a writer, maybe I really will get a book published one day, maybe it won't matter that I can't seem to keep a job, maybe I haven't just been screwing up my life irresponsibly all these years, maybe my boys will eventually think I'm all right for all this, maybe all those humiliations rejections denials have meant this. It is hard to believe. I'm a construction worker, a carpenter, again next week. Much as I wish I could like it, Mrs. Jackson's remark makes me smile more that bloat out.

Handshaking. One a pretty woman. I'm saying it seems to me that I've accomplished more as a construction worker really, but no, I haven't been writing that long. I tell the story about being a carpenter at the museum at UTEP and sneaking over at my lunch break with what I thought was a Great Novel chapter and asking a writer I'd heard of who'd won this fiction prize and then one day, spackled with fresh concrete over my army surplus pants and tank top and shades, she's telling me I should go talk to the chairman of her English department and I've got this very used brown bag with my burritos from home and a scratched up bottle of Fanta orange drink this guy would bring cold from Juarez every day and sell to us and when I get downstairs, through the office doors, the secretaries crack up when I say I guess I have an appointment with the chairman. When I go in, he's kinda cocked in this swivel chair, above him's this photo of William Faulkner who like him is from Mississippi. Next thing I know I'm teaching English part-time and writing a novel which turns out to be shit but I learn that maybe the way to get novels read is to write short stories that are published. That's my current state of history—why I'm writing short fiction now. The woman I'm telling this story to is pretty, but I've decided I better control myself, act cool, not do something like hooting from a car at a prostitute on Sunset and make civil people think I'm not. Professor Hart says I knew you were all right when you opened your notebook—where my story is placed, where there's that bumper sticker *Carpenters for Mondale Means Jobs*. I know he's all right too because he says this. Wendy's about to leave but I stop her— please, I wanna take you out to dinner before I go and do you know of some good place I could stay? She gives me a phone number and an address of a hotel.

We cable car back to the foundation office. Finally I see it: There's this cool weather haze of intelligence around. I don't notice any new wave haircuts, no young women with red slip-ons and white pants and red checked blouses and bright red-framed sunglasses and platinum hair or purple hair or purple clothes. Sophistication. No poor people. Of course, maybe we're in that part of town. But in LA there's no part of town without poor people. Uh-oh. My mistake. There is that whole west side that I forget about. That's another city to me. Off the cable car we are separating. The pretty woman's going to Berkeley and much as I like to hang out with pretty women, I don't say please come with me, though I think in my always deluding desires that the possibility was possible, but I think I better be cool, I just won a Literary Award. I pick up my Olympics 1984 Levi-Strauss souvenir carry-on bag at the foundation office and stuff my plaque inside and Susan's given me a xerox of a map with stars where I am, where I'm going.

A writer, I stop where this laborer is working behind a screened-in jobsite. How's the work situation around here? Lots better, he says. Bad for a while. The same in LA, I say. What I've been thinking about for the past two years is settling my family back in El Paso and me going out to earn my six-months a year money on my own where wages are high and I'd been thinking why not SF? I have my own personal problems in LA.

I stop another guy walking on the street, a construction worker, and ask the same. Real bad for a while there, but better now. It's hot in LA. I like to work up sweats on cool days. This year I had a heat stroke. It was a 97 degree day above the pit and I don't think about sweating, but at about two I knew I was in trouble and at a quarter to three I had to get down off the deck because I was afraid I wouldn't be able to in moments. There's shade below the deck. I'm delirious and there's some guy telling me I better go back up there, I can lose my job. I get this incredible charley horse which stoops me over, and then, stooped over, gets in my stomach. I can barely speak. My own steward's busy (that culo who burns me later) but the laborer's steward helps. I don't want to be hauled up in the basket by the crane, I prefer to walk across the job. A very long walk. I changed colors a few times. When my check came the next week, I'd been docked a half hour for that day. So I'm thinking I might like San Francisco summers. Change makes me much less surly. I gotta go back to work next week. Sure I have an attitude problem. I don't like being treated like a dog and run off for it. I always try to make it clear at the beginning that I won't listen to any shit. One day the foreman came up to me and said they want us to pick up the pace. I said, look, this is how I work. I do my job, and if you or they think you can get somebody better . . . He says, I'm not talking about you, I'm telling everyone the same thing, I'm just telling you what they want in the office. In truth, I am one of the better carpenters. That's cuz I'm not stupid and I'm large and many construction workers, it may surprise you, don't combine the two. God's gift and curse because it also means I stick out and I don't even have to go without my false front tooth to get attention. So like this owner of the company one day likes the way I'm working. He's an older man with Nazi blue eyes and one of those accents too, and my foreman informs me that the old man has told him he likes me cuz I talk back, but, the fore-

man says, you can be sassy but don't be wrong. Fact was that I
didn't know I talked back to him. He was wrong about a few
things and I told him that and showed him on the plans but that
was it, it wasn't attitude. My grandpa, guys are teasing me, cuz
he likes me so much. But then one day a month or so later that
old man's yelling at me about something I'm not responsible for
building but I happen to be near with four other carpenters, which
is the other thing he's mad about, them. I'm not the foreman, I
say, I don't know what the plan is right there. So he's pissed.
Whadu I pay you for?! he's screaming. And I don't even say shit
to the old fucker or nothing, though I tell the foreman that I
don't think that should happen again. For a week the old man
doesn't speak to me. I'm working with an apprentice Carlos who's
a 1st period and the old man goes talking to him, not directly to
me, Tell your friend to come over here when you're done, stuff
like that's going on. Then the foreman brings me that lay-off
check. I don't know what you did in the office, he tells me, but
I couldn't talk em out of it. I go up to the carpenter's superintendent, a little fucker who likes to use his mouth for cussing
out and screaming at men and for smoking cigars because he's
the boss, and I ask him who and why. He says, snarly, *me* and
because I'm tying it up and we're laying off, just reducing the
workforce. This is how the workforce was "reduced": They laid
off this black guy who was suing the union and hadn't paid dues
in six months who had a horrible splinter up his ass and didn't
work and who the local business agent came out that day to tell
the company to lay off or else, a white dude who was hired as a
working foreman the day before but who didn't work and didn't
seem to know much about carpentry, and me. That's called, "a
reduction of the workforce." What I'm getting at is that maybe
changes of geography would be good for me.

    Finally I find the hotel that Wendy has recommended. It
doesn't open for hours, which is seriously discouraging since I

feel like making an honest writer of myself and working on a story I'd been working on and told myself to finish before I went back to work next week. What could I do? I looked for a bar to lay down my Olympics souvenir bag and I saw one, red letters, the Macao. It reminds me more of Texas or El Paso or Juarez, a long mirror like counter from the door light, red vinyl stools, the surrounding décor Chinese red and one small really black velvet painting of this woman who looks white with maybe a touch Asian or maybe even Spanish holding up her pretty breasts with one arm. There's a TV in the corner with bad reception and bad color, high up on that corner. My bag goes on one stool and me on another and the barmaid leans into her side, behind her the upside down stepping up "v" technique for bottle display, at the top another woman statue Giacometti-like except for her good hips and chichis. The bottom case is two or three straight lines of hard liquor. I order a Bud Light, not being much for Heineken or Coors or Bud regular, the only others, and the barmaid and I go through the usual breaking through the silence routine. She talks about how the place picks up at night, but it's so cold outside now and that's why we're alone and she talks about having to work fourteen straight hours, no overtime, no double time, she's not union like me. She's Korean, hangs out with this friend in Koreatown when she's in LA, near Olympic Blvd, which is a great place inside, she says, but is ugly outside. I buy her a drink, that's a Remy-Martin shot with a sparkling water chaser. We're loosening up, she's talking about LA's stupid Chinatown, but at least there's neighborhoods there, Koreatown, Chinatown, Little Tokyo, about how ugly Hollywood is, all those nigger pimps dressed like they are, she says. She was so disappointed. All those years she thought Hollywood was some beautiful place. Her name's Rose, she says. We're drinking and talking now and, well, she's pretty and I'm not so drunk to say that, she already knows it, more or less told me a few times already about the men always saying or doing—and look, I say, I'll show you what I'm doing here, you won't believe this, and I pull out the framed certificate or plaque whatever you wanna call it and show her where it says Literary Award. I'm probably smiling pretty big about it. Putting it back in my Olympics bag, I'm probably still smiling pretty big too, cuz my bet is that even if she reads English, which is maybe maybe not, she probably can't know what a Literary Award is. Which makes me even more happy to buy more rounds for she and I, cognac with beer chaser for me now. Rose and I are getting a tiny bit drunk and she lets me use the bar phone to call these friends. There's no answer to either of the phone numbers I've pulled from the information operator and behind me, in the TV set, they're laughing. Rose is laughing too. Some talk show with some familiar host. Pretty soon it's Pat Paulsen talking about his run for president. That is particularly funny back in the studio there in Hollywood and in the speaker of the TV. The empty bar's filled with this hilarity and Rose and I are drinking. She's telling me about a woman who came in and how she was nice to her. She's this white lady with lots of bracelets and she puts her hand on Rose's hand and is saying she'd like to come back and so Rose says sure, great. Later that night there's an argument going on at the table behind her. Some man and woman. They're screaming, so Rose has to go over to settle them down and says what's the problem with you two, it can't be that bad. But the man tells her to get fucked and to suck him if she doesn't like it and so Rose gets a little mad about this, saying I think you should leave sir and just as she's going on about it, that woman walks in. Hiii, Rooose!! but now she's a man. She couldn't believe it, that's San Francisco, men are women, women are men, how can you know? All these guys asking her what she's all about, what she's been doing. Rose and I are looking into each other's eyes a lot more now, maybe that's cognac and beer, but it seems to me she's leaning on the liquor case dif-

ferently now, notices I'm noticing that, and Password is on, or
something like it, contestants from Hollywood and Glendale,
winning more money than my Literary Award for filling in blanks
like the best way to happiness is through the and guessing the
most popular word. Rose says she's been in the states for five
years and I tell her how good it is, her English, and she says some
people ask me if I'm an American-born Korean and I say I'm a
Korean American. Not that many Koreans, she says, not here,
better in LA, here all these Chinese. They say, why don't you
learn Chinese Mandarin and I say I live in the United Sates why
don't you learn English! But if they talk Korean, I talk Korean.
Now it's the Match Game. Another man's walked in and she
saw him in a bar the other night when all these men were bother-
ing her. She gets him a beer and talks I guess Korean. I'm thinking about a hotel room again. But first I feel one of my headaches
and I swallow headache pills. All the sudden she changes the
channel with remote control and we're watching the Olympics.
Too much flag waving, I say, and both Rose and the man burst
out with equal remarks how disgusting it's all getting. There's a
boxing match. Koreans and Mexicans are the best, I remark, they
have the best fights at the Olympic Auditorium, and Rose says
yeah, that would be a good fight to see right now, and she says
let's change it, none of us like this. The Match Game again. I'm
thinking about what Diane Johnson told me after I said Faulkner
had published *Light in August* when he was 33. You're on schedule, she said, but I hadn't heard it at that moment because I'd
seen her face on this book she'd written, *Terrorists and Novelists,*
and her face was exactly like the photo except she was so small.
A little woman with this huge mind. And she says to me how
I'm on schedule.

    I'm telling Rose I'll be back and I mean it. I go over to the
Hotel Obrero, the one Wendy recommended, and push the button because it's supposed to be open by now and the buzzing

back says the door's open. Up the stairs and it's mostly a restaurant. Tablecloths and flowers, place settings. They've just gotten a phone call, somebody else is coming and now they have to make more space somewhere. It looks so much like San Francisco to me, and I say nice name for a hotel, how about a room? We're booked up, she says. I about collapse with disappointment. I'm drunk, Rose is across the street, it'll be getting dark, I've got this bag. I think the place must be the gourmet flowering of the hippie era. The women who are running it have those lines in their faces and the clothes run that hippie direction except now, in the eighties, they're washed and even ironed. Natural foods inevitably lead to gourmet concerns about taste and freshness. It all makes so much sense. Here I am, I am here, you gotta be kidding, I say. I'll do anything, so I tell the one running around with the plates, I just won this Literary Award, I ate at the Mark Hopkins, I hobnobbed with the famous, and Wendy Lesser, editor of the powerful Threepenny Review, recommended your place to me. I don't wanna look for another, please! This woman looks up at me and she says to the other, who's already calling around for another place for me to stay, he just won a literary award, she says what is it? and I say feelan or the fellan or the faylan I can't remember how it's exactly pronounced. The woman in the office gives me a card and starts telling me which buses will take me there. Once I hear the word transfer I'm real depressed, and then to top it off, she's saying something about it being about only so many blocks from there. Maybe it's just that I'm just used to buses in LA, and I don't know where I am in SF.

Like any red blooded American boy I decide I better go smoke a joint and think things over seriously. I'd seen this great street, not too far from the packed humanity of Chinatown, that looked strangely deserted, maybe even deadend and so vertical nobody'd hang out on it. I find this step there and light up this really awful stuff. There's this whipping wind and I have to keep puffing and drawing furiously. I sit for a few minutes pondering my fate and watching these kids at the corner. They're jiving and bullshitting, acting bad, though they carry books. Good ole American kids whose parents are Chinese. I decide to go to this cocktail lounge not too far away, just so I'm sure I haven't been too premature and quick to fall in love with Rose, and have a gin and tonic. There's no comparison. I drink up and go.

I've decided that I'd seen some old dive hotel somewhere near here when I'd walked from the foundation and that I'd consider that. Except the contrast to the Mark Hopkins might be too enormous and here I am dressed fancy in my Zody's dress shirt. It's not like me. I've stayed in some pretty sorry joints before, like that Grand in El Paso, near it the McCoy, which was, in fact, nice to me, cheap too for the weekly rate, but never could be after a lunch at the Mark Hopkins Hotel. It didn't feel right, and as things go, when I stopped at this light, and as I crossed the green, there was a taxi cab I'd have to loop around in the crossing zone to avoid. So I just get in and hand him the card the woman at the Obrero gave me.

I tell him about the situation. There's nothing like public transportation to spoil a good buzz, he says. He tells me he's been here for a few years now but is from LA, went to Santa Monica High. That's a pretty neighborhood now I say, definitely high rent high chic. It was always like that, he says, always real snooty. In a lot of ways it's like here. I say, what it seems like to me is there's no sleaze. I don't think I realized how dumpy LA is, how many bums and freaks there are, how dirty everything looks. Yeah, you're right about that, he says. Like look here, this is about the sleaziest part of San Francisco and people actually think it looks bad. There's this man asleep on this well-groomed bench, maybe he's a bit raggedy, but nothing like you see on LA Street, or like the dude always leaning against a telephone pole outside the place I live. I say, well I guess LA's got the Olympic bums.

USA! I say. Fuckin Olympics, he says. Can you believe that shit, I can't stand it anymore. It sure makes me feel good to hear that, I say. I was starting to feel like maybe I was a communist. We saw that torch in Hollywood and I heard these people saying how this was one thing that anybody would proud to be American for. Which made me feel real bad, since I really do not understand that nationalistic fervor It's pretty scary, he says. Speaking of scary, this place isn't in the uh gay area is it? Well, he says, every bar on that street is, and maybe every on this other one. I say Jesus. He laughs. I get out and I pay him and look at the card. The best in the European Tradition. It's got the look. Plants, nouveau old. I go in. It's squeally boys all right, tight little hairdos, tight little mustaches, tight little shirts, etc. This does not sound liberal, but there's lots of things I'm not liberal about and one of them is considering this, but what I can't believe is those people would send me here like I wouldn't care. I got nothing against gays, but sorry, I like girls. I go across the street and think this one over and look for a cab. These are the times. I'd miss two weeks of work to watch the Olympics—course I'd miss two weeks of work for any passable excuse—and I'm not enjoying them like I want to. I win the Literary Award and somebody, without one indecent or humorous thought, sends me over to a place like this to spend the night. It makes you think.

I got to think on it what seemed like a long time. Finally I got another taxi. One of the things that came up in my meditation was what Susan had said earlier, that there was a Holiday Inn right up the street, up the street being Chinatown, which is where I figured I belonged for the night at the very least I figured out that anybody'd be confused wearing dress shirts and dress pants and winning Literature Awards and eating papaya and tuna fish for lunch and then thinking he or she could always stay in a fleabag hotel someplace. It also didn't seem appropriate to carry my new souvenir bag up to one of those squeaky beds either. I think it would've been too much for anybody. This sort of reasoning made me feel much better. Famous writers should stay in well-known hotels, and besides in some place like that if I wanna talk about literary awards they'd understand me. I started having fantasies about beautiful businesswomen on business trips to San Francisco staying at the Holiday Inn and going down to the bar for a little cocktail and running into a newly famous author. If they didn't know anything about LA, I could say I lived in Hollywood, cuz I do, otherwise I'd just say Los Angeles and let it go at that. I was thinking what's forty-five or fifty dollars anyway. I just got this money and I'll make it up when I go back to work next week, so I'll have a good time now. If the place has a swimming pool, I might even consider another night. All the great athletes, straight up from the neighborhoods, as soon as they get some coin, go right to these places, their old style thinking goes to the Salvation Army with the winos and the less endowed. I felt much better about the situation and I was telling the taxicab driver about it. Fern bars, he says, that's what they call those places. Gays can be a little bitchy sometimes, he says, but they'll spend the money and then tip too. And I can't complain about that. I told him about this neighbor I had who came over worried about having the electric meter in his apartment read. He didn't know when they'd be coming and he didn't know if he'd be home and could I keep my eye out for him? I'd said, who gives a fuck if they read your meter? Which I meant but was gonna say, okay just leave a key here or somewhere, except he got so offended by my first remark he just left in a huff. He never forgave me for being such an *aw*ful man. The taxi driver and me are having pretty good laughs now. He's also from LA and asks me what I do. Construction, I say, I'm a carpenter, but you won't believe this, and I tell him about the Literary Award and he cracks up and says, as we get to the Holiday Inn, so what's your name? Gilb I say. G-I-L-B. In my family they took a good Germanic name and misspelled it. Even Professor Hart noticed that and said lots of people have trouble with vowels, he laughed, and I say, it just shows how I was born to be a speller.

The Holiday Inn has a big screen TV at the bar area which isn't too far from the check in and out desk. It looks mostly like Chinese, I assume, businessmen and a few from the polo shirt crowd watching. Men's gymnastics and the first image I see is of an American standing there with his muscular arms spread out like a happy Jesus in a gym suit. There's incredible cheering and then a flash to the flags. The biggest flag gets the biggest TV attention. Finally the guy at the counter's asking me if he can help me. That's for sure, I say. How about a room, do you have any? Yes, I think we do. He looks at something. Yes. He looks up at me guiltily. It'll be seventy-eight dollars, for one night. He's a young guy, my age or maybe a few years younger, and I appreciate his guilt but wonder what's giving me away, the bag or my shirt or my scuffed up cowboy boots. I don't think it's the pants. I don't give a shit anymore, and pull out a wad of twenties, I just wanna be done with the bullshit for the night I count out four twenties and hold some others for the inevitable this and that and the other and he seems relieved and takes my name and all and says do I have my driver's license or a credit card. I didn't drive up here, I flew up here. I don't have any credit cards. But I have cash, dollars, twenties. Look. I'm supposed to have an i.d., he worries. I just won this I say, stooping to anything at this point, and I don't wanna write a check! He agrees but thinks to ask the manager. She's this fat woman who I can tell immediately has no respect for The Arts but would willingly wiggle her jowls for the right business suits. No, she says. What? This is American currency! U-S-A!! U-S-A!! U-S-A!! The crowd's waiting for the judges' point decision. No, I'm sorry sir. You *can't* be serious? It's the law, sir. You're sure of that. are you? I'd like to pick her up by her fat cheeks and hold her in the air and belch in her face.

All hotels and motels in the city require the same thing, it's not just our policy. She's not looking me in the eyes anymore. She's looking down at some paperwork. I wanna appeal to her. I say how about manuscripts with my name on it, a notebook? How about this plaque, this has my name! I'm digging in my bag and I take it out but she's shaking her head and leaving. Team USA is doing pretty good in the bar if the happiness of the sportscasters is any indication. I sense the young desk clerk feels bad about what's come to pass, his eyes telling me he thinks she overeats too. He recommends some street where there's all these motels, but I don't pay any attention. I tell him thanks anyway and head for the door, thinking about fleabags again. Also I've written down that there's flights every hour until 9 pm. It's probably about 8. I also think about how those days of walking in and signing Mr. and Mrs. John Sancho being dead. That's real depressing.

God's always playing with my head, getting His omnipotent laugh out of me, and so He plants this airport bus in my face off of which steps this absolutely astonishing, in this light as a spring breeze, white, damn near transparent dress, looking like Miss America the Playmate of the Year Susie XXX Lollipops and damn she's carrying *a book* man! and it looks as though, pleasant as her face is, she doesn't think of herself as a sex object but just as some modern day working woman earning her living on a business trip. Maybe all this snorting sounds sexist and let me apologize here because I don't like to think of it that way. I believe women should work anywhere and at anything they want and get paid the same as any man. I've worked construction, for instance, with women who I think were better than many culos I've had to spend days with who in fact, because they weren't men, were tons easier to get along with and almost invariably did an equal share and had brains besides. On the other hand, it's true, I like women, they are the objects of my terrible sinful sexual thoughts, I'm even miserable if there's no woman in my life and I do love my wife, she's so pretty and so good to me, most of the time, maybe not good enough, haha, I'm joking! but it's like this guy who liked Harley-Davidsons and belonged to the Bandidos told me once—it's not my fault, it's that women put off this scent and we just react to it biologically and respond instinctually, we are animals you know, civilization or not. So it was equally her fault that I reacted like I did, thought and am saying the things I'm saying. And I think Geraldine Ferraro's great and not because of her sex and also because of her sex.

It was, simply put, too much for this young writer. I asked the bus driver if he was on his way there, to the airport. He said, not for a while, I'll be back here in twenty minutes or a half hour, but if you wanna take a ride, hop on. Which I do. First thing he wants to talk about as he's working his papers is that woman who just got off. No bra, he says. Says she's a clothes buyer and gonna spend the weekend here for a weekend vacation after the work's done tomorrow. He sounds like he's panting and I don't need to hear this. I start thinking about getting off the bus and begging the hotel, crawling in supplication, not just because of the woman mind you, but because I'm losing my moment, this woman like the symbol of that, the fleeting moment of a youthful Literary Award winner. Maybe I won't get another shot until the Nobel then I'll be some old fuck with more mind than muscle, the young women of success and fame hanging around for only my warm words not nights, and as soon as I'm on that plane it'll back to anonymity, to photographers taking photos of me only because there's sweat running down my nose and I'm wearing a hardhat and I'm in the construction hole and there's this crane nearby. That happened days before the workforce was reduced, and as that man above me, leaning intense into the wooden rail, his automatic rewind on me, click click click click, I'm thinking, you're taking a picture of a *writer,* you only *think* I'm a construction worker! It was gonna be the Museum of Contemporary

Art after all, and it is something, men working like that, in that heat, in that huge pit, but back in LA those women who shop on Melrose or go to art galleries won't look twice at me. I probably won't even be wearing my Zody's dress shirt or if I am they'll know it's from Zody's and there are lots of men with Mercedes and Jags, and I do have a beautiful woman, I do have two happy kids, and I'm not thinking about leaving them, this little snatch of a dream come true will be in the past, will fade like some bright colorful painting by Gaugin, or maybe by my union carpenter friend Claude Fiddler.

So I don't get out of the airport bus. I sit behind the driver and he's talking about his wife and them going out the other night and how hard it was to find one of those instant teller machines and we're driving. I'm seeing the San Francisco maybe I've never seen before even though I'd say and have said I've been there a couple times, but it's another world, this great clean wash of beauty, the bay, the harbor, tall beautiful buildings, so many more than LA's civic center, all this so sharp and clear it feels like cocaine, it's as rich as that, and I think of Los Angeles, how it isn't like this, even on those days after a rain, in fall, when the sun isn't so white and overexposing, LA isn't at all like this, the LA I know, never like this. I'm remembering myself, my friends my dates time passing my wife my babies, driving the streets, that's what I like to do for my entertainment, roll down the window, nothing ever like this, the soot of smog all over everything like it is, graffiti, poverty, anger, hate, racism, I see that everywhere in LA, or when you try to move away from that then snobs, better-than-thous, in-er than thous. Yeah, it's only the LA I know but that's what I'm talking about, that's what I'm seeing in the view of San Francisco that I have and it's just like in my stomach so fucking sick of all that, I just want all that to stop because it has been starting to feel too much like me, it's taking me too and I don't want it to I don't like the taste of that bitterness like exhaust fumes.

The plane is delayed so I got time and I figure what's really wrong with my stomach is hunger and headache pills. I eat a cheap hot dog and drink milk and buy the Chronicle. I wait. There's a woman there and she's looking at me. She's small with big eyes and she's showing cleavage. An hour ago maybe it'd be love at first sight. She's not far away. I don't think I'm imagining it, but I think a conversation could start up easily. Finally I look over and yes, she smiles. I smile back, but, though days from now maybe I'll be calling myself a stupid fool, I want this to end. I wanna get on the plane in peace, the subdued, mature peace I'd been aiming for all day but never found. And pretty soon, the plane full, talk of far off places all around me, we are up and San Francisco is below. There's a guy next to me in the plane, an empty seat between us. Every time I look over he's looking at me, or I see him looking at the envelope that says San Francisco Foundation on it where I kept the tickets that were mailed to me. I'd laid it there on top of the newspaper. I don't put it anywhere else though I think of turning it the other way since it seems he can't move his eyes from it. He keeps looking at me or it and then I start thinking he must be homosexual, that's gotta be what's up with the guy, then I'm thinking he's just gotta be weird, then I'm thinking he's just fucked up, then I'm thinking he's gonna drive me nuts, and then we're landing. He smiles over at me when I look at him, without moving my head from the aisle seat, while I look out over the plain of lights that is Los Angeles. I hate landings at LAX.

It's late enough, but I call Becky to see if maybe she can pick me up at the hotel, but my babies are asleep and she's asleep too. I tell her it's all right, we'll talk in the morning—did Tony lose his tooth? No. I buy the bus ticket to the Bonaventure and I wait with so many others, people who are from everywhere in the world and country, you can see all these colors and shades, the lines noses eyes, the clothes. LAX is impressively organized,

these buses and vans clearly marked, everybody excited about
which one it is, all of them moving smoothly without confusion, all these in the past distant locations in the LA sprawl dealt
with like the conscious city it has finally become. People, lug-
gage. I wait over a half hour closing in on an hour, I must have
just missed that last one, and all the sudden I see LA in an image:
a big plastic banana. Exotic like that, chic like that, funny and
fun like that, stupid like that. I imagine this huge banana, big as
that Oscar Meyer hot dog vehicle I used to see on television as
a kid, this one created better by those Japanese plastic food imi-
tators, those ones that make entire replicas of Little Tokyo restaurants menu for the customer to see a lifesize version in actual
color and size of whatever it is they might want to slam down
their throat. A perfect reproduction of an actual banana done
huge. LA's tropical just like that—bananas can be eaten fast and
are healthy and fill you up and are cheap and they're imported,
they aren't from here, just like nothing is from here, white people
aren't from here, black people aren't from here, yellow people
aren't from here, brown people aren't from here though Indians
are really brown and maybe they are from here but I doubt it,
they were probably just passing through, cruising the beaches.
Everything in LA is like the plastic banana, the palm trees, the
water, and the city boundaries. Maybe it's the light that makes
me think of it, the yellow light all around, but now I see that big
fat banana everywhere I look and when I get on the bus it gives
me something to feel happy about because I like bananas and I
would feel real sad if bananas got as expensive as cherries or even
grapes. LA, in other words, is extremely dependent on Latin
America if it wants to maintain its plastic banana image. It's as
profound as that.

　　I got this on my mind in the bus but I do notice the blond
man who's short and wearing glasses sort of lurking around near
me as he searches for an empty seat on the bus. Searching empty

seats wouldn't be noticeable usually but in this case it is since
there's maybe only seven or eight people on the whole thing,
and it must seat like seventy-five. The guy's dressed a little dumpy
too, not even K-Mart let alone Zody's, and I'd swear he'd sit
right there next to me if it hadn't been for the San Francisco
Chronicle I had taking up the seat, but finally, after much feint-
ing, he takes one over my shoulder. Then he leans forward, do
I speak Spanish? I don't like to say yes, I say, because then when
I make all my mistakes you'll think I'm a liar. He says, I look
like I must have, well maybe a father or mother. That's right,
exactly, I say. Are you Spanish? I swear I detect Castilian, and
the man is as blond as bleached hair. He moves to the seat next
to me. No, he says, people always think I'm a gringo because
I'm so white, he smiles, but I'm Mexican, from Guadalajara. He
pulls out this airport bus map with stars at the different hotel stops
and wants me to tell him which one to go to and how they all
line up relative to the downtown area and but I stop him there
saying this really isn't a map, you can't even look at this like a
map, this city's so big that well maybe it's better you just go with
me but you're planning on staying at one of these hotels? He
nods. Okay, I say, I'm sure the Bonaventure is as good as any.
It's maybe the prettiest hotel I've seen in Los Angeles. Don't
worry about it, it takes more than a half hour to get there. So we
talk about LA, how big it is, how it goes all the way down to
Tijuana, which is the border, I'm surprised he doesn't know, and
one thing's for sure, a map won't do you that much good here if
you don't have a car. I ask him if he's here for the Olympics and
he says yes and says yes I have some friends—he names some street
which sounds like in Highland Park but it could be a lot of places
but he doesn't wanna call there so late. He's a mechanical engineer back there I tell him I'm a construction worker. I've dropped
the literary stuff now that I'm back in LA, and he just stares out
at the city, onto the freeway. I give him names of things, say no

not yet, you'll see it. He's still kid eyed. This is just one free-way, there's lots of them. I'm looking at Los Angeles with him, lots of people and cars, I say. I'm sort of surprised by it just like him, and I mention the prices of the hotels and he says well maybe there's others? I feel like oh no and say well yes but they're not real close. There's cheaper ones downtown, in Hollywood, there's probably some in East LA. He just wants to go where there's someone who speaks Spanish. I say that's no problem, LA's language is Spanish most places, East LA's just like Mexico, you won't have any trouble at all. It won't be long, I'd say in the next ten years, and the mayor of Los Angeles will be a Chicano and the mission bells will ring, and then he's smiling about this. It is fun and I say look, just stay with me, I'll get you straightened out. If we have to, I have a car at home and or maybe you can stay at my place, my wife won't mind. It may not be the greatest, but it'll be someplace, it's even in Hollywood. I can tell that makes him feel better and it makes me feel better too. He says that would be fine, if we can't find some place else. I say of course, and he says yes there it is, and there it is, the downtown buildings so vertical when you come on them in the night, so wall-like and skyward. He's impressed. I show him where my jobs were, which ones I worked on.

He sticks to me like Ricky does when we're alone, jumps up worrying about getting off. and I say I just have my bag. He only has a briefcase, which is a little ragged looking too, but how's that my business and we walk over to the taxi line where this driver yells, Oigan hombres, quieren uno taxi? We both laugh about this and also because, together, the two of us look have to look as Mexican as two Czechoslovakians. I think maybe it's my Zody's shirt giving us away but I don't tell him. This Arab taxi driver does pretty good with his pidgin Spanish, this funny sound to the words, but he understands my man's slight Castilian lisp quickly and without hesitating and he even tells him where the address of his friends is and shows him on a map and says but of course I know where a good hotel is, one that's not expensive, it isn't too far from where they live either, it'll cost maybe five six dollars to get there. We say good-bye and good luck to one another.

I wave over another cab, make the comment that I've been in more taxis today than probably I've been in my whole life. He asks me where I was and I tell him and he compares taxi driving in San Francisco to taxi driving here, how much better it is up there, people so much more used to using them. No, he says, he's only visited there once years back, but I know because I hear stories from other taxi drivers and I can tell when I get fares from people from up there. We're on the Hollywood Freeway going north going to my home now and I say yeah those drivers were telling me that their best fares are from gays and he says oh yeah they like to get in the back seat, I've seen lots of crazy stuff in the backseat. I've seen men and women doing it lots of times, some woman yanking her skirt up and jumping right on top, or blowing him right there, right where you're sitting. I look at the vinyl upholstery under me. Lots of crazy stuff, but, he says, gays are the wildest, they just can go crazy, and there's lots of taxi drivers that like it because these gays like to drive around the city or on the freeways for an hour or two, big fares. Some drivers let gays do anything, some drivers will do anything for money. They'll unzip for them right while they're driving or go anywhere they want with the meter running. It's really something, you can't believe it. So aren't you married? he asks me. Yeah, the wife's at home. She wouldn't come out to pick you up, huh? She's asleep and I didn't wanna bother her. I say, so at least you're getting better business right now, with the Olympics? No, no, he says, it hasn't changed any, it didn't turn out like everyone thought it would, it's just the same. I tell him how to get to my place once we get off the freeway, and as we near he says, so you're gonna go straighten it out with the wife now, aren't ya? Gonna get some kind of agreement between you, gonna pick a bone with her, ain't that so? I pay him, say thanks. He says, well don't do anything I wouldn't do.

I don't know what Hollywood's supposed to look like. but I guess it looks like this—a small Spanish courtyard with a blue-green porcelain fountain in the middle of it, a naked, pubescent girl-like boy holding something that's been kinda broken off in time right at or near his groin. The water's supposed to have run over the top dish but now it would land in the dirt where our Armenian neighbor has his much tended to eggplant bushes. The half moon's above this, which makes you notice how pretty the place is even with the glass dropping out of the rotting window frames. At one time the building was a beauty and it still looks good now. When the gays move in, after all the mejicanos have lived here a while as the rent prices drop down, they'll make this place a high class building.

Everybody in my apartment home is asleep. Becky's sleeping with Rick in his bed because he cries so much when he's alone and I don't think he should sleep with us and she's just like that, likes to not let him cry. I dump out the stuff from my souvenir Olympics bag onto the bed and out drops my diploma plaque saying something about literature. I put it on this typewriter. I warm some flour tortillas on a pan and melt cheese onto it and roll them, two of them. I gulp the milk that's never cold enough in this refrigerator we bought used. A few hours later I'll be waking up from my sleep.

IV

WORKING LIFE
AND LA FAMILY

Spanish Guy

Two sons, one wife, no job, I've driven my squeaking '62 Chevy II wagon across three deserts from my happy—and rent due every month—home in El Paso, where there's no work, to Long Beach, where, I'm told, there's so much. So what if I see only two tower cranes in a moon's skyline. In the morning, it doesn't matter to me that the business agent at the union hall could care less that I, a journeyman carpenter, have arrived from Texas. I sign the long out-of-work list anyway and after that pull over to one of the job-site holes and ask. The superintendent there gives me the old "check back in two weeks," which might mean check back in two weeks or be a kind no, but when you're not working, you have to keep positive, and you tell the man, thank you very much, and you shake his big, crusty hand firmly. You feel like in two weeks, you will be working there. You feel that if you think like this, he will, too.

So I drive around L.A. and Orange counties, two eyes out for cranes. I spend very little to stay in an old hotel that I won't describe except to say "stinky." I sleep on couches, imposing on any friend (a few nights) or acquaintance (one night). Another two weeks pass. In that time, the super in Long Beach has told me twice more to check back in a couple of weeks. Positive, I ignore subliminal snickers of doubt. From a tenementlike motel on the banks of a freeway, I am confidently circling the want ads, comparing prices for weekly rooms.

One fine morning, positive happens. Yes, a job! Okay, only a promise of a week, possibly two, and there's something not right, because the job-hungry locals won't take it. So what if it means they know something I don't. It's not my usual highrise work. It's on a university campus, even, perimeter HARD HAT ONLY fence or not, look, women carrying books are walking not that far away. No cranes picking or landing, no cement trucks groaning. My crew begins with a Wally and a Dave and a Jorge and a Roger and an apprentice, Lumpy. The afternoon of the day I come on, Wally and Jorge are handed checks good-bye. Then Dave, in charge day two, tells us that Roger quit. That's because Brad, our foreman who's away, thank you Lord Jesus, got too much authority too young, and that's what's wrong with this job. What an incredible dickhead, he explains.

Brad is back on day three. I hear him screaming around the job site. I map escapes when I see his hard hat moving toward us, wanting to avoid the inevitable, but which comes before break time morning of day four.

"Now *why* would you guys think you'd have to do it *that* way?" He has taken off his hard hat, running his fingertips over his old-fashioned flat-top.

I want to say, Because you so so *esmart* and we so so *estupid*. But I don't. It's just me and Dave. Brad starts shaking his head. He decides to make it me.

"I *told* you," he claims with a disgusted sneer.

"I don't want you talking disrespectfully to me," I say.

"I'm not even raising my voice," he says, a little surprised that I can speak.

"Okay, then explain to me what it is you want."

He explains, though not really, and it's in that Like I Told You Dumb Fucks voice. My partner Dave has backed away, pretending to do something else, his ears all satellite dish.

I don't care now, so when Lumpy walks up and asks what's wrong, I say, "Who knows? We're supposed to *divine* these things."

"You mumbling?" Brad asks.

"No. I just said I'll take my time now." I stuff my tools and bags into my box.

I insist on being positive: I'm still on the out-of-work list in Long Beach. That check-back-in-two-weeks job is, really is, getting close to needing men. And a day later I find an ad: "Furn room. Quiet priv. home, by P.C.H. for working male. Prefer nondrinker. $125 dep. $95 wkly."

A Spanish guy, she calls me. Her name is Judy. She is Danish, too talkative, and uses hip language like "guilt trip." Her ex-husband was a drunken cop, in A.A. now, a bastard still, and her son is a junkie. She's supposed to take four Valiums a day, but she takes only one because she "knows her body." She has bursitis in the shoulder. She pulls her blouse down over the bra strap, showing me where. It's a four-bedroom house, and I pay a week plus the deposit.

There are two other boarders, both kids from Oklahoma—Steve and one who I call Tim but whose name, he tells me several times, is Mark. They are selling the L.A. *Times* and excited that it's, like, five dollars an hour with a ten-cent commission on each sale. They are so smiling happy, having a so wild time. They sit at the kitchen table and listen to Judy tell Big Jim stories. Big Jim is her husband. Big Jim, hyperactive, at the motels at the end of an all-night shift, having enough for two floozies. Big Jim cracking three heads in a fight. Big Jim, so mad, picking up that refrigerator and heaving it.

Judy is a neat maniac. Even if you're a grease monkey, she says, there's no reason you can't keep your fingernails clean. I am afraid to acknowledge mine when she makes this pronouncement. She doesn't like it when the bed isn't made in the morning. She likes the pillows fluffed out just so, like this, and the bedcover under, then over, like this. And the decorative pillow goes centered. One time I didn't wipe down the tile in the shower stall. Another time I forgot to dry the bathroom sink after I brushed my teeth. It's not so hard, she tells me. She had to unreverse the sliding closet doors in my room.

She goes out on Bingo nights, which is every other. Those nights I don't go to a bar to watch sports or whatever they've got on. I sit, cautiously, on a flowery couch in her living room and smell the cleaning fluids and sprays everywhere, drinking unstaining tap water from a mug with Danish names on it. There are bad oil paintings of sailboats and a needlepoint, framed, of a sailor from somewhere else and another time. Clocks, two to a wall, tick and chime, reminding endlessly. I don't like to be unpositive, but I hate clocks. I have not one of these clocks at home. I miss home. I want to go home.

At the beginning of the second week, I tell her I am leaving at the end of it. Take the week out of the deposit money, I tell her. She gets really mad. She talks about the law. She talks about contracts. She shows me what I signed: "Diposit refundable as last weeks Rent after 90th ninety days." I don't back down, but I never discuss the thirty-dollar difference. I go to the union hall in the morning. No jobs. I don't want to look for jobs. I go to a coffee shop and I read a newspaper for too long, considering non-union and nonconstruction work, but I don't want to do it. Or I read a book, though I don't even want to do that. I look around, thinking instead to talk to someone different, to see something new, but no, I don't feel like it. I don't want to be doing any of this ever again.

Victoria

I'll even blame the heat that summer for my inability to remember which year it was—1986, give or take. It was hot like never before, my skin so porous it was hard to distinguish the side of it I was on. Like I could sweat and become a puddle. A dirty puddle, because I'd absorbed that construction site. And because this was Los Angeles, and it was smoggy, too. But you know what, it wasn't the smog or the hole dirt or the cement dust, it was heat that seemed to drain all the color into an overexposed gauze. It was so hot. I'm talking about three digits, so don't think I'm exaggerating. It was so hot. It was so hot everybody had to say it again and again. Not hot as in longing but as in insomnia. So hot I don't remember if the heat lasted three weeks, a month, two, three. It was day-and-night hot, as forever and endless as boredom.

I remember the fan. That's what I had going in the apartment when I got back from the job. I can still hear the shuddering fizz as it rotated, the clacks as it teetered at far left and far right until it shifted. I'd rigged together electrician's tape and number nine tie-wire to keep the plastic base joined to the plastic stem, worried it would come apart, too cheap to buy a new one. I carried the delicacy with me wherever I sat because I wanted it close. Right after work, that was on the couch, near the tube. I'd have already downed one beer, and I'd have already put three cans of an already refrigerated six-pack in the freezer, and I'd be almost done with the third when I turned on my show to drink two more almost frozen: *Dallas* was on every weekday evening. It was going around probably a second time, so I'd seen some of the episodes, but maybe you know how it goes, and who knows why you hook on to a particular TV program. For me it had always been cop shows, so I can't explain my deal with *Dallas*. I didn't like the city of Dallas, did not want to live there and never had. There was nobody I identified with and nothing these Ewings owned that I dreamed of having. Besides Pam. That is, besides Victoria Principal. You see, I didn't watch television much, and when I did, it was reruns, not prime time. I didn't flip through *Star* or *People* and I knew nothing about Hollywood, even if my apartment was a few blocks from it. Obviously a woman as stunning as Victoria Principal had a past that brought her to the show, obviously everybody knew how beautiful she was. But since I'd never seen or heard of her outside either *Dallas* or my own television set, my brain didn't register obvious. And of course it didn't matter. I alone saw and discovered her, how sweet and gorgeous she was. I wouldn't even joke to my wife about my infatuation with her. Pale as she was, I wanted her to have Mexican blood—you know, like Rita Hayworth, Raquel Welch, even, I thought I heard, Vanna White. And if she didn't, well, I didn't care that much.

The job was called a class-A high-rise, and it was a steel building going several stories up and a few down. We were pouring decks and nonstructural beams and wrapping columns. It was in Beverly Hills, and it was on Rodeo Drive. Which sounds good but isn't. It meant that, because of Beverly Hills's noise ordinances, starting time was an hour later than a job anywhere else. Because of L.A.'s morning traffic, it meant getting there at the same time as any job and leaving an hour later than usual, right in the worst evening traffic. I needed the money bad. My first days—or was it weeks?—were at the bottom level, in dirt, sharing space with a bobcat—a miniature backhoe, like a go-cart compared to the real thing—whose purpose, as I recall, was to fuse abused earth and unfiltered exhaust fumes into, first, a paste that lathered my sweaty arms and face into black, and, second, a dyeing agent for snot and phlegm whose blow-and-hack audiovisual description you don't want to read.

It was down there where I first met the guy I remember only as Pretty Boy. He was sent to assist me a couple of times. I'm fairly sure we were doing the same work, together, those hours, but you wouldn't know it by looking at him. I think he maybe perspired some, but he did it in such a way that it could have been a spray-on. You know how they use those little misting bottles on wealthy beaches to keep cool, or on a movie set, where they dapple a "V" on the gray T-shirt between the pecs and shoulder blades? Pretty Boy had puffy blond hair like an Aryan, like a surfer, like a New York model. If he didn't have to wear a hard hat, I'm sure a head twitch would send a cute curlicue off his forehead. He loved Reagan. He had an apartment in Santa Monica. He was single. That is to say, he did not live with a wife, he did not have two children. He smiled much more than was acceptable and, unlike me and everybody else panting in the L.A. basin, said he didn't mind the heat. He'd admit it was hot, it was hotter than anything he'd lived through, but . . . But *what*? He just shrugged his shoulders, a smile more a wink—he treated himself to colder air-conditioning when he got home, turned it *way* down. That is to say, he had air-conditioning. Do I remember that remark, its surrounding image lingering dreamy. He was such a short, thin pretty boy. What good would it do for me to reply? What good to beat him with my steel Estwing hammer?

My hammer brings up Modesto Rodriguez, he of somewhere a hundred kilometers or so from Acapulco, Mexico, where he was a *mero mero,* a big cheese, in a village where he was not, as in Los Angeles, mostly unemployed and struggling. And a lot of that struggle was with the English language. He had been working with a young laborer on the job, Matthew, who was related to someone and so was allowed to do all kinds of jobs laborers aren't supposed to, like this union carpenter's work with Modesto Rodriguez. I'd been brought up from the darkness below to set beams on the first level because, though Matthew spoke Spanish, Modesto's wasn't the same—the suggestion being that his was "Mexican," not "Castilian"—and therefore they were having trouble communicating. The other laborers on this job were a Polish guy from Poland and a black guy from Compton. Modesto was very happy to be with me, because the other two spoke the same depth of this "Castilian" Spanish as Matthew. That is to say, their fluency was at the level of saying *no problemo* a lot. What nobody ever understood, thinking Spanish alone was a lot to have in common, was how little Modesto and I had to talk about—unlike, for instance, me and that laborer from Compton. Modesto had great enthusiasm, though, and he wanted to know everything. If someone did come up to say something, he wanted it translated. He wanted everything anyone said translated, everything I said back translated. Once I started not doing that, it was often the topic of discussion while we were working. I had to tell him that it was too hot for me to talk even in English most of the day.

I do remember clearly the beginning of the end of this job for me. It was before lunch, and the super was standing there. Modesto barked words of greeting in an overly voweled English, wagging energetically. The super was shaped like a heavily mustached and bearded and eyebrowed cantaloupe. You wouldn't be able to tell by staring if he smiled or not. Take that back. He didn't smile. He never smiled around me anyway. It could've been the heat. It was hot and wouldn't stop being hot. But then sometimes, for reasons unknown, or instinctual, or born of karmic resentments from previous lives, people don't like you. It could be the nose. Could be a hard hat worn backward, the bandana under it. Could be the laugh. Could be the teeth, though not the silver ones in Modesto's mouth—I thought they were too glary in the sun, wondered if they got too hot when he grinned— because the super wasn't bothered, looking right at them when he wanted to know what we were doing. And he continued to as I translated and then stepped forward, skipping the Spanish. He did not want to look at me while I explained why we were going about our project the way we were, which was not how it was being done before I got there. It's true, I make decisions, and I made one about installing these beam sides. I was a journeyman, and sometimes I knew what I was doing, and this saved time and made the work easier on us. The super heard me explain. He knew it wasn't wrong, because we were putting them in and stripping them out much faster. He didn't like it anyway, because, probably, of my nose type.

It was just hot, I knew it. It was so hot. Nobody was in a good mood. Well, Modesto was okay. At lunch, we went up on the roof, where some Pacific Ocean breezes might pass by. Modesto would have another T-shirt and change into it and let the sweat-soaked one dry, then eat. A great idea, which I copied. Pretty Boy was up there, too. Miserable as it was, he was always in a good mood. Why shouldn't he, all those breezes going to him alone? Even his depressing stories didn't make him feel bad: he went to a nightclub on the Sunset Strip called Coconut Teasers. I'd been there once. It was one of those bright, pink-decorated places male and female people who had their hair styled went, who wore clothes with names and worked out in gyms with names on machines with names and drank colored drinks with names. Men as beautiful as Pretty Boy, buttons done and undone just so. Women with lots of ample cleavage and revealing thigh. A place, in other words, I went to once for a short visit. Pretty Boy liked to go there because he liked to sleep with lots of pretty girls and that was the place for him. He said he took pictures. What kind of pictures? You know. No, what kind? Of the women. Everyone you slept with? Yeah. He brought a photo another day to show me. A Polaroid. She was lying on a bed, and she didn't have anything on. She let you? They all do. Whadaya mean, they *all* do? I take pictures of them all. I have a collection. And they all have their clothes off? Sometimes not their bottoms. You just ask them? He nodded. And they do this? He nodded, smiling. And you have a collection? In a binder. He smiled.

Sometimes I didn't want to be there and watch the cool breezes billowing into him. And I was with Modesto all day. Sometimes I'm grouchy. I wanted to eat lunch alone sometimes. So I found a bench at the edge of the site, on a driveway at the back entrance of the I. Magnin department store—maybe we were building an addition to it. I liked sitting there, watching the rich ladies step out of their Jaguars and Mercedeses and BMWs, all dressed like it was an opera night, then high-heel clicking those twenty-five feet into the autumn climate of the luxury store. The red-coated attendants sprinted up and down the parking structure, whistling like birds, those radial tires squealing like peacocks. I sat there one lunch break with my feet up on the bumper of a Bentley. I was sitting there this other lunch break when Victoria Principal came and sat next to me.

Victoria Principal of *Dallas*. She sat down a yard from me. Maybe less, when I think of it. Yes, less. Expert with a carpenter's tape, I assure you, reconsidering now, it was less. Her precious hips were between sixteen and twenty inches from mine once she sat down. I saw her coming before she sat. She seemed like a mirage at first, bad eyesight. And I didn't want to stare while she sat there. I was eating. I can't remember what I was eating. Tacos? Yogurt? I think of both when I strain to remember. I said hi. She turned and she said hi back. Victoria. She was very pleasant about saying hi, not self-conscious or worried in that unnatural heat about sitting next to me, a sweaty, dirty construction worker. Of course I wanted to talk. We both watched the boys in the red coats sprinting, whistling. Did I want to offer her my food? I don't remember that. I didn't want to tell her I was a fan. I didn't want to tell her I watched the reruns. I almost did say something. All I could think of: I'm a carpenter here. That would've been the opening. Once we got to talking, I would tell her more about me, that I wasn't *just* a carpenter, but a writer. Really. I never told anybody that, but I would want her to know, to know that my working poverty wasn't without value—artistic, or spiritual, some higher implication like that. I would have to talk both casually and with sophistication. Instead I sat there. I did peek over at her a few times. I didn't want her to think I was a weirdo, but I couldn't resist. She was beautiful. And then her Jaguar Mercedes BMW appeared and she was getting up and I said bye. She turned to me and she said bye back. She was nice. Nice like a kiss is nice. Like a kiss that, even when you can only imagine it, makes you remember, right then, that you are happy to be alive.

Modesto didn't know who Victoria Principal was. Pretty Boy said he said hi to Kareem Abdul-Jabbar when he walked by a couple of weeks before and that Kareem waved to him. What did Pretty Boy know about love? My brain was swollen with the vision of her, of her and me sitting there, saying hi, saying bye. I couldn't get it out of my mind.

Modesto and I had to haul some long sticks of 2 × 4 up several levels of stairs. This was a laborer's job, but Matthew didn't have to do this sort of thing. Somewhere along the way, my hammer fell out of its sling, and when we were done, I went up and down trying to find it. That's when the super decided to look me right in the eyes. What are you doing? he asked. I'm looking for my hammer, I told him. Why? Because I lost it some-

where. Where did you lose it? I couldn't believe he was actually
staring at me either. And I didn't know what else to say except,
if I knew where I lost it, it wouldn't be lost.

And that was the end, though I don't remember what happened after this incident. Nothing specifically dramatic, I don't
mean to imply that. I simply cannot remember whether I got
my check, whether I quit, whether it was a day later or a week
or two. I've had so many jobs, and I've been laid off and fired
and quit so many that no unimportant details stick. Just that it
was the hottest, most miserable summer ever, and I hated this
job. That on a bench near Rodeo Drive, at lunch, I sat so close
to Victoria Principal we could have been holding hands, we could
have been sharing tacos, or yogurt, talking, getting to know each
other.

I Want to See
a Fortune-teller

It was several months ago when my friend M—an intelligent, highly skilled Chicana professional—first suggested I speak to her psychic. I had just arrived in Austin, and I must have looked as psychologically damaged as I was feeling. My friend M has been voice-trained to persuade in smooth, comforting tones, and while my sentiment lingered over a loving altar she'd assembled in memory of her deceased *madrecita,* I listened. This psychic could reveal amazing things, my friend M confided, and I'd be in for a special experience—so special it had to be arranged, I had to be recommended.

Visiting a psychic isn't normal advice, I don't think. I didn't say no, but I thought it was better to settle down, to both rest more and work harder, if you know what I mean. I wanted to tough it out solito, you know? Hook in to a meditative self-reliance and discipline, apply the rugged, cattle-driving, gusher-spouting spirit that made Texas. I was also afraid I was going broke, and I didn't think I should waste money.

I thought my approach was succeeding, I really did, until one day a month ago, yet another Chicana, from Laredo but who lives in Boston, called me. She's a friend of a friend, and I hardly know her. Call her Y. Still, Y closed the gap between her mouth and the telephone, excusing herself for getting so personal, and told me how I should visit this psychic she knew in Austin. Though Y always hoarded the phone number for her own self-ish reasons, she thought I was someone who needed it.

For a week, I pondered my condition, so obvious to every-one else. Looked deep into my messed-up self: okay, I would go, I would spend the money.

I bumped into my friend M. I was feeling a little . . . how do I say? Like I was going to talk to a psychic because I needed to. Which feels sneaky, something like that. Maybe that's only me. Anyway, I was curious: was her psychic the same one whose phone number I now had? Not only was it the same, my friend M wanted us to have an hour appointment together. We could take notes on each other's reading. I wasn't so sure. How would my future come out in half an hour? And maybe I wanted to go alone. Then again, there was the money. Half the expense now. Okay, I told my friend M, yes.

After two weeks, she hadn't gotten back to me. I was feeling shaky. That sneaky psychic haze was everywhere. Why *wasn't* M calling me? Maybe she sensed my uncertainty, my want for privacy, my initial desire to exclude her. I felt I intuited some unspoken change in her intentions.

So I dialed the psychic's phone number myself. I'm sorry I can't give her name. I'll just call her Señora Equis.

She answered. She had an accent, though it was like every-body's in my neighborhood.

"Y gave me your number," I said. "She told me how good you were, and I wondered if you could fit me in."

"Y," she said, "Y." Though you can't tell from this, she repeated a different name than I gave her. "I haven't heard from Y. Where is she now?"

I told her. In fact, the feeling was that I *had* to tell her every-thing I knew. How my friend was the Y from Laredo, how she'd been here, how she was going back to Boston, where she lived now. Actually Cambridge.

"And what is your name?" she asked.

"Dagoberto," I told her.

"Dagoberto," she said, thinking to herself way out in that unknown at the other end of the telephone line. "I have been so busy, Dagoberto, I have so many appointments this week."

"Whenever you can fit me in." I tried not to sound needy, but I wanted her reading bad.

She took my number. She assured me she'd call back.

But she didn't. I called again. I left a message on her answering machine.

I bumped into my friend M. She was embarrassed. I was right. She'd taken her sister with her. Her sister *really* wanted to go. And it was, M exuded, amazing. I explained that I'd contacted la señora Equis on my own. You *spoke* to her? M asked me. Well, yeah. She shook her head, impressed, I think, I wasn't sure. But she never got back to me, I told her. I wish I'd given her your name, I told M, because maybe she didn't remember who Y from Laredo was.

My friend M called her on my behalf. I heard her talk into the message machine. She gave la señora Equis my name and number.

Señora Equis didn't call me back. What did she pick up on that made her not want to speak to me? Did she read my doubts? Did she feel I wasn't being serious enough? Was it because I'm a man? Was it because she saw how I'd been too cheap about her labor and skill? What was it she knew about my future that she wasn't willing to tell me?

I had to leave Austin. I drove ten hours, wondering and worrying about all that I didn't know. When I got back to El Paso, a card was in my post office box. It said, *Listen to me! You are about to enter into a period of your life with incredible potential for vast achievements. Major wealth, good fortune and the end of financial worries are about to come to you.* It wasn't from la señora Equis, and it wasn't addressed to me. It had been misdelivered.

Bullfight, Vegetables, Death

The last time I went to a bullfight, I took my oldest son, Tony, around back to show him an event few see. Three donkeys, yoked and harnessed, had dragged a dead bull from the dirt basin of the arena, up a tunnel, and to the door of a nearby building that resembled a garage. A chain was cinched under the front legs of the bull, and a motorized hoist lifted him. His eyes were empty, though his body—especially his teeth and legs—still seemed alive, even dangerous. Just fifteen minutes earlier, in the ring, his tongue looked as white as his horns, but it was now scarlet with blood, drooping from the side of his mouth. He was being pulled upright and heaved onto the bed of a pickup truck which had backed up to the door.

I had a camera with me that I assumed, wrongly, was loaded with film. I'd already snapped off some powerful shots, in my amateur opinion, when a young boy, maybe only a year older than my son, standing on the pickup bed, directed a sharp knife between the bull's legs. When he was done, he held the big black sack in his other hand and looked at me. "Aquí señor, here, mister!" He raised the bull's cojones high and smiled as if they were a shiny trophy. I clicked.

That unprinted photo was of my son Tony becoming a vegetarian. And he hated vegetables, too. I used to make jokes about his conversion: he was donut-tarian, a churro-tarian. But he hasn't eaten a burger since that day.

Bullfights have never been a conscious interest of mine, either as art or sport. They're just something to do, something different, very different, something in the neighborhood I go to at the last minute. Juárez's Plaza Monumental is only a ten-minute drive from my home. I go as spectator, not participant. I'm not critical or supportive, only curious.

I noticed the ad for this weekend's bullfight the day before. Obviously I didn't even have to ask Tony, but this time my younger boy, Ricardo, had mysteriously decided he wouldn't go, either. He just turned thirteen, the same age Tony was that last time. "Why not?" I asked. "Tired," he said. "Not in the mood," he said. The fact is, he loves meat too much, and he was afraid what happened to his brother might happen to him. "I really think you should go," I told him. "It'd save a lot on food money if you became a vegetarian, too." He wasn't sure I was joking.

So when I went without my sons, while a group of men in aqua shirts rushed the arena to rake away the broad, almost rutted trail that the killed bull leaves in the dirt as he's dragged away, I followed him, again, to the back. It was the same scene: same thick chain, same hoist, and a pickup truck. The bull had those same eyes that, motionless as they were, I swore could still see. As always, I felt his power hovering there even if nothing moved, felt he was looking back, listening.

This time two boys—I imagined them as brothers, and I think they were—watched near me. First the older boy would touch the coarse, matted black hair of the bull's enormous torso, then the young one would. Older brother, then younger, touched the head, an ear, a horn, a tooth. They both knew that this was an animal, they both knew he was dead. They were gentle and respectful but not afraid. The pickup began to move out. The younger boy had been standing eye-level to the bull's face as it slumped on the bed of the truck. As the bull stared straight at him, he waved good-bye as only a little kid can.

Poverty Is Always Starting Over

My youngest son, Ricardo, began this baseball season really excited because last year his team, the Blazers, won the city world series. He had the dream-come-true year during the play-offs, when he scored the winning run that took them to the championship. His slide into home, coming like it did in the bottom of the last inning, made the front page of the sports section. In color, no less. As if that weren't enough, the very next game, the first of a best-of-five series, was against the Cobras, a team so dominating they hadn't lost a single game. Ricardo came up with the bases loaded, at the top of the ninth, and drove a pitch so hard that when it hit the chicken wire above the left-field fence, the ball rode up. Pitching at the bottom of that inning, he struck out two, and the Cobras scored nothing. After this win, the series was history. The Blazers were the champions.

But you and I both know it wasn't my son. It wasn't the other good players on the team, either. It was the coach, Junior. The kids loved him, and he knew what he was doing. Junior had been a star athlete in high school. He was around thirty years old, divorced with two daughters, one twelve. If anything, Junior put in too much time with the team. He didn't have a job, unless you counted the occasional weekend gigs when he dressed

223

up as a mariachi. He also took a couple of classes at the community college. But mostly he was unemployed. What he wished for was a job with the parks, because he loved sports so much—he coached basketball as well as he did baseball. But Junior couldn't coach this year because he was in hiding. He owed a lot of money. The kids on every team sell candy, and Junior didn't turn in the money for three different teams. Like $1600, give or take. He'd been having personal problems. I knew his truck had been stolen.

So this season begins without Junior. And without baseballs, bats, helmets, catcher's equipment, practice bases, uniforms. And the champion Blazers are starting over again. The new coach doesn't have a telephone. The new coach works for maybe a dollar more than minimum wage where the nuts you eat on airplanes are packaged. He works strange hours, so there haven't been many practices. When there are, they aren't much. Mostly he yells at the kids, frustrated, for making mistakes. They don't like him. He has eight all-star-level players—Carlos and Freddy, Raúl, Roger, Adrian, David and Bobby, and my son Ricardo—but they're looking at a .500 record. The one other team in the league with equal talent, the one that has the newest, coolest uniforms and the top-of-the-line equipment, is the team that has something else, too: the same coach, the same coaches they've had for several years. They get into the play-offs almost every season.

In the neighborhood where the Blazers practice, walls are for graffiti fights. Most of the players live in modest, unattractive homes on wider streets that people drive past on their way to work. Most of their parents graduated from high school. One mother is going to a business college to become a medical secretary. Another just got a job as a clerk at the prison, where her husband works. Several are single parents. They are the only ones who attend the games. All speak Spanish, and several only Spanish. Their other children, if they are just out of high school, are married or are about to be. Nobody talks about college to the younger ones.

Poverty is often seen for its brutality, for what it absolutely denies. But common poverty isn't about not getting started, it's as much about *only* getting started, about *always* being at the beginning. Poverty is about starting over again and then yet again. It's about talent fully shaped, but which, unencouraged, discouraged, lasts the briefest moment.

The Blazers aren't talking much about baseball anymore. The parents say how next year, if their sons want to play, they'll find some other team. I want to let you in on a secret that the commissioner of our league told me not to tell anyone else: our new coach hasn't turned in his candy money, either. Over $500. The story goes, the coach's wife had it in her purse at a grocery store, and then it was gone. Lost, or stolen, or something like that, the commissioner told me, and he shook his head.

Rite of Passage

My son Ricardo is thirteen years old. That's the age when so many things matter. He wants to be looking good: the hair cut not too little and not too much, the pomade to furrow and shine and hold back and down *right*. He wants the shoes to have a squeak to them, the shirts ironed, tails out, the pants new and baggy. He just got braces. He wanted to get them as much as his mom and I did. He's looking up the road, and he's seeing pretty girls walking.

It's the age when music first begins to matter, when that sound *means,* when it separates who knows from who doesn't. Lots out here in El Paso still listen to the oldies—Ben E. King, the Four Tops, Mary Wells. But mostly that's boyfriend-girlfriend music, for those nighttime dedications: *for La Cindy, thinking so much of you esta noche, from Edgar.* Like kids everywhere, my son is into watching MTV and learns what music he likes there. It's the hit sound heard in every city, even by Chicanitos like my boy—Alanis Morisette, Ace of Bass, Collective Soul, Natalie Merchant. He works hard following this music, too, making mix tapes of his favorite singles from the radio and his and his friends' handful of CDs and cassettes.

I had told Ricardo that the time would come when he and I would go off somewhere together alone, no mom or big brother, and more recently, I promised him that the next time I got to stay in New York City, I'd fly him out for a few days. Last month I kept my word. We did all the things you're supposed to: ride taxis and subways, foot-cruise Soho and the Lower East Side. Eat Jewish deli at Katz's. Boat to the Statue of Liberty and climb to the top of the crown. Elevator up the Empire State Building. Spiral the Guggenheim for abstract modern art, walk and walk the Metropolitan for Egyptian-mummy tombs and armor from the Middle Ages and a quick stare at Cézanne and van Gogh.

I wanted us to hear music together. I love nightclubs, no less now than I did as a boy. I was fourteen when I heard the Yardbirds on Sunset Boulevard, and a world opened. So I imagined a rite of passage, my son and I sharing live music, *real* music—the first time for him. I told him we'd try, though he shouldn't count on it because I wasn't sure about clubs and liquor laws and minors.

One night, down some nearby stairs, I heard a stylishly flat woman's voice, dissonant but sweet with youth, and a punky-folk electric guitar. We'd just eaten, gotten too much food, were carrying a doggie bag, but why not? The door was open. They were warming up, setting up the stage, testing sound. She had shoulder-length platinum hair, flowery clothes, while the guitar player dressed studded punk and swung his pale head with Neil Young hair. We went in. It was a small nightclub, the classic: black walls and ceiling, purple curtain, blue lights on one side, red on the other. It was very small, an intimate club. Soon another band warmed up. Another woman lead singer, her cropped hair so silvery it was white in the stagelight, and black black black clothes. Tables in the club weren't even set up yet, but there was a big patent-leather couch right in front of the bar, the best seat in the house, and Ricardo and I took it.

We settled in and relaxed. Finally, the club manager came around to ask the few people inside, Are you in a band, are you with a band? Around us, but not a word to us. Weren't we visible? The most obvious of all? A thirteen-year-old boy and his big old dad sitting on the only couch. He shut the door, pocked with band and instrument and studio stickers, snapped no at people who pounded to come in too early. He set up tables inches from us, slid chairs so close I had to move my legs. And even then, he didn't make eye contact with me or my son. The soundman, New York to the bones, in purple spandex, gold jewelry, long and frizzy brown hair, and tinted shades from ear to ear, looped back and forth around us. The bartender wandered in, started setting up behind us. Ricardo and I whispered. He sat close to me. Years earlier, I'd shown him and his brother how to sneak into Dodger Stadium. I could explain the how and why of that, but not this. I said, Not until they ask us to leave.

The nightclub doors opened to cover charges. We sat comfortable. He drank Sprite, I had a gin and tonic. The shortest person there, he went next to the stage when he wanted, came back. We stayed for hours, and when he was ready to leave, he grabbed the doggie bag, and we excused our way through the hippest crowd.

Books Suck

Imagine this: one day you're pronounced a writer. I'm not talking about a book being published, even after all those years and years of waiting for that, but when they—you know, *they*—say you've won an award for it and they fly you above the Chihuahua Desert, across all of Texas and over the Mississippi River, and then above all these roads and highways you've never driven on, never seen a single billboard for from the airplane window, to a city as expensive-sounding as Boston, Massachussetts. And *they're* paying. You've decided to take your son, who's fifteen. Fifteen, one of those jerk years. The years when you can look at him, once a soft, sweet baby, as tender as your first true love, and be faced with the age-old fatherly question: does he want me to kick his ass? Is it *right* to kick his ass? Despite internal and external protestations to the contrary, would it be *good* to kick his ass?

But you're taking him because you've always promised yourself that this day would come. You imagined it differently. You imagined that you and he, just the two of you, would hike up Glacier National Monument, that sacred Indian place of emerald lakes beneath pearl mountains of ice, risking the hazards of sudden snowdrifts and grizzly bears. You got real, though. You are a city guy. You have to wait for some nature friend to take the two of you sometime, or something like that.

So, instead, Boston. As a writer. That's official language, upheld by a panel of wise judges. You take your son because that right moment has come. Father and son, dad and boy, pops y m'ijo. The two of you together. And he's gonna see *this* you, the writer you. That you whom you were those years he pointed to his empty mouth and bare feet and wondered why you weren't *really working* right then. It's like a rite-of-passage thing for him to go with you to Boston.

Here's the secret part, the worm at the bottom of the bottle: your son says—he says often, very often, so often it doesn't sound as funny as it does when you say it just once or twice or so—he says, Books suck. Try meditating on that for about a day, and you'll get the impact. I mean this. For one full day, every time you see or hear about a book, you utter it. Whenever you think of a book, think, Books suck.

Imagine how it is if you write books. And that voice is your son's. Your first son's, the cute baby all grown up. And you don't think he's kidding.

And so when you get to Boston, you decide to sneak over to Annie, the Pulitzer Prize *and* National Book Award winner, who you admire so much, and warn her beforehand. You don't know her well yet, so you're a little worried about impressions. Annie, you whisper, I want to tell you so that it doesn't come as too much of a shock—my boy, my handsome son over there, if he happens to say books suck, well, you know, please forgive me, forgive him. How old is he? she asks, and she nods when you tell her. She says she understands. She has two sons. But do you believe her? N'hombre! You think she probably had sons who liked her for being a writer. She doesn't realize that your boy means it.

So one day your son comes home from the mall with a friend. They saw a movie, and guess what, he bought a book. A *book*? You are a little suspicious. It's called *This Book Sucks*. A magnum opus featuring Beavis and Butt-Head.

How do you like that, Dad? he asks, and he's smiling sarcastically, as proud as if he wrote it.

You look at the price. Twelve bucks! He spent twelve bucks on this book? Of his hard-earned money? Money he soaked from you, now that you think about it. Easy money, you might say. But . . . his own money.

So whadda you think, Dad?

It's a tough call, a real tough call. You ask if he'll let you read it. Sure, he says, and for the moment, he's actually pleased with you.

M'ijo Goes to College

My son Toño called me. Let me say that again. *He* called *me*. He said, "Dad, I'm kind of hungry." It was a Sunday night, when there are no meals at the dorm, so I know it might seem like, you know, big deal, wow, the kid's digging for free eats off the old man. But don't you see? I didn't call him, he called me. Think of how it was when you were a teenager, when that certain he or she first called, compare it to that. So I said, "You're hungry, huh? How about in a few hours?" He said, "Okay"—his voice is a gentle whisper, nothing like mine—"but . . . I'm studying. For that history test? And I needed a break. And I wanted to come back . . . and study some more?" He's *studying,* too? For his first big test at the university. What else could I say? "I'll be right there, m'ijo, cuz I guess I am kind of hungry, too."

Just a few weeks ago, it seemed like I'd be the last person he'd call. That was because of me, my own life, and because of him, the two different kinds of males we are, and because I was the father, and he was the son, and even a few days before he was going to leave our home in El Paso for a dorm at the University of Texas, we were having the usual classic confrontation: "Since I'm paying all this money for your education," I made clear in tone only, "and since I'm driving you and your stuff over five hundred miles," I said out loud, "I think you can be ready, have it all packed up in those boxes right now." He'd maintained this smug, spoiled look that I was supposed to understand as yeah yeah, he knew. And so the evening before we were supposed to leave, when there was only one half-filled box, I had to track him down.

"How'd you get this number?" he demanded to know.

"The CIA, what else?" He wasn't amused. But many hours later, he was finally packed. I was about to load my pickup and was searching the boxes to find his computer's CPU, to stack it the most carefully, when he stormed in. "What are you *doing*?!"

That was it for me. I wasn't driving ten-plus hours across West Texas with him. His punishment? Since he doesn't drive, his mom bought him an airline ticket, an hour-and-a-half flight. I drove out without him, those five hundred and something miles. Which gave me a lot of time to feel like everything was my fault, my lack of understanding: he was scared. None of his friends was going away to college. He'd never been away from home alone. He was young. He grew up in El Paso, in a poor neighborhood that I, and the uneven life that I led, raised him in. I never did anything like live in a dorm. I never had to compete against the smartest college kids when I was seventeen or eighteen or even nineteen or so on. I'd forgotten to show my enormous pride in him—he'd gotten good grades, he wanted to go to a good school, and he was doing it.

The first time he called me, I was staying at a friend's. I'd gone over and picked him up, and we were in the truck, stopped for a red light. "Look, Dad," he said, pointing to the driver of a hulking, oxidized American sedan, circa 1975. "A cholo!"

I laughed. "There are gangs in Austin, you know." Where Toño grew up, just about everyone is Mexican-American, and he couldn't get over how different living in Austin was.

We got the green light, we were moving. "You know," Tony said to me, "I think I'm even starting to miss graffiti."

I couldn't believe it. Not even a week, and he was missing the culos who spray the walls of our very own house year after year. Already romanticizing the gang kids he, like 99 percent of the other Chicanos in high school, never hung with. Pretty soon he'll be telling me how tagging is art, describing it like a well-paid academic who does not live in the neighborhood. But I know what he's talking about, and what he means, too, and yeah, it makes me feel good: he misses home. And he's proud of who he is and where he came from.

One thing, though. I don't want him to know about this piece. I don't want anyone to tell him how much I've liked it when he's called, when we've gone out to dinner together, talked, even did a movie. I don't want him to hear that I said any of this.

Letter to My Sons

Dear Antonio and Ricardo,

Many people think hard about whether or not to have children. These are conscious people, usually better off, older, and they make a choice. Many don't think enough about having children. These are people not conscious enough, usually poor, usually way too young, who don't understand what choice they are making. I was between these worlds when each of you was born. And—you will both come to understand this too well, too soon—I would have said no, not now, not yet, but because of my love for your so-beautiful mom, our love, I also would think yes, want yes, because I wanted to have babies with her. There was no plan, no preparation. When each of you was born, there was no bedroom to paint blue for you. In El Paso, on an apartment porch, I made a crib with a skilsaw for you, Toño, though you never slept in it once. In Los Angeles, we bought you a simple, inexpensive (though not for us) department-store crib, Ric. You took daytime naps in it. At night, both of you slept against your mom and only near me. Someday, if not now, you'll remember the rentals you grew up in, the poor neighborhoods, the landlords and landladies, the used furniture. What you can never remember, won't even know until it occurs to you as fathers, is the joy, which, like all mysteries, is wordless, impossible to describe unless you know it. The joy, the pleasure, you both are to me. How to try? Something we can share. The photo album. Too many, too much. Little Tony dressed up in blue overalls, a hammer in his hand, one of my old hard hats on, playing construction. At the beach, in a sand-castle hole, you're looking at the camera as I take your picture, a hat that says "My Dad Is a Union Carpenter," a hat that falls over your eyebrows, and you can't see over the brim, and you have to hold your chin up to look, your mouth open. You wore hats like that for years, wouldn't have them another way. There's my baby Ricardito, sitting on a white table in Ensenada, a diaper on, a smile that's never left. And there you are running through the pigeons on Olvera Street, arms wild, laughing. There are the two of you leaning over the couch, pulling back the curtains, your serious faces against the windows, watching and listening to the garbagemen and the garbage truck. Another of your Hot Wheels plastic bikes, one red and blue and yellow, the other all black, streamers on the handlebars (they were so noisy, and that's what you liked), parked in the driveway of the apartments in East Hollywood, when the giveaway L.A. Dodger batting helmets were racing helmets, and the red-framed glasses without lenses were goggles. There are the three of you, your *mami* and you two all wrapped up warm, one evening when we went to *las posadas*. But every time I page through these photos, I have to stop. The joy is too painful, brings me to tears. I've sneaked things. Watched you at lunchtimes in your school, on the playground. Petted your soft hair when you slept. Remember the snow days in El Paso? The gloves and extra socks and little wool hats. When I hit those fly balls to you? I did it selfishly, so I could be with you, to feel your strength when the ball hit my glove on that hard throw back. I've sneaked reading your school papers. So good, so much better than anything I ever did. Sometimes I still wake up and see your faces, my babies, you, so vividly. I wouldn't have wanted any others, wouldn't want to change any details. As short as it all is, I've missed out on nothing with you, never once thought it was going too fast. My only complaint is the complaint about life itself, that other mystery, that there is change, your growing, change that is the very source of all the other joys as well. Passage is all of ours, and we've gone together. I miss your childhood like it was my own, no more, no less. I do miss you as my babies, and I worry, worry and worry, because I love you both. What I'm trying to say, now that I see you, tall, muscular, smart, ready to fly, able, what I'm saying is thank you, and listen to me: always be there for your mom, who loves you more than God, and always be there for each other, be close, stay close, and remember, I'm your pops, I'll always love you, I'm so proud, and whatever cash I can give you, you know that I will, but you've got to pick up your room at least once a month, please?

Love,
Dad

Work Union

From the richest high school to the poorest high school in America, students are being told that employment in the computer industry is nothing less than salvation from the indignities of the jobs those others have to do to survive. If you don't learn your computer skills well, if by some chance you're bored sitting in front of that screen, day after day under buzzing fluorescents, pecking at a vanilla keyboard, clicking a mouse, it's your problem, and there will be no excuse for your fate in this new economy: you will be doomed to menial, manual labor. That dirty, anybody-can-do-that work. Poor income, low prestige. Pues, así va la vida, compa, that's life if you don't get your stuff right.

But if every young person did learn software programming or Web-page design, if everybody was taught to be so good at these and the rest, there simply wouldn't be enough of those jobs to go around, and the current high income associated with that employment would, as we know, fall dramatically. What is being taught is not only these skills but a justification for keeping an imbalance of power between the new high-tech workers and jobs that will always be necessary—building the offices, highways, bridges where those others do their business through modems and cell phones.

There was a time when work, a man who worked, a man who worked hard, who sweated, got dirty, even, who built things with tools in his hands, was looked upon with respect and honor. And it was the union that made for more personal dignity and real wages.

Not everybody wants to sit at a desk for a living. So many of us come from cultures where it is expected that we will move our bodies in the wind and sun, at dawn and into dusk. Many of us have been taught by family that physical work feels good and is good—when the day is over, we know what we did because we see it, we feel the efforts in our feet and hands and bones, and when we go home, when the wife puts food on the table and the family sits down and eats, there is unmistakable pride that all of it is because we have done our job.

It is human to work, to bend and grip, to lift and pull. It's never about getting tired or dirty. There is nothing wrong with sweat and toil. It is only about conditions and decent wages that there can come complaint. This is what so many people don't understand, especially those who sit in chairs in offices. They see us tired, they see us worried. They say, Well, if you don't like your situation, why don't you get a better job? Because it isn't the job, the kind of work. The job is good. Being a carpenter, an electrician, a plumber, a ironworker, a laborer, those are all good. What isn't good is to be earning a living that can't bring in enough money to raise a healthy family, buy a home, go to a dentist and doctor, and be around comfortably for grandchildren.

A writer from Detroit who worked years for the Fisher Body Plant in Flint, Michigan, has recently been profiled in the newspapers because he won a prize for his writing. In the exultation of winning, he has been quoted often about those years he worked on the assembly line, saying, "I can't stress to you enough how much I hated it." This writer, he is certainly a good man, but like so many, he simply forgot what a joy employment is, what a job means to people and their families. There is only good in work, and the very best people are those who work hard.

◻I◻I◻◻

Preface: I know it's no big secret, and everybody's heard the rumors about it by now but I still won't talk too loud. That's not so easy for me, because I always talk too loud. The thing is—listen—I don't want to cause anything. Even as I write this, I feel like keeping my peripheral vision open a little wider, make sure what's coming at me on either side. I'm nervous. It's that people are saying all kinds of things. Like, did you hear that hiss of whispering? Maybe get a little closer to the page.

My credentials: I've been through a few earthquakes. In bed once, I watched an electrically engaged, spinning ceiling fan swing from its long-neck stem above me, unsuspecting and innocent, nearby breakable items falling and breaking. It was a disturbing event, yet more important is that it was psychologically empowering. I've watched streets being taken over by radicals, those whose uniforms were not uniforms. Watched them throw bottles of gasoline and lit-up rags. I've seen tanks roll in. No, I'm lying there, got carried away with a visual leap. But honest: twice, a couple of jeeps and covered two-tons. Those other dudes, in the green uniforms and helmets, were carrying rifles. What I'm getting at is that I also have the experience of civil ruptures. Also, I have a relationship with a psychic. I don't go often, not like I would to a therapist. I don't mean I'm seeing a therapist now. That was only a particular and unique problem that—believe me—was not so intriguing. Well, maybe it would be to some. My difficulty was a knockout, you wouldn't believe, and I was pretty polluted with doubt as well as blocked. But the point is, I have seen this psychic. She has told me things, very personal things, which are mostly none of your business. Sorry, I am trying to keep it down. The psychic has not told me any specifics about the thousand-year plan, and she did not have much to report about what was going to happen in general when those computer-programing digits line up, but by exposing me to her process, she has taught me things about myself, and when one examines oneself, as Socrates exhorts, when you look inside, therein lies all the wisdom of saints and mystics. As a person alert and attuned, I have been studying other forms of insight, as in meditation, and prayer, and dancing crazed and slow, as well as inducing both the Dyonisian and Apollonian ecstacies. Finally, I've been reading *The New York Times* business section, keeping up with less wild mutual funds, primarily, though I remain not unaware of the rush of Internet stocks.

The visions: insomnia-driven or not, who wouldn't appreciate the architecture of these mangled, gargoyled highrise buildings tilting any direction during the dark hours? It might reflect an exploding economy, but it is more logically a form of post-traumatic stress disorder. Sights of those sweating men clawing nests of rebar, wobbling on aluminum beams being plywood-decked, fatslob bosses who look similar to friends you have who are screaming at you to shut up, a mother no longer alive but shaking her head, fathers you don't really know walking the other direction, lovers and wives who hate you so that you feel major guilt and major regret, children you can't reach who need money. There is broken discussion, as though in a distant cell-phone call, about the intoxicating juices of fertility, of the biologically ineluctable, and of the blind Darwinism of reproduction.

Los indios: down from montañas, up from un valle, from the driest desert and the wettest jungle and into the American sporty outdoors draining the so-filthy oil of German Beamers, into the tasty indoors sprinkling decorative shavings of the indigenous chocolate onto French pastry. They are openly swabbing the most highly successful corporate floors, maintaining the chemical freshness of the most competitive graduate school urinals. They are dispensing the latest in folded brown hand wipes and rolled toilet paper. Their children are sneaking about. Playing. Laughing. Learning idiom. A nongig, low-megahertz, outdated machine is in a Dumpster. *Un abuelo,* working for an independent contractor, finds it at four A.M. on the route. Quien sabe, he says, putting it aside for the chavalitos. On it still is SimCity 2000.

Revelation: close the eyes. Smell. A haunting perfume of dust in that first desert rain. Open them. Brown or green. Or red like a rose, or purple like a sage blossom. There will be wind that whisks leaves. Light will shine like a mystic crystal. Darkness will lay still the night like the sweetest sleep. It is an earth, which is in outer space, up and down like a roller-coaster ride, all that joyous, thrill screaming despite the inevitable peril, taking on and off the throb of a Christmas Day like a star that is also reflected against an orbiting moon. What will be called days, and weeks, and months, and years will pass and pass.

Pride

It's almost time to close at the northwest corner of Altura and Copia in El Paso. That means it is so dark that it is as restful as the deepest unremembering sleep, dark as the empty space around this spinning planet, as a black star. Headlights that beam a little cross-eyed from a fatso American car are feeling around the asphalt road up the hill toward the Good Time Store, its yellow plastic smiley face bright like a sugary suck candy. The loose muffler holds only half the misfires, and, dry springs squeaking, the automobile curves slowly into the establishment's lot, swerving to avoid the new self-serve gas pump island. Behind it, across the street, a Texas flag—out too late this and all the nights—pops and slaps in a summer wind that finally is cool.

A good man, gray on the edges, an assistant manager in a brown starched and ironed uniform, is washing the glass windows of the store, lit up by as many watts as Venus, with a roll of paper towels and the blue liquid from a spray bottle. Good night, m'ijo! he tells a young boy coming out after playing the video game, a Grande Guzzler the size of a wastebasket balanced in one hand, an open bag of Flaming Hot Cheetos, its red dye already smearing his mouth and the hand not carrying the weight of the soda, his white T-shirt, its short sleeves reaching halfway down

243

his wrists, the whole XXL of it billowing and puffing in the
outdoor gust.

A plump young woman steps out of that car. She's wearing
a party dress, wide scoops out of the top, front, and back, its
hemline way above the knees.

Did you get a water pump? the assistant manager asks her.
Are you going to make it to Horizon City? He's still washing
the glass of the storefront, his hand sweeping in small hard circles.

The young woman is patient and calm like a loving mother.
I don't know yet, she tells him as she stops close to him, thinking. I guess I should make a call, she says, and her thick-soled
shoes, the latest fashion, slap against her heels to one of the pay
phones at the front of the store.

Pride is working a job like it's as important as art or war, is
the happiness of a new high score on a video arcade game, of a
pretty new black dress and shoes. Pride is the deaf and blind confidence of the good people who are too poor but don't notice.

A son is a long time sitting on the front porch where he
played all those years with the squirmy dog who still licks his
face, both puppies then, even before he played on the winning
teams of Little League baseball and City League basketball. They
sprint down the sidewalk and across streets, side by side, until
they stop to rest on the park grass, where a red ant, or a spider,
bites the son's calf. It swells, but he no longer thinks to complain
to his mom about it—he's too old now—when he comes home.
He gets ready, putting on the shirt and pants his mom would
have ironed but he wanted to iron himself. He takes the ride with
his best friend since first grade. The hundreds of moms and dads,
abuelos y abuelitas, the tios and primos, baby brothers and older
married sisters, all are at the Special Events Center for the son's
high school graduation. His dad is a man bigger than most, and
when he walks in his dress eel-skin boots down the cement stairs
to get as close to the hardwood basketball-court floor and cere-

mony to see—m'ijo!—he feels an embarrassing sob bursting from his eyes and mouth. He holds it back, and with his hands, hides the tears that do escape, wipes them with his fingers, because the chavalitos in his aisle are playing and laughing and they are so small and he is so big next to them. And when his son walks to the stage to get his high school diploma and his dad wants to scream his name, he hears how many others, from the floor in caps and gowns and from around the arena, are already screaming it—could be any name, it could be any son's or daughter's: Alex! Vanessa! Carlos! Veronica! Ricky! Tony! Estella! Isa!—and sees his boy waving back to all of them.

Pride hears gritty dirt blowing against an agave whose stiff fertile stalk, so tall, will not bend—the love of land, rugged like the people who live on it. Pride sees the sunlight on the Franklin Mountains in the first light of morning and listens to a neighbor's gallo—the love of culture and history. Pride smells a sweet, musky drizzle of rain and eats huevos con chile in corn tortillas heated on a cast-iron pan—the love of heritage.

Pride is the fearless reaction to disrespect and disregard. It is knowing the future will prove that wrong.

Seeing the beauty: look out there from a height of the mountain and on the north and south of the Rio Grande, to the far away and close, the so many miles more of fuzz on the wide horizon, knowing how many years the people have passed and have stayed, the ancestors, the ones who have medaled, limped back on crutches or died or were heroes from wars in the Pacific or Europe or Korea or Vietnam or the Persian Gulf, the ones who have raised the fist and dared to defy, the ones who wash the clothes and cook and serve the meals, who stitch the factory shoes and the factory slacks, who assemble and sort, the ones who laugh and the ones who weep, the ones who care, the ones who want more, the ones who try, the ones who love, those ones with shameless courage and hardened wisdom, and the old ones still so alive, holding their grandchildren, and the young ones in their glowing prime, strong and gorgeous, holding each other, the ones who will be born from them. The desert land is rock-dry and ungreen. It is brown. Brown like the skin is brown. Beautiful brown.

Acknowledgments

So many thanks. To those who encouraged and made these essays appear: Lou Dubose, Michael King, Wendy Lesser, Amy Salit, Naomi Person, Phyllis Myers, Cressida Leyshon, Ben Metcalf. To the ones whose grititos have mattered so much to me: Armando Villareal, George Keating, Bill Timberman, Rudolfo Anaya, Annie Proulx, Rose Reyes, Tish Hinojosa, Pat LittleDog, María Martin, Denise Chávez, Tom Grimes. For this book's practicals: Bob Pomeroy, Jon Marc Smith, Deb Seager, Judy Hottensen, Morgan Entrekin, Daniel Maurer, and César A. Martínez. Of course, for so much of what's in here, Ricardo, Antonio, and Rebeca. And a few special ones: Warren Perkins, Lydia Contreras, Elva Treviño Hart, David Rice, Abraham Verghese, and Amalia Ortiz.